Praise for

DEFENDING THE HOMELAND

"Hicks, Keeney, and their colleagues have produced a volume that will expand our knowledge of terrorism, militancy, and political violence. Addressing themes such as U.S. experiences with combating domestic terrorism, foreign intervention and international relations, gender and terrorism, comparative studies on European and African terrorism and radicalization, and historical and conceptual matters, the book will enhance and enrich insights into the complexity and diversity of political violence, and the obstacles that states experience confronting these challenges. *Defending the Homeland*—as a whole and through its individual chapters—will be of interest to general readers and to students and academics from a range of disciplines. This book is bound to be included on many syllabi and reading lists, as well as among the sources cited in scholars' publications."

DR. PETE LENTINI,
DIRECTOR, GLOBAL TERRORISM RESEARCH CENTRE,
MONASH UNIVERSITY, AUSTRALIA

"*Defending the Homeland* is a must-read collection of essays that position contemporary questions of security in the wider historical and socio-political context of radicalism. The essays demonstrate the wide-ranging and innovative research that is currently being conducted into how radicalized groups justify the use of violence. At the same time, the contributors also show how there is a precarious relationship between state responses to radicalized violence and an increase in the use of violence against the state. To understand current security problems, *Defending the Homeland* offers students of foreign policy generally, and students of security and terrorism studies specifically, a framework for moving away from mono-causal explanations of political violence to a much needed appreciation of the complex interplay between group motivations, historical context, and security measures."

JEANNIE GRUSSENDORF, GEORGIA STATE UNIVERSITY

"*Defending the Homeland* captures the breadth of transformation that national security thinking has undergone in the United States. The collection of essays covers the conceptual range and remarkably broad spectrum of "national security" concerns—from internal threats of labor unrest to Cold War proxy conflicts to the current global threat of terrorism. *Defending the Homeland* makes clear that a domestic vs. international divide in strategic thinking is neither useful nor appropriate to the modern study of national security politics."

DONNA M. SCHLAGCHECK, WRIGHT STATE UNIVERSITY

"This book is a *tour d'horizon* of the many and variegated types of radical assault on established 'orders', both just and unjust, and the reactions and repression such assaults can engender. It is a useful and unusually wide-ranging compendium of disparate case studies. Taken together, the constituent parts of *Defending the Homeland* suggest the breadth of the contemporary challenge and the need not only for study but for vigilance as well."

JASON PARKER, TEXAS A&M UNIVERSITY

"This thoughtful collection of essays reveals the complexities of defending the state from real or perceived threats while determining to what extent civil liberties must be set aside in the name of national security. The changing face of modern terror also comes under consideration as governments and citizens struggle to understand the motivations of today's terrorist. *Defending the Homeland* is a worthwhile addition to the increasing body of literature on homeland security and terrorism, one that students, scholars, and general readers should peruse and consider carefully."

GREGORY MOORE, NOTRE DAME COLLEGE

"Terrorism is not a new phenomenon, but terrorism remains the major threat to democracy and world peace for the foreseeable future. The tragic events of 9/11 have focused U.S. awareness on the fact that there are many facets of terrorism posing a threat to national security, at home and abroad. The essays collected in *Defending the Homeland* identify some of those aspects, which students and academics may wish to explore further."

BRIAN F. KINGSHOTT, GRAND VALLEY STATE UNIVERSITY

DEFENDING THE HOMELAND

DEFENDING THE HOMELAND

HISTORICAL PERSPECTIVES ON RADICALISM, TERRORISM, AND STATE RESPONSES

EDITED BY

MELINDA M. HICKS

AND

C. BELMONT KEENEY

MORGANTOWN 2007

West Virginia University Press, Morgantown 26506
© 2007 by West Virginia University Press

First edition published 2007 by West Virginia University Press
Printed in the United States of America

15 14 13 12 11 10 09 08 07   9 8 7 6 5 4 3 2 1

ISBN-10 1-933202-16-5
ISBN-13 978-1-933202-16-7
(alk. paper)

Library of Congress Cataloguing-in-Publication Data

Defending the homeland. Historical perspectives on radicalism, terrorism, and state responses. / [edited] by Melinda M. Hicks and C. Belmont Keeney.
p.   cm.
1.Terrorism—Political aspects. 2. Terrorists. 3. Radicalism. I. Title. II. Hicks, Melinda M.
III. Keeney, C. Belmont.
IN PROCESS

Library of Congress Control Number: 2007932031

Book design by Than Saffel
Image research by Alison Sanfacon
Printed in USA by BookMobile

CONTENTS

ACKNOWLEDGMENTS
C. Belmont Keeney and Melinda M. Hicks   VII

FOREWORD
Jeffrey H. Norwitz   IX

PART I – THE U.S. AND NATIONAL SECURITY

NATIONAL SECURITY: A PRETEXT FOR REPRESSION?
Ellen Schrecker   3

RANK-AND-FILE REDNECKS:
RADICALISM AND UNION LEADERSHIP
IN THE WEST VIRGINIA MINE WARS
C. Belmont Keeney   20

THE OVERLOOKED SUCCESS:
A RECONSIDERATION OF THE U.S. MILITARY INTERVENTIONS
IN MEXICO DURING THE WILSON PRESIDENCY
Mark Mulcahey   43

NO MORE CUBAS! THE LESSONS OF COUNTERINSURGENCY
David Lauderback   74

THE RHETORIC OF NATIONAL SECURITY:
THE GEORGE H. W. BUSH ADMINISTRATION
AND THE NEW WORLD ORDER
James DePalma   107

PART II - INTERNATIONAL TERRORISM

BEYOND VICTIMS AND PERPETRATORS:
WOMEN TERRORISTS TELL THEIR OWN STORIES
Jamie H. Trnka 133

WHEN DO WOMEN KILL? LIFE AND DEATH IN TSARIST RUSSIA
Jean K. Berger 155

A TROUBLED PAST, AN UNCERTAIN FUTURE:
RADICAL ISLAMISM AND THE PROSPECTS FOR NIGERIA'S STABILITY
Josh Arinze 179

IS TERRORISM UNIQUE? A TACTICAL AND IDEOLOGICAL APPRAISAL
Benjamin Grob-Fitzgibbon 204

ACKNOWLEDGMENTS

The idea for this book originated when we began reviewing submitted papers for the 2005 Senator Rush D. Holt History Conference at West Virginia University. Our theme for the conference, Defining Security in an Insecure World, invited a wide spectrum of research pertaining to terrorism, radicalism, and national security issues. While the conference itself produced a variety of excellent presentations, some of the scholarship stood out and, we felt, deserved a broader audience than the occupants of a few small conference rooms. The expanded papers included in this volume offer a fitting representation of the spirit of the conference itself and, hopefully, will become a welcome addition to the ever-expanding body of literature on terrorism and national security. Throughout the process of writing, researching, and editing, we have been exceedingly fortunate to receive a great deal of invaluable assistance. We would like to thank Pat Conner, Than Saffel, and Sara Pritchard at the West Virginia University Press. Our thanks also go out to Robert Blobaum, chair of the Department of History at West Virginia University; Steve Zdatny; Ronald L. Lewis; Ken Fones-Wolf; Ken Sullivan, executive director of the West Virginia Humanities Council; Eugene Vansickle; Katharine Antolini; Mark Myers; Mike Buseman; Rudolph Almasy and the Eberly College of Arts and Sciences; and, of course, the hard work and patience of all our contributors.

C. BELMONT KEENEY AND MELINDA M. HICKS

FOREWORD

....

Jeffrey H. Norwitz

T HIS COLLECTION OF NINE ESSAYS, expanded from presentations giv-
en at the 2005 U.S. Senator Rush D. Holt History Conference in
Morgantown, West Virginia, is a rich source of thoughtful, analytical,
and often provocative papers demonstrating that history and national security strategy are inseparable. All strategy must be studied in the context
of historic considerations. Failing that, significant mismatches between
policy goals and strategy will emerge. History informs the development of
national security strategy. Implementation demands it.

National Security Strategy

Strategy, particularly at a national level, can be considered a linkage of
ends and means. Ends are objectives—often referred to as national interests—that a country believes are vital. Means are the resources and capabilities a nation possesses. Formulating national security strategy begins
with the questions "What does a nation want to accomplish?" and "What
resources does the nation have?"

Dr. Donald Nuechterlien, former professor of international affairs at
the Federal Executive Institute, described national interests in four categories: defense of the homeland, economic well-being, favorable world
order, and promotion of values. If each category of interest is given equal

emphasis, it follows that keeping the *United States safe* while *promoting democracy* abroad cannot be accomplished unless the U.S. *economy is strong* and worldwide *chaos is minimized.*

Creators of strategy must also identify the means and resources available to accomplish national interests. Political scientists often refer to strategic means as "elements of national power." Diplomatic, economic, and military elements of power are the three most often cited. Many feel that information, as a separate element, deserves its own category. The argument holds that national security is inextricably tied to how a nation is perceived by the world community. The term *strategic communication* captures the essence of how a nation uses information to shape its reputation. Calculated use of information as an element of national power is a means by which interests can be achieved.

When it comes to threats, like terrorism, those who craft national security strategy cannot simply assert that the world is a dangerous place when making a case for spending resources. To protect everything is to protect nothing. Priorities matter. Therefore, assessing what protection to buy necessitates consideration of risk, threat, vulnerability, and consequences. Specifically, the term *risk* can be thought of as the outcome of a comprehensive assessment of threat (what's out there to hurt me?), vulnerability (where am I weakest?), and consequences of occurrence (what level of suffering will I experience?). Risk assessments are essential components of the national security debate so strategists can prioritize where and how to spend limited resources. Yet, risk assessments can never be perfect. Thus, the consequences of getting it wrong must be studied. Exercises are effective vehicles for testing theories of preparation, response, and recovery against real-world scenarios. Done correctly, priorities emerge and strategic alignment of resources is achieved. However, governments have other duties besides creating strategy. Leaders must also execute and implement strategy.

Homeland Security—Past and Future

Expectations of the American public, as they pertain to homeland security, were redefined in the aftermath of September 11, 2001. Twenty-eight days after the attacks, President George W. Bush signed Executive Order 13228, establishing new government offices to deal with homeland security. Planning fell into six different mission areas: detection, preparation, prevention, protection, response, and recovery. More than simply address-ing terrorism, the federal government consolidated disaster preparedness into one cabinet-level agency. Four years later, Hurricane Katrina roared ashore in Louisiana, Mississippi, and Alabama, testing the Department of Homeland Security. Secretary Michael Chertoff described the aftermath of Hurricane Katrina as "probably the worst catastrophe, or set of catas-trophes"[1] in the country's history. According to some in Louisiana, the federal, state, and local governments failed miserably in all six mission categories. Only the military was given high marks.

In a post–Hurricane Katrina world, many demand a greater role for the armed services in homeland security. Even the president suggested as much. Writing in the *Wall Street Journal*, Daniel Henninger noted, "The question raised by the Katrina fiasco is whether the threat from madmen and nature is now sufficiently huge in its potential horror and unaccept-able loss that we should modify existing jurisdictional authority to give the Pentagon functional first responder status."[2] This is troubling and imme-diately conflicts with issues of states' rights and federal intervention into what has been the purview of independent citizenries. Managing the con-sequence of catastrophic destruction, where government ceases to func-tion and anarchy erupts, is a frightening prospect but one that the United States now confronts. What happens when first responders can't respond? Who manages the turmoil, establishes order from disorder, brings leader-ship and experience where none exist? These questions frame a profound discussion that America must have with itself.

Consider, for a moment, what the armed forces bring to a situation. The essence of military professionalism is a set of unique skills, based on a culture and value system that holds duty, honor, and sacrifice above all else. Military leaders are, in the words of Harold D. Lasswell, profession-als in "the management of violence."[3] Dealing with an array of complex challenges in an environment of extreme confusion and disorder, literally

---

1   Michael Chertoff, Homeland Security Secretary, interview on CNN Live Saturday, *The Aftermath of Katrina*, September 3, 2005, available at http://transcripts.cnn.com/TRANSCRIPTS/0509/03/cst.04.html.

2   Daniel Henninger, "Who Calls the Cavalry?" *Wall Street Journal* online, September 9, 2005, available at http://www.opinionjournal.com/columnists/dhenninger/?id=110007230.

3   Harold D. Lasswell, quoted in Samuel P. Huntington, *The Soldier and the State*, (Cambridge, MA: Harvard University Press, 1957), 11.

making life-and-death decisions, military professionals apply reasoned leadership to accomplish missions in the face of crises that would paralyze lesser managers. Moreover, military professionals master complex logistic, communication, medical, transportation, and security needs. It is easy to see why the armed forces have been so successful in countless hurricane-relief operations, firefighting missions, and disaster-response scenarios. But there are serious consequences if, in lieu of elected officials, America begins to depend upon the military as domestic-problem solvers.

One of the foremost thinkers and writers on matters of civil-military relations is my Naval War College colleague Dr. Mackubin Thomas Owens. He observes that the United States military consist of "fighters, not first responders" in a *Weekly Standard* article by that title. "If we are looking for efficiency and respect," says Owens, "the military outshines most other agencies. After all, generals and admirals become generals and admirals because they are good at getting things done."[4] However, Owens argues that increasing use of the military for domestic purposes will adversely affect its ability to wage war. Moreover, healthy civil-military relations would be undermined. History suggests as much, and I strongly agree.

Some authors suggest changing the law in order to make using military forces easier for law enforcement and civil-unrest situations. They point to apparent lawlessness in New Orleans as evidence of societal breakdown. Only the military, they argue, can restore order in a feral region devastated by calamity. In my opinion, changing the law is dangerous and unnecessary. Section 1385 of Title 18, United States Code, is commonly referred to as the Posse Comitatus Act. It states:

> Whoever, except in cases and under circumstances expressly authorized by the Constitution or Act of Congress, willfully uses any part of the Army or Air Force as a posse comitatus or otherwise to execute the laws shall be fined under this title or imprisoned not more than two years, or both.

Owens correctly points out that the Posse Comitatus Act does not constitute a bar to the use of the military in domestic affairs. It does, however, insist that such use be authorized only by the highest constitutional authority: Congress and the president. Owens warns against changing Posse Comitatus: "Our nation should not return to the days when lesser author-

4   Mackubin Thomas Owens, "Fighters, not First Responders," *The Weekly Standard* 11, no. 6 (October 15, 2005).

ity than the president could use the military for domestic purposes." He asks, "Do we really want the American public turning to the military for solutions to the country's problems? If we do, we will find that we have involved the military in the political process to an unprecedented and perhaps dangerous degree."[5] He is, of course, correct. Furthermore, the unique role of the National Guard, captured in Title 32, United States Code, gives state governors adequate military leverage without tasking the active-duty forces. In sum, looking to increase the role of America's armed forces to solve domestic security challenges is bad national security strategy.

Definitions Matter

Problem solving begins with problem definition. The struggle to define terrorism has triggered an infinite number of essays and books. It has provided incalculable opportunities for debates among scholars, politicians, and anyone remotely paying attention to world events since 2001. In 1998, Dutch political scientist Alex P. Schmidt surveyed internationally and identified 109 definitions of *terrorism*. If the use of terror by those determined to change the political landscape is indeed a threat to national security, then those who feel threatened *must* define the term. For, if a strategy is to have any chance of succeeding, then the end state—what we are trying to accomplish—must be unambiguous. The general opinion is that it's hard, nay impossible, to define *terrorism*. But that's an unacceptable answer.

Israeli terrorism expert Dr. Boaz Ganor, author of *The Counter-Terrorism Puzzle: A Guide For Decision Makers*, and director of the International Policy Institute for Counterterrorism, proposes to define *terrorism* as "the intentional use of, or threat to use violence against civilians or against civilian targets, in order to attain political aims."[6] This definition touches on three important elements: the essence of the activity (violence), the aim of the activity (political), and the targets of the activity (civilians). Ganor writes:

> The statement, "One man's terrorist is another man's freedom fighter," has become not only a cliché, but also one of the most difficult obstacles in

---

5 Owens, "Fighters, not First Responders."

6 Boaz Ganor, *Defining Terrorism: Is One Man's Terrorist Another Man's Freedom Fighter?* (Herzlia: ICT Papers, The International Policy Institute for Counter-Terrorism, The Interdisciplinary Center, 1998), 1, available at http://www.ictconference.org/var/119/17070-Def%20Terrorism%20by%20Dr.%20Boaz%20Ganor.pdf.

coping with terrorism. The matter of definition and conceptualization is usually a purely theoretical issue—a mechanism for scholars to work out the appropriate set of parameters for the research they intend to undertake. However, when dealing with terrorism and guerrilla warfare, implications of defining our terms tend to transcend the boundaries of theoretical discussions. In the struggle against terrorism, the problem of definition is a crucial element in the attempt to coordinate international collaboration, based on the currently accepted rules of traditional warfare.[7]

What about world opinion on the definition of *terrorism?* Indeed, the United Nations is boldly trying to come to consensus on this exact issue, yet to date, there is no definition of *terrorism* that 191 nations can agree on. Speaking of the UN work in this area, Secretary General Kofi Annan said:

> The (high-level United Nations) Panel calls for a definition of terrorism which would make it clear that any action constitutes terrorism if it is intended to cause death or serious bodily harm to civilians and non-combatants, with the purpose of intimidating a population or compelling a Government or an international organization to do or abstain from any act. I believe this proposal has clear moral force, and I strongly urge world leaders to unite behind it.[8]

The significance of this courageous effort by the UN cannot be overstated. Will it be difficult? Of course. Is it necessary? Absolutely. For without a universal definition of *terrorism*, solutions will be nearly impossible to achieve.

A final thought regarding solutions to dealing with terrorism: Let us remove emotion and politics from the equation for a moment. Terrorism has always been, and will continue to be, criminal activity. Regardless of the intent of the perpetrator or the status of the victim, events labeled *terrorism* are, in actual fact, a series of criminal acts. Murder, destruction of property, kidnapping, extortion, assault, possession and manufacture of

7   Ganor, *Defining Terrorism*, 6.
8   Kofi Annan, UN Secretary General's keynote address to the Closing Plenary of the International Summit on Democracy, Terrorism, and Security, "A Global Strategy for Fighting Terrorism," Madrid, Spain, March 10, 2005, available at http://www.un.org/apps/sg/sgstats.asp?nid=1345.

explosives, illegal possession of certain weapons, and conspiracy to commit these crimes are each covered by criminal law and international agreements resulting in arrest and extradition. Many experts and scholars argue that terrorism is best treated as a criminal act or series of crimes—thereafter, prosecuted by a legal system with all its transparency, rights of the accused, and rule of law.

On the other hand, ineffective, endless judicial processes seem painfully protracted and are fraught with legal machinations. The counterargument claims that "this is war" and that courtrooms are not the proper battlefield. The military element of national power is the only adequate way to pursue and prosecute a global war on terror. Many say the stakes are too high, the enemy is too ruthless, the geographic boundaries are too cumbersome, and criminal investigations are too slow to effectively keep terrorists on the run and deny them sanctuary from which to plan and organize. Only the military, the argument goes, is agile enough, trained, equipped, and skilled in deadly combat to defeat terrorists wherever they hide.

The Way Ahead

Shortly after September 11, 2001, I published an article entitled "Combating Terrorism: With a Helmet or a Badge?" in which I explore the tension between military and criminal approaches to fighting terror.[9] More than five years later, the same debate still frames philosophical disagreement in dealing with terrorism and national security. Furthermore, passionate discussion concerning liberty vs. security fuels rancorous dissent among well-read, articulate thinkers. The Patriot Act, often misunderstood and poorly explained to the American public, serves as a catalyst for heated discourse, possible only in our democracy. For the time being, fear of terrorism is the driving force behind a national security dialogue. Yet our country, and those nations similarly threatened, will survive this struggle. But what of the Constitution?

I suggest the greatest battle is to remain a nation of law in the face of a ruthless enemy who would consider this our weakness. We cannot allow the next serious terrorist attack—and there will be one—to unleash reactionary forces corrosive to what defines American freedom and liberty.

....

9   Jeffrey H. Norwitz, "Combating Terrorism: With a Helmet or a Badge?" in *American Defense Policy*, 8th ed. Paul J. Bolt (Baltimore: Johns Hopkins University Press, 2005), 424–32.

Jeffrey H. Norwitz

In August 2006, the British disrupted well-coordinated terrorist attacks which, if successful, would have destroyed ten trans-Atlantic commercial airplanes bound for America. Seventeen suspects were charged with conspiracy to murder. The threat is real. Cogent, reasoned, and rational dialogue *now*—about national security and terrorism—will reinforce our resolve never to lose America's unique identity in the face of today's threats and tomorrow's calamities . . . whether they result from the wrath of nature or man. This book is part of that dialogue.

JEFFREY H. NORWITZ, PROFESSOR
NATIONAL SECURITY DECISION MAKING
U.S. NAVAL WAR COLLEGE

SECTION ONE:

....

THE U.S. AND NATIONAL SECURITY

T HIS COLLECTION BEGINS WITH an examination of how the United States has defined and addressed national security issues in both foreign and domestic policy throughout its history. The first two essays explore how the United States government has reacted to internal threats while the remaining three essays examine foreign policy from Woodrow Wilson's administration through the post-Cold War era. Combined, these studies not only demonstrate the necessity of safeguarding national security but, more importantly, illuminate the need to understand the nature of threats to democracy, lest our democratic institutions and ideals suffer due to misguided policies.

Ellen Schrecker begins the discussion of domestic policy with the argument that political repression has often existed under the guise of national security issues. Her sweeping essay, spanning the whole of American history, demonstrates how civil liberties may sometimes be sacrificed on the altar of national security. Expanding on this theme is C. Belmont Keeney's discussion of the West Virginia Mine Wars, which serves as a microcosm for understanding the misconceptions and consequences that arise when the State fails to understand the motives behind violent radical movements. In light of the national security issues facing the United States in the war on terror, both of these studies serve as a warning: freedom and liberty can be endangered when a society feels its national sovereignty threatened and reacts in a reckless fashion.

Turning to foreign policy, Mark Mulcahey's examination of U.S. military intervention in Mexico during Woodrow Wilson's presidency concludes that a moral imperative and realistic, limited goals are necessary prerequisites to armed intervention in a foreign country. As the twentieth century progressed, armed intervention often took the form of counterinsurgency. In his study of U.S. intervention in Latin America during the Cold War, David Lauderback spotlights American attempts to contain communism in the Western Hemisphere. While the United States successfully prevented the spread of communism in Latin America, it failed to foster a climate under which democracy could thrive in the region. James DePalma goes beyond the Cold War in his essay on the George H. W. Bush administration and the New World Order, effectively reconstructing the problems that arise when military intervention fails to meet the lofty language of political rhetoric. Taken as a whole, the themes of realistic military and diplomatic goals, counterinsurgency, and misguided political rhetoric offer up valuable lessons to be applied to the fragile and volatile international climate of the early twenty-first century.

NATIONAL SECURITY:

A PRETEXT FOR REPRESSION?

Ellen Schrecker

ROM THE SPEAKER'S PLATFORM in a Canton, Ohio park, Eugene V. Debs, the Socialist Party's perennial presidential candidate, could actually see the local county jail across the street, where three of his comrades were serving time for opposing the First World War. He referred to them in his speech when he noted that, because of the Wilson administration's crackdown against opponents of the war, "it is extremely dangerous to exercise the constitutional right of free speech in a country fighting to make democracy safe in the world."[1]

Debs knew that the sentiments he was expressing in his two-hour jeremiad against the depredations of capitalism might lead to his own incarceration. He even said as much, though he insisted he was going to "be exceedingly careful, prudent, as to what I say, and even more careful and prudent as to how I say it." Accordingly, he did not directly attack America's participation in the war or urge his listeners to oppose it.[2] But he did not mute his criticism of the wartime violations of free speech or conceal his hostility to the ruling class, which, in his only—and rather oblique—reference to the conflict, he claimed "has always declared the

1 Ray Ginger, *Eugene V. Debs: The Making of an American Radical* (New York: Collier Books, 1962, 1st ed., 1949), 374.

2 Ginger, *Eugene V. Debs*, 375–7.

wars" while "the subject class has always fought the battles" and "has had nothing to gain and all to lose—especially their lives."[3]

Such language, though indirect, was enough for the federal authorities to indict him for violating the 1918 Sedition Act's prohibition against "uttering, printing, writing, or publishing any disloyal, profane, scurrilous, or abusive language" about the government. Despite an eloquent defense, Debs was convicted and sentenced to ten years in prison. This was not unexpected. After all, he *had* criticized the government and had intentionally defied the authorities to prosecute him. He assumed he would be convicted and planned to appeal to the Supreme Court on the grounds that the Sedition Act violated the First Amendment.

The Court's unanimous decision, delivered on March 10, 1919, by Justice Oliver Wendell Holmes, upheld Debs's conviction.[4] Holmes disposed of Debs's First Amendment claim by referring to his previous week's opinion in the case of another antiwar Socialist, Charles Schenck. In that decision, the Supreme Court's first explicit interpretation of the First Amendment, Holmes famously stated, "The most stringent protection of free speech would not protect a man in falsely shouting fire in a theatre." More significantly for our purposes, however, Holmes went on to explain that:

> When a nation is at war many things that might be said in time of peace are such a hindrance to its effort that their utterance will not be endured so long as men fight and . . . no Court could regard them as protected by any constitutional right.[5]

Holmes's formulation—that wars and other national emergencies provide an exception to the Bill of Rights—elicited little opposition. It was expressing what was then—and still is—the standard wisdom.

Although Americans pride themselves on their heritage of freedom, the kind of repression that landed Eugene V. Debs in the Atlanta Federal Penitentiary was no aberration. American authorities had been suppressing dissent during crises ever since the Native American coalition that launched King Philip's War in 1675 seriously threatened the survival of the Massachusetts Bay colony, driving the Puritan elders to protect themselves

3   Ginger, *Eugene V. Debs*, 376–7.

4   *Debs v. U.S.*, 249 U.S. 211 (1919).

5   *Schenck v. U.S.*, 249 U.S. 47 (1919).

from what they viewed as God's wrath by cracking down on Quakers and other heretics.[6] Political repression (by which I mean the use or threatened use of coercive power to inhibit or eliminate those individuals, groups, and movements that are perceived to endanger the nation's political and economic rulers or its cultural and moral well-being) is, alas, as American as apple pie. Besides the prosecution of Debs and the other opponents of World War I, think of the Alien and Sedition acts, the anti-abolitionist "gag rule," the post–World War I Red Scare, the internment of Japanese Americans, McCarthyism, Guantánamo, and the Immigration and Naturalization Services' (INS) post–September 11 roundup of Arabs and Muslims. The list is long and dismal. Moreover, in almost every instance, when the United States cracks down on political dissenters and unpopular minorities, it does so in the language of national defense.

Surprisingly, despite the all-but-ubiquitous connection between emergencies and political repression, few commentators have paid much attention to the role of security in limiting political freedom. Perhaps they assume that the concept of security is so self-evident it needs little analysis. That may, in fact, be true. But because security has been so routinely invoked as a justification for violating people's rights, it may be helpful, at least for now, to give it some scrutiny.

Of course, the invocation of security as a justification for suppressing dissent is not unique to the United States. Even authoritarian regimes claim that they are protecting themselves when they seek to silence or marginalize their opponents or specific minority groups.[7] Still, despite the similarities, the way in which the United States approaches the discussion of national security does reflect this country's particular cultural and political traditions. For example, when we talk about national security and civil liberties, we tend to do so in terms of the need to strike a balance between safety and freedom. That conceptualization stems, I think, from the traditional American predilection for framing difficult issues in the adversarial language of the law and may well bear little relationship to what the nation's protection actually requires.

Not every discussion of national security, however, contains two sides. Some limitations on personal freedoms are universally recognized. No one,

6 Edmund S. Morgan, *Roger Williams: The Church and the State* (New York: Harcourt, Brace & World, 1967), 83–4.

7 Robert Gellately, *The Gestapo and German Society: Enforcing Racial Policy 1935–1945* (Oxford: Oxford University Press, 1990), 140.

for example, would disagree with Supreme Court Justice Robert Jackson's 1949 remark that the protection of civil liberties should not "convert the constitutional Bill of Rights into a suicide pact."[8] Self-preservation, the ability of the state to ensure its own existence, takes precedence over everything else. This is not a startling observation. From the dawn of the modern state system, it has been generally recognized that when the nation is at risk, the rights of its inhabitants may have to give way. In language that today's American leaders would no doubt endorse, the seventeenth century's most pragmatic practitioner Cardinal Richelieu explained, "In normal affairs, the administration of justice requires authentic proofs; but it is not the same in affairs of state . . . There urgent conjecture must sometimes take the place of proof; the loss of the particular is not comparable with the salvation of the state."[9]

"The salvation of the state." That is the bottom line. Though various in nature and changing over time, the threats to that salvation have usually comprised either foreign wars or domestic insurrections or some combination of the two. That has certainly been the case in this country. At such moments, it is assumed that dissent threatens the internal unity of the nation and thus needs to be put down if the polity is to be preserved. Moreover, as Cass Sunstein observes, during wartime, citizens must "have a degree of solidarity and . . . believe that everyone is involved in a common endeavor" in order to convince "the enemy that it faces a unified adversary."[10] If such solidarity does not exist—and, as we shall see, it seldom does—it must be created: either by the consent of propaganda or, more commonly, the coercion of repression.

Unfortunately, because *national security* is such an inherently malleable term, problems arise when what one set of elites or political leaders views as a threat to the nation's survival, others may see as a legitimate disagreement over policy or a demand for social justice. As the historical record reveals, it has almost always been the case that during moments of real or supposed crisis, the authorities have overreacted, exaggerating the danger of domestic dissent and imposing unnecessary injustice on individu-

8   Justice Jackson, dissent, [337 U.S. 1 , 37] TERMINIELLO V. CITY OF CHICAGO, 337 U.S. 1 (1949).

9   Richelieu, quoted in Robert J. Goldstein, *Political Repression in Modern America* (Urbana-Champaign: University of Illinois Press, 2002), xxxi.

10   Cass R. Sunstein, *Why Societies Need Dissent* (Cambridge, MA: Harvard University Press, 2003), 81.

als. Moreover, because the repression that occurs often benefits powerful economic or political groups, it is easy, especially with the historian's twenty–twenty hindsight, to accuse its perpetrators of hypocrisy, of taking advantage of an emergency to weaken or eliminate their enemies. In some instances, such was the case; in many others, the fears, though exaggerated, were genuine. The authorities believed that the dissent they were repressing, though seemingly limited and ineffectual, could be the spark that set off a cataclysmic conflagration. And, as we shall see, this emphasis on its precautionary nature constituted a regular component of American political repression.

So, too, was the insistence that the repressive measures were just for the duration. The authors of those measures knew that they were limiting people's freedom, which, for a progressive politician like Woodrow Wilson, was much to be regretted. And, in fact, one of Wilson's most effective arguments for suppressing his administration's critics was that it was a temporary measure.[11] Once the crisis ended, the repression would, too. And most of the time it did, though not without having done considerable damage to American democracy.

From the start, the nation's leaders cited dangers from abroad to justify political repression. In the 1790s, the French Revolution forced the hitherto suppressed divisions among the founding fathers into the open and provoked the first serious attempt to suppress dissent. As relations with the Napoleonic regime soured, the Federalist administration of John Adams began to prepare for war while at the same time blaming the French for encouraging internal opposition to those preparations.[12]

Already jittery about retaining power, the Federalists took advantage of that war scare to enact measures—the Alien and Sedition acts—designed to silence their foes by deporting politically undesirable foreigners and making it a crime to "write, print, utter or publish . . . any false, scandalous and malicious writing or writings against the government of the United States, either house of Congress . . . or the President."[13] Naturally, the Federalists denied that they were acting from partisan motives. The Sedition Act was necessary, Alexander Hamilton explained, because the

11   Paul L. Murphy, *World War I and the Origin of Civil Liberties in the United States* (New York: Norton, 1979), 252.

12   James Morton Smith, *Freedom's Fetters: The Alien and Sedition Laws and American Civil Liberties* (Ithaca, NY: Cornell University Press, 1956), 17.

13   Smith, *Freedom's Fetters*, 66.

nation's security required protecting its leaders "by preserving their reputations from malicious and unfounded slanders."[14] The seriousness of the situation required preventive action. "The times are full of danger," a leading Federalist warned his colleagues, "and it would be the height of madness not to take every precaution in our power."[15]

The Federalists' political opponents, members of the newly formed Republican Party (now the Democratic Party), correctly realized that the Alien and Sedition acts were aimed against them.[16] And, just as they feared, the government took advantage of the new laws to prosecute the nation's leading Republican editors.[17] Even so, despite the obviously partisan nature of the Sedition Act and its clear violation of the First Amendment's guarantee of a free press, both judges and juries went along with it. The rest of the country, however, did not and essentially rendered the measure moot by electing the Republican Thomas Jefferson president in 1800. The Sedition Act left a legacy: for more than a century, the federal government refrained from outlawing any form of speech.

State legislatures, however, felt no such compunctions and, in the South, where the protection of slavery seemed a matter of extreme urgency, they imposed all manner of restraints on abolitionist propaganda. Especially after the Nat Turner rebellion of 1831, the region's plantation owners were terrified that such literature might encourage another slave revolt.[18] Thus, even though there was no evidence that the early abolitionists were addressing the slaves (they wanted to appeal to the conscience of their masters), the southern authorities passed laws imposing the death penalty for circulating incendiary publications while others made it a crime to subscribe to or receive an abolitionist paper. Congress, at the behest of the South's national representatives, refused to address the issue of slavery. And, finally, it became illegal to teach slaves to read. In every case, it was a matter, as one of the leading southern journals put it, of "public safety."

---

14   Smith, *Freedom's Fetters*, 154.

15   Smith, *Freedom's Fetters*, 53–54.

16   Levy, *Emergence of a Free Press*, 298. For a detailed discussion of the gestation of the Alien and Sedition acts, see Smith, *Freedom's Fetters*, 35–155.

17   Smith, *Freedom's Fetters*, 185–87.

18   In 1831 the Virginia slave Nat Turner led an abortive revolt that killed about fifty whites before he was captured and killed along with about two hundred of his followers and other slaves.

Otherwise, "slaves would have placed in their hands those 'other documents, books, and papers,' inculcating insubordination and rebellion."[19] Ironically, of course, it was the slaveholders, not their slaves, who would eventually rebel.

The Civil War posed the most serious and the most direct threat to the U.S. government—and to the nation's civil liberties. Like wartime presidents before and after, Abraham Lincoln did not worry about the Bill of Rights. When hostile Baltimore mobs threatened to cut communications to the nation's capital, he ordered the military roundup of some Confederate sympathizers and then asked Congress to suspend the writ of habeas corpus.[20] As he sought to justify his actions in what may well be the single most justifiable suspension of individual rights in wartime in the nation's history, Lincoln questioned whether "such extreme tenderness of the citizen's liberty" might not destroy the Union. "To state the question more directly, are all the laws, *but one,* to go unexecuted, and the government itself go to pieces lest that one be violated?"[21]

Since many of the Civil War's later incursions against individual rights lacked the immediacy of that early crisis, the authorities justified their repressive behavior by claiming that they were taking precautionary measures. Such, in fact, was Lincoln's rationale for his administration's seizure of the antiwar congressman Clement Vallandigham. "The military arrests and detentions, which have been made," he explained in June, 1863, had been for *"prevention,* and not for *punishment*—as injunctions to stay injury, as proceedings to keep the peace—and hence . . . , they have not been accompanied with indictments, or trials by juries, nor, in a single case by any punishment whatever, beyond what is purely incidental to the prevention."[22]

----

19   Quote from "DeBow's Review," in Russel B. Nye, *Fettered Freedom: Civil Liberties and the Slavery Controversy, 1830–1860* (East Lansing: Michigan State College Press, 1949).

20   Mark E. Neely Jr., *The Fate of Liberty: Abraham Lincoln and Civil Liberties* (New York: Oxford University Press, 1991), 4–12. See also the relevant chapters in William H. Rehnquist, *All the Laws but One: Civil Liberties in Wartime* (New York: Knopf, 1998), and Geoffrey R. Stone, *Perilous Times: Free Speech in Wartime* (New York: Norton, 2004).

21   Lincoln, address to Congress, July 4, 1861, cited in Neely, *The Fate of Liberty,* 12.

22   Neely, *The Fate of Liberty,* 174.

The end of the Civil War did not end the threat of insurrection; this time the dangers came from a generation of Socialist revolutionaries and anarchists who called for overthrowing the government and sometimes even built bombs to do so. When such a device was thrown into the ranks of the Chicago police at a demonstration in Haymarket Square on May 4, 1886, the local establishment panicked. The authorities quickly rounded up the city's most prominent anarchists and put them on trial for their lives.

Individual guilt was not at issue. "Law is on trial. Anarchy is on trial," the prosecutor explained in his summation to the jury. "These men have been selected, picked out by the grand jury and indicted because they were leaders. They are no more guilty than the thousands who follow them. Gentlemen of the jury, convict these men, make examples of them, hang them and you save our institutions, our society."[23] Even though the government could produce no evidence that any of the defendants were involved with the bombing, the jury saved society by convicting all of them and sentencing several to death.

The prosecution also satisfied the city fathers' need to appear to be in control. As often happens when the authorities face a situation they can do little about, they fulfill the demand for action in the aftermath of a catastrophe by cracking down on members of unpopular racial or political groups, whether or not those people had any connection to the event in question. This was the case in Chicago where, according to a contemporary observer, the judge who ran the Haymarket trial "manufactured the law" and "disdained precedent in order that a frightened public might be made to feel secure."[24]

Although the repression that followed the Haymarket massacre decimated the anarchist movement, the nation's rulers continued to evoke its alleged threat to national security as a justification for taking action against union organizers and other radicals throughout the early twentieth century. Thus, when the Supreme Court acquiesced in the government's refusal to admit a British anarchist to the country in 1904, it reiterated the traditional line: "as long as human governments endure they cannot be denied the power of self-preservation."[25] Emma Goldman posed a similar menace. The Philadelphia authorities were only exercising their "right of

23   Paul Avrich, *The Haymarket Tragedy* (Princeton, NJ: Princeton University Press, 1984), 284.

24   Avrich, *The Haymarket Tragedy*, 263.

25   Chief Justice Fuller in *Turner v. Williams* 194 US, 279 (1904).

self preservation," a Pennsylvania court explained. If the city let her speak, she would "advocate ideas which, if carried out, would naturally lead to the destruction of government."[26] Elsewhere, local governments barred members of the Industrial Workers of the World (IWW) from speaking in public.[27]

The repression that accompanied America's entrance into World War I built upon those earlier precedents. The radicals who had previously threatened the nation's internal security were now designated the accomplices of its external foe. That some of the same groups and individuals who had been repressed earlier came under attack during the war reveals a continuity with regard to the private interests involved. Antiunion businessmen could—and did—wrap themselves in the flag, while the government's rhetoric stressed the overarching dangers abroad and the desperate need for unity at home.[28]

In order to obtain that unity and prevent dissenters from interfering with the war effort, the administration got Congress to pass the Espionage and Sedition acts in 1917 and 1918. By the time the fighting stopped, the Justice Department had rounded up and prosecuted Eugene V. Debs and over two thousand other people under these two laws. Meanwhile, the postmaster general banned what he considered "seditious" literature from the mails, effectively proscribing most of the nation's left-wing publications.[29]

Vigilantes augmented the official repression by harassing and occasionally even lynching draft dodgers, German Americans, and other opponents of the war. Given the government's massive propaganda campaign to demonize the enemy and its willingness to enlist private groups in its efforts to enforce the Selective Service and other wartime measures, the Justice Department's claim that "the major part of our energies went in stemming the tide of intolerance" was unconvincing, especially since the

26 David M. Rabban, *Free Speech in Its Forgotten Years* (New York and Cambridge, MA: Cambridge University Press, 1997), 144.

27 William Preston Jr., *Aliens and Dissenters: Federal Suppression of Radicals, 1903–1933* (Cambridge, MA: Harvard University Press, 1963; rev. ed., University of Illinois Press, 1994); Patrick Renshaw, *The Wobblies: The Story of Syndicalism in the United States* (Garden City, NY: Doubleday, 1967), 85–95.

28 Murphy, *World War I and the Origin of Civil Liberties*, 249.

29 The best single survey of the political repression spawned by the First World War is Murphy, *World War I and the Origin of Civil Liberties*.

measures it took to stem that tide hardly bolstered the right to dissent.[30] In some parts of the West, for example, the army rounded up and detained members of the IWW to protect them from mobs ready "to inflict serious, perhaps, fatal injury" on them.[31] The government's main solution, however, was legislative—the nine amendments to the already repressive Espionage Act incorporated into the 1918 Sedition Act, designed, so its proponents insisted, to outflank the vigilantes by enabling the Justice Department to prosecute anyone who made "disloyal . . . scurrilous or abusive" remarks about the government or said anything to bring the armed forces into "contempt, scorn, . . . or disrepute."[32] The administration was, in historian William Preston's words, "in effect eliminating mob violence against IWW's and other nonconformists by removing the enraged citizen from the mob and placing him in the jury box."[33] The Wilson administration's attempt to preempt the unauthorized violence was a common phenomenon. Governments often rationalized their repressive actions by claiming that they were actually protecting unpopular groups and individuals by depriving them of their rights.[34]

The end of the war did not end the repression. The Bolshevik Revolution, a massive strike wave, and a spate of anarchist bombings, including one on the front steps of Attorney General A. Mitchell Palmer's own home, prompted a frenzied wave of arrests and deportations during 1919 and 1920. Again, the repressive measures of this first Red Scare were advertised as precautionary. Palmer hoped to forestall a Bolshevik uprising by cracking down on the fledgling Communist party. As he explained to a Senate committee, he did not think "that the Government must stand idly by and wait for the actual throwing of the bomb or the actual use of arms in military operation before it can act to protect itself against such onslaughts."[35]

....

30   Rabban, *Free Speech in Its Forgotten Years*, 327.

31   Preston, *Aliens and Dissenters*, 106–07; Murphy, *World War I and the Origins of Civil Liberties*, 85–91.

32   Michael Linfield, *Freedom under Fire: US Civil Liberties in Times of War* (Boston: South End Press, 1990), 44; Murphy, *World War I and the Origins of Civil Liberties*, 68, 201–2.

33   Preston, *Aliens and Dissenters*, 122.

34   Preston, *Aliens and Dissenters*, 107.

35   Beverly Gage, "The Wall Street Explosion: Capitalism, Terrorism, and the 1920 Bombing of New York" (Ph.D. dissertation: Columbia University, 2004), 330.

There were political advantages as well. Palmer was under consider-able pressure from Congress to do something. He planned to seek the Democratic nomination in the 1920 presidential election and assumed that a vigorous response to the Bolshevik menace would promote his candidacy.[36] It did not. After all, despite their revolutionary rhetoric, the few thousand radical and not-so-radical foreigners snagged during the Palmer raids on some minor left-wing organizations hardly posed a threat to the American government, while their mistreatment at the hands of the law turned into a public relations disaster.[37]

A few years later, the authorities echoed Palmer's argument about the dire consequences of inaction when they arrested the Communist party's leaders who were gathered at Bridgman, Michigan, in 1922. A wave of labor unrest had just swept the country, coal miners and railroad workers were still out on strike, and the government claimed that the crisis required a crackdown on communists to keep them from adding fuel to the already inflammatory situation.[38] This was an argument that the Supreme Court's traditionalists readily accepted. Justice Edward T. Sanford's majority opinion in the 1925 case of Communist party official Benjamin Gitlow passionately defended the need for preventive action against the advocates of class warfare:

> They threaten breaches of the peace and ultimate revolution. And the im-mediate danger is none the less real and substantial, because the effect of a given utterance cannot be accurately foreseen. The State cannot reason-ably be required to measure the danger from every such utterance in the nice balance of a jeweler's scale. A single revolutionary spark may kindle a fire that, smouldering for a time, may burst into a sweeping and de-structive conflagration. It cannot be said that the State is acting arbitrarily or unreasonably when in the exercise of its judgment as to the measures necessary to protect the public peace and safety, it seeks to extinguish the spark without waiting until it has enkindled the flame or blazed into the conflagration. It cannot reasonably be required to defer the adoption of measures for its own peace and safety until the revolutionary utterances

36 Robert J. Goldstein, *Political Repression in Modern America* (Urbana-Champaign: University of Illinois Press, 2002), 154.

37 Currently the definitive book on the Red Scare is Robert K. Murray, *Red Scare: A Study in National Hysteria, 1919–1920* (Minneapolis: University of Minnesota Press, 1955).

38 Gage, "The Wall Street Explosion," 464–66.

lead to actual disturbances of the public peace or imminent and immediate danger of its own destruction; but it may, in the exercise of its judgment, suppress the threatened danger in its incipiency.[39]

A similar imperative about the need to take preventive action suffuses the Roosevelt administration's treatment of the Japanese Americans on the West Coast in the early weeks of World War II. Though many factors played into the president's decision to intern both the Issei and the Nissei, one of the most powerful was the desire to prevent them from engaging in sabotage. Though we now know such fears were groundless, at the time, in the aftermath of the shock of Pearl Harbor, even such a level-headed observer as Walter Lippmann subscribed to the widespread rumors that Japanese sympathizers had been sending radio signals to enemy submarines in the Pacific and would threaten the heavy concentration of defense industries and aircraft factories on the West Coast where most Japanese Americans lived.[40]

Racism was a major element in the decision to relocate the entire community. The state's big growers were eager to eliminate the competition they faced from the Japanese farmers who had been making inroads into the state's produce markets, and they took advantage of the wartime emergency to do so. "We should strike now, while the sentiment over the country is right," the chair of the Santa Barbara County Board of Supervisors explained in February, 1943, as he urged the adoption of a measure to expel the Japanese after the war. "We don't want to see the time return when we have to compete with the Japanese again in this valley."[41] There was no national security fig leaf involved. "We're charged with wanting to get rid of the Japs for selfish reasons," the director of the Grower-Shipper Vegetable Association admitted. "We might as well be honest. We do. It's a question of whether the white man lives on the Pacific coast or the brown man."[42]

....

39 *Gitlow v. People of State of New York*, 268 U.S. 652 (1925).

40 Peter Irons, *Justice at War* (New York: Oxford University Press, 1983), 53–61; Greg Robinson, *By Order of the President: FDR and the Internment of Japanese Americans* (Cambridge, MA: Harvard University Press, 2001), 101–102; Rehnquist, *All the Laws but One*, 196–97.

41 Michi Nishiura Weglyn, *Years of Infamy: The Untold Story of America's Concentration Camps* (Seattle: University of Washington Press, 1976, 2nd ed. 1996), 152.

42 Irons, *Justice at War*, 39–40.

Other formulations that were invoked to justify the internment program were considerably less crude, though ultimately just as racist. The most common asserted that because they clung to their traditional culture, the Japanese Americans were, to use a term FDR employed in the 1920s, "unassimilable."[43] Their inscrutability, therefore, made it impossible for the government to implement a loyalty program that would deal with them on an individual basis. As he shepherded his recommendation for a mass evacuation through the bureaucracy, the military lawyer who was shaping the program explained that:

> as you cannot distinguish or penetrate the Oriental thinking and as you cannot tell which ones are loyal and which ones are not . . . it is, therefore, the easiest course (aside from the mechanical problem involved) to remove them from all the West Coast and place them in the Zone of Interior in uninhabited areas where they can do no harm under guard.[44]

When Attorney General Francis Biddle reluctantly signed on to the relocation scheme, he explained in a February, 1942, memo that Roosevelt's action:

> cannot be considered as any punitive measure against any particular nationalities. It is rather a *precautionary measure* to protect the national safety. It is not based on any legal theory but on the facts [sic] that the unrestricted movement of certain racial classes, whether American citizens or aliens, in specified defense areas may lead to serious disturbances. These disturbances cannot be controlled by police protection and have the threat of injury to our war effort [italics mine].[45]

The prospect of what Biddle called "serious disturbances" supplied an additional rationale for the Roosevelt administration's action. Just as the Wilson administration had incarcerated the Wobblies for their own protection, the Roosevelt administration was uprooting the Issei and Nissei to frustrate potential lynch mobs. The threat to the nation's well-being, in other words, came not only from the potential sabotage that the Japanese Americans might engage in, but also from the unauthorized violence of

43   Robinson, *By Order of the President*, 42.

44   Karl Bendetsen, quoted in Weglyn, *Years of Infamy*, 95.

45   Biddle memo, in Weglyn, *Years of Infamy*, 71.

their Caucasian neighbors against them. This was not a chimera; vigilante incidents did occur. As Mike Masoaka, the Japanese American community's most prominent spokesman, told a congressional committee:

> If the military say 'Move out,' we will be glad to move, because we recognize that even behind evacuation there is not just national security but also a thought as to our own welfare and security because we may be subject to mob violence and otherwise if we are permitted to remain.[46]

Even after it was clear that the military crisis had passed and the threat of sabotage had been grossly exaggerated, the government still argued that the internment program was necessary to avoid subjecting the detainees to violence at the hands of their fellow citizens.[47]

Nor should we ignore the partisan political pressures involved in the government's decision to relocate the Japanese Americans. It was a decisive action that not only responded to the insistent demands of West Coast politicians and business groups for taking care of an unpopular minority but also allowed the Roosevelt administration to appear in control of the situation.

Times were, after all, grim in the immediate aftermath of the devastating American defeat at Pearl Harbor when the Japanese military was sweeping from one victory to another and the United States was not yet militarily engaged on any front.[48] But, even after the crisis ended and it had become completely clear to everybody within the administration that there was no longer (if there ever had been) any military necessity for the relocation, politics still determined the Japanese Americans' fate. The White House refused to end the program because of the impact it might have on the 1944 presidential elections. "I just came from the President a while ago," Undersecretary of War John McCloy explained to the general who was hoping to end the internment. "He put his thumbs down on this scheme. He was surrounded by his political advisors and they were harping hard that this would stir up the boys in California and California, I

---

46   Masoaka quoted in Irons, *Justice at War*, 80. Weglyn, *Years of Infamy*, 70; Irons, *Justice at War*, 24–28.

47   Irons, *Justice at War*, 179, 195; Weglyn, *Years of Infamy*, 221–26, 299; Robinson, *By Order of the President*, 118.

48   Weglyn, *Years of Infamy*, 70; Irons, *Justice at War*, 24–28.

guess, is an important state."[49] Once the election was over, Roosevelt let the Japanese Americans leave the camps.

Again, as was so often the case, the judiciary went along with the administration. Acceding to the administration's argument that the exclusion of Japanese Americans from the West Coast was a matter of self-defense, the Supreme Court refused to question Roosevelt's actions as Commander in Chief.[50] Because of their desire to present a united façade during wartime, even the Court's most liberal members went along and in 1943 unanimously upheld the curfew conviction of college student Gordon Hirobayashi. Noting that the "war power of the national government is the power to wage war successfully," Chief Justice Harlan Fiske Stone explained that "[w]here, as they did here, the conditions call for the exercise of judgment and discretion and for the choice of means by those branches of the Government on which the Constitution has placed the responsibility of warmaking, it is not for any court to sit in review of the wisdom of their action or substitute its judgment for theirs."[51] It was "the military urgency of the situation," the Court explained in its 1943 *Korematsu* decision, that made it legitimate to exclude Japanese Americans from the West Coast. "Temporarily."[52] Again, the assumption that the violations of individual freedoms would abate once the emergency passed seemed to make the otherwise nasty business more palatable.

The judiciary's willingness to let the government override individual rights continued into the Cold War era as well. Again, it was the invocation of an emergency—this time the face-off with international Communism—that led to the widespread political repression we now call McCarthyism. Once again it was claimed that preventive action was necessary. It would be intolerable, Chief Justice Fred Vinson explained in his 1951 opinion that affirmed the conviction of the nation's top Communists, if "before the Government may act, it must wait until the putsch is about to be executed, the plans have been laid and the signal is awaited."[53] A similarly precautionary rationale suffused the FBI's surveillance of thousands of

---

49   Robinson, *By Order of the President*, 222.

50   Rehnquist, *All the Laws but One*, 191.

51   *Hirabayashi v. United States*, 320 U.S. 81 (1943); Rehnquist, *All the Laws But One*, 199.

52   *Korematsu v. U.S.*, 323 U.S. 214 (1944).

53   *Dennis v. United States*, 341 U.S. 494 (1951), 515.

Americans who, J. Edgar Hoover determined, might have to be incarcerated in an emergency. Communists were so dangerous, one of Hoover's top aides explained, that "any members of the party occupied in any industry would be in a position to hamper the efforts of the United States by individual action and undoubtedly the great majority of them would do so."[54]

In order to prevent such a threat from materializing, the federal government and the main institutions of civil society implemented a massive program of loyalty checks and investigations. One authority has estimated that 20 percent of the nation's workforce was affected by these anti-communist programs in one way or another.[55] Members and former members of the Communist party, as well as men and women whose only connection to communism had been to attend a meeting or sign a petition in the 1930s, found themselves under suspicion and fighting for their careers and reputations.[56] Today it is hard to see how firing unfriendly witnesses or blacklisting entertainers could become matters of national security— and yet they were. "One never knows," Supreme Court Justice Tom Clark insisted in 1956, "just which job is sensitive. The janitor might prove to be in as important a spot security-wise as the top employee in the building."[57] Actors could slip Soviet propaganda into their scripts; federal meat inspectors could poison the nation's food supply.[58] When the *New York Times* fired one of its copy editors for refusing to cooperate with a congressional investigating committee, it claimed that it had done so because he worked on the foreign-news desk. Had he been assigned to the sports page, he could have kept his job.[59]

Whether that was the case is, in a sense, irrelevant. By the late 1940s and 1950s, the invocation of national security had so much legitimating

---

54 Ellen Schrecker, *Many Are the Crimes: McCarthyism in America* (New York and Boston: Little, Brown, 1998), 207–8.

55 Ralph S. Brown Jr., *Loyalty and Security: Employment Tests in the United States* (New Haven, CT: Yale University Press, 1958), 181.

56 The most comprehensive account of the scope of the McCarthy era purges can be found in David Caute, *The Great Fear: The Anti-Communist Purge under Truman and Eisenhower* (New York: Simon and Schuster, 1978).

57 *Cole v. Young*, 351 U.S. 536 (1956).

58 Ellen Schrecker, *The Age of McCarthyism: A Brief History with Documents* (Boston: Bedford Books, 2nd ed., 2002), 185–86.

59 Schrecker, *Many Are the Crimes*, 189–90.

power that it took years for the nation's mainstream institutions to extricate themselves from their collaboration with McCarthyism's violations of individual rights. Until the anticommunist furor receded in the late 1950s, the nation's judiciary, for example, was willing to allow the federal government to fire civil servants on the unsubstantiated testimony of anonymous FBI informants.[60] And it did nothing to curtail the violations of civil liberties indulged in by the congressional investigating committees.

Fast-forward to the present and the current war on terror. In so many ways, it seems like "déjà vu all over again." Since September 11 has been likened to Pearl Harbor, could it be possible that the Bush administration rounded up and incarcerated thousands of Muslims from the Middle East and South Asia within a few weeks of that catastrophe in order to look decisive and in control? Moreover, while there is certainly a need to be proactive in rooting out potential saboteurs, given the historical and (so far) contemporary willingness of both the legislative and judicial branches to concur with whatever measures the executive undertakes in defense of national security, one cannot help but wonder whether a hidden scenario of executive aggrandizement undergirds the administration's evasion of all constitutional constraints on its electronic surveillance of domestic communications. Once again the government wraps its activities in the cloak (or should I say "shroud"?) of national security. The rights of individuals cannot, the Bush administration claimed, impede its war on terror. We have heard this kind of talk before. The detainees of Abu Ghraib, Guantánamo, as well as the unknown number of prisoners the CIA has "rendered" into the hands of third-party torturers are but the latest, albeit perhaps the most extreme, victims of the American style of political repression. In almost every case that we have looked at, the passage of time has shown that the dangers were exaggerated and that protecting America's security did not require the destruction of people's rights. Will that be the case today? The historical record does not encourage optimism.

---

60   *Bailey v. Richardson*, 182 F.2d 46 (DC Cir. 1950).

RANK-AND-FILE REDNECKS:

··

RADICALISM AND UNION LEADERSHIP IN THE WEST VIRGINIA MINE WARS, 1912-1933

C. Belmont Keeney

I N THE YEARS FOLLOWING THE FIRST WORLD WAR, many Americans felt that the world had grown increasingly insecure. Revolutions in postwar Europe and labor upheaval at home helped feed the Red Scare in 1919 and 1920. In West Virginia, this labor upheaval took an extremely radical and militant turn. In the last days of August 1921, thousands of West Virginia coal miners, armed and organized for war, left the state capitol in Charleston and marched south. Their objectives were to lift martial law in Logan and Mingo counties, free imprisoned coal miners, and destroy the hated mine guard system that ruled the southern portion of the state. To identify themselves in the dense woods and hillsides, the miners wore red bandannas around their necks. Soon thereafter, the *New York Times, Washington Post,* and *London Times* referred to the miners as the "Redneck Army." As August gave way to September, these rednecks clashed with mine guards, state police, and volunteer middle-class militia at Blair Mountain in what Robert Shogan has recently called "America's largest labor uprising."[1]

····································

1   See Robert Shogan, *The Battle of Blair Mountain: The Story of America's Largest Labor Uprising* (Boulder, CO: Westview Press, 2004), ix–ii. Shogan's book is the most

Since that time, much regional attention has been given to the West Virginia Mine Wars and the Battle of Blair Mountain. Historical studies, novels, and movies have all chimed in to tell this story of violence and industrial conflict. What is notably interesting about this conflict is how the militant radicalism that threatened the established economic and political order was not shaped by national labor leaders such as John L. Lewis, Samuel Gompers, or Eugene Debs, or even by the national organizations associated with these leaders. Instead, the radicalism of the miners in southern West Virginia began and ended with the local rank and file. Historian David Corbin ably put it this way:

> Any uprising of the southern West Virginia coal diggers would begin with the miners themselves and . . . the union spirit that evolved in southern West Virginia—and the ideas and ideals the miners formulated about unionism and about what unionism should represent—would reflect the character and values of the rank-and-file miners, not the international union.[2]

While a number of historians have studied the nature and the causes of industrial violence in West Virginia during the mine wars, surprisingly little has been published about the rank-and-file leaders who played such a dominant role in the uprisings and unionization of the coalfields from 1912 to the passage of the National Industrial Recovery Act in 1933. If David Corbin is correct in his assertion—and I believe he is—that the union movement during the mine wars was directed locally and not by the international United Mine Workers of America (UMWA), then a study of the key rank-and-file leaders during the Mine Wars would be essential to understanding the nature of industrial conflict, radicalism, and unionization during the period. A study of the motives and nature of radicalism in the local union leadership during the West Virginia Mine Wars will broaden our understanding of the forces that shape radicalism and the responses such radicalism receives by government and society.

recent work covering the West Virginia Mine Wars. For use of the term *redneck* in association with the media's coverage of the uprising, see the *New York Times*, *London Times*, and *Washington Post*, August 26 to September 4, 1921.

2   David Alan Corbin, *Life, Work, and Rebellion in the Coal Fields: The Southern West Virginia Miners, 1880–1920* (Urbana and Chicago: University of Illinois Press, 1981), 52.

This essay will focus on the roles, motives, and ideals of Frank Keeney, Fred Mooney, Bill Blizzard, and other important leaders during the West Virginia Mine Wars. This study will conclude that, while the Mine Wars began as a struggle influenced by outside social and economic forces, they became a struggle dictated, from the miners' side, by the rank-and-file leadership.

The Socialist beliefs and militant actions of Keeney, Mooney, and Blizzard dominated the agenda of the UMWA in West Virginia for two decades and contributed greatly to the industrial violence of the conflict. The West Virginia Mine Wars represented a class conflict led by a militant, Socialist rank and file using direct action in an attempt to achieve economic justice for the working class. The national press, the captains of industry, the state, and even the local middle class branded these men as radicals and rednecks who posed a threat to the economic and social order of the day. They were correct.

From the beginning, the unionization of the southern West Virginia coal miners was destined to be a bitter struggle. Aside from the company towns and the mine guard system, national influences laid the foundation in southern West Virginia for a more violent struggle. In 1898, the United Mine Workers successfully organized the coal miners of Pennsylvania, Ohio, Indiana, and Illinois, a group of states also known as the Central Competitive Field. Over the next ten years, the UMWA attempted to gain a foothold in West Virginia but met with very little success. As West Virginia became one of the leading coal producers in the country, its nonunion mines sold cheaper coal and took away from the unionized markets of the Central Competitive Field. Also, due to more favorable locations of the coal seams, the cost of coal production in West Virginia was considerably lower than in other states. Nonunion miners of West Virginia earned less than those in other states, further lowering production costs. By 1912, cheap West Virginia coal took a tremendous toll on the Central Competitive Field, endangering union contracts established in the area. If the UMWA was to survive as an organization, it had to establish itself in West Virginia. The West Virginia coal operators, on the other hand, felt the necessity to keep the union out in order to compete with states closer to large industrial markets. For the operators and the UMWA, the unionization, or the prevention of unionization, in southern West Virginia was critical to the prosperity of both sides. Thus, from the very beginning, the labor clashes in southern West Virginia began as an extremely intense struggle because the stakes were so high.[3] The West Virginia Mine Wars began with these high stakes not because of the state's isolation—a common misconception about Appalachia—but because of its *connection* with the national labor movement and industrial economy. National dictates made the conflict nearly inevitable.

When the miners of Paint Creek and Cabin Creek walked out on strike in the spring of 1912, the UMWA and the coal operators dug in for a fight to the death. The companies fired miners and evicted their families from their homes. The UMWA supplied tents for the miners to live in at Eskdale and Holly Grove, two nearby places still not owned by the coal companies. The coal operators hired over three hundred Baldwin-Felts detectives and brought them into the area. The mine guards patrolled the streets and prevented miners and their families from walking on company roads or crossing company bridges. Thousands of miners tugged their families and belongings across the creeks and into the hills.[4]

As the spring blossomed into summer, the UMWA national and state leadership faltered. The union had little money to fund the strike and now faced the burden of supporting approximately 7,500 strikers. Many of these, from Cabin Creek, were not originally a part of the strike call but decided to strike for union recognition as well. Thomas Cairns, president of District 17, and International Board member Thomas Haggerty ran the union's activities in West Virginia. During the summer of 1912, they tried to negotiate a settlement with the coal operators. The operators, believing they could crush the union in Paint Creek, as well as keep it out of Cabin Creek, refused to compromise.[5]

It was during this moment that the West Virginia Mine Wars took a decisive turn. A Cabin Creek miner, seeking more union aid in the strike,

....

3   Clipping from the *West Virginia Federationist*, August 18, 1921, The Felts Papers, West Virginia Regional Coal Archives, Bluefield, WV; Richard D. Lunt, *Law and Order vs. the Miners: WV 1906–1933* (Charleston, WV: Appalachian Editions, 1992), 14–15; Fox B. Maier, *United We Stand: The United Mine Workers of America, 1890–1990* (Indianapolis: Allied Printing Company, 1990), 50–60.

4   Howard B. Lee, *Bloodletting in Appalachia: The Story of West Virginia's Four Major Mine Wars and Other Thrilling Incidents of its Coal Fields* (Parsons, WV: McClain Printing Company, 1969), 20–21; Corbin, *Life, Work, and Rebellion in the Coal Fields*, 88–89.

5   *Bluefield Daily Telegraph*, August 13, 1912.

arrived in Charleston. Frank Keeney, having lived in a tent at Eskdale since the beginning of the strike, decided he could stand by and watch no longer. His children were sick with smallpox and his wife was eight months pregnant.

Bursting into District 17 headquarters, Keeney confronted Cairns and Haggerty, asking them to accompany him to Cabin Creek to organize the miners. They refused. Furious, Keeney told them that he would take charge of the strike himself and went on to say, "I will find someone with nerve enough to go with me, for if you men are afraid to make the trip, there is a woman who will go!"[6]

Keeney stormed out of the office and tried to learn the whereabouts of Mother Jones, who had been sent by the international office of the UMWA to Charleston, and had just arrived. Mother Jones later recalled the meeting:

> I remember one awful night when [Frank Keeney] came to see me at one o'clock in the morning. It was in 1912. He came to me with tears in his eyes and said nobody would come to them. He asked if I would come. I was thinking it was about time to break in there anyhow, so I said I would go. He said, "But they might kill you." I said I was not afraid, that I could meet no more glorious death than fighting those thieves and robbers. We went up [to Cabin Creek] that *morning.*[7]

6   James and Geraldine Jackson, interview by author, tape recording, Charleston, WV, August 1993; Fred Mooney, *Struggle in the Coal Fields: The Autobiography of Fred Mooney* (Parsons, WV: McClain Printing Company, 1967), 27. James Jackson was Frank Keeney's grandson. Geraldine Jackson was Keeney's daughter and was born in the Eskdale tent colony in 1912. It should also be noted that Keeney never left behind any personal papers. In fact, he gave specific instructions to his son, Belmont, that his papers were to be burned after his death. Belmont did as he was told and destroyed what would no doubt be highly useful information. However, in his later years, Frank Keeney spent many evenings sharing stories about the mine wars to his children and grandchildren. While the validity of the accuracy of oral history is disputed by some, the stories Keeney left behind are among the best information at hand. It is encouraging to note that I asked a number of the same questions to Keeney's children and grandchildren at different times and apart from one another and found the answers and accounts from different interviews to be consistent.

7   Edward M. Steel, ed., *The Speeches and Writings of Mother Jones* (Pittsburgh: University of Pittsburgh Press, 1988), 206.

When Frank Keeney returned to Cabin Creek with Mother Jones, the entire struggle altered dramatically. Mother Jones made speeches and rallied the miners. More importantly, she endorsed Frank Keeney as their new leader. The miners would not forget that Frank Keeney, not President Cairns or Thomas Haggerty, brought Mother Jones to Cabin Creek. Keeney enlisted the aid of his friend and fellow striking miner Fred Mooney to help him lead.[8] Together, these two men spearheaded a movement from the bottom up to wrestle away control of the strike, and eventually the union itself, from the district officials. Frank Keeney and Fred Mooney were radical, militant Socialists, and what began as a strike with national union interests quickly evolved into a social movement, meticulously led by Keeney and Mooney. Historians have debated the extent of Socialist influence on the southern West Virginia miners. The prevailing view maintains that southern West Virginia miners like Keeney only turned to the Socialists for help after the UMWA turned its back on the striking miners in 1912. The rank and file, according to this view, flirted with Socialism but never fully understood or accepted Socialist ideology. According to Corbin:

> They did not speak in a Socialist vocabulary, nor did they call for the establishment of a "Socialist commonwealth" . . . there is little indication that they understood Socialism as a way of life and government and as a means of social salvation.[9]

In his recent book on the Battle of Blair Mountain, Robert Shogan reiterated Corbin's analysis and wrote the following:

> By the time they reached the leadership of District 17, Mooney and Keeney had rejected the ideologies of the left both in theory and practice . . . Keeney, though he had once joined the Socialist Party, after his experiences in dealing with Socialists in the Paint Creek-Cabin Creek Strike, he came to regard them as ineffective and unreliable allies.[10]

While the majority of the coal miners in southern West Virginia were not registered members of the Socialist Party, the rank-and-file leadership ad-

---

8   James and Geraldine Jackson interview.

9   Corbin, *Life, Work, and Rebellion in the Coal Fields*, 240–241.

10   Shogan, *The Battle of Blair Mountain*, 224.

hered strongly to Socialist ideals. Frank Keeney did understand Socialism. His commitment to Socialism began even before the Paint Creek and Cabin Creek strike and continued well into the Great Depression. Keeney first became involved with the Socialist Party in 1904. In 1903, the UMWA attempted an organizing drive on Paint Creek. Keeney, while not participating in the strike, saw the evictions and tent colonies and witnessed the union fire cooling in the winter snows of 1904. The mine guards soon stamped out what sparks of the union remained. While the union went away, the Socialist Party beckoned. The Cabin Creek district contained one of the highest concentrations of Socialist voters in the state. Keeney's hometown of Eskdale, with a Socialist mayor, was at the center of this radical activity. Thus, even before he became a union man, Frank Keeney became a Socialist man.[11]

It was also during these early years that Frank Keeney met a tall, white-haired, radical Socialist by the name of Harold Houston. These two men began a close friendship that would endure the rest of their lives. Houston, for many years the state secretary of the Socialist Party and twice its nominee for governor, believed the only thing preventing Keeney from becoming a great man was his lack of education. Houston became somewhat of a mentor to Keeney, gave him books to read, and encouraged him to study law.[12] By the time of the Paint Creek and Cabin Creek strike, Mooney had also joined the Socialist Party, and both men regularly voted for Socialist candidates.[13]

Keeney and Mooney's involvement with the Socialist Party was a marriage, not an affair. In 1916, Keeney regularly wrote editorials for a Charleston Socialist newspaper, the *Argus-Star*. In a 1916 letter to Keeney, Mooney referred to him as "Comrade Keeney" and ended the letter by writing, "Yours for the Revolution, Fred Mooney."[14] A year later, in step with other Socialists such as Eugene Debs, Keeney, then president of

---

11   Winthrop Lane, *Civil War in West Virginia* (New York: B. W. Huebsch, Inc., 1921), 86; *Labor Argus*, August 25, 1910.

12   Kathleen Keeney and Donna K. Lowery, interview by author, tape recording, Alum Creek, WV, August 14, 1992; Fred Barkey, "Fritz Merrick: Parkersburg Rebel with a Cause," *West Virginia History*, July 1998, 85–87.

13   Fred Barkey, "The Socialist Party in West Virginia from 1898 to 1920" (Ph.D. dissertation: University of Pittsburgh, 1971), 113–118.

14   *Argus-Star*, February 10, 1916, March 30, 1916, and April 13, 1916. Mooney's letter to Keeney appeared in the April 13, 1916, edition of the *Argus-Star*.

District 17 of the UMWA, privately condemned America's declaration of war on Germany. He said, "I hope that any troops that this government sends overseas to fight this rotten war are killed. That is the only thing this country will understand."[15]

Keeney's Socialist views continued on through the Great Depression. In 1931, Keeney formed his own union, the West Virginia Mine Workers, and told his miners that "[t]he tools of production must be returned to the worker and a complete socialization of industry take place before we can have justice." Of the other parties, Keeney said, "If a miner asks you to vote with either of the old parties, ask him to take you to his home. If he does so, look into the starved eyes of his wife, examine his underfed and ragged children. Let him show you what else he has gained by voting for either Republicans or Democrats."[16]

As the 1932 election approached, he told his striking miners, "Now, you all know Norman Thomas. He's a Socialist and we reckon we'll vote for him for president." Someone in the crowd responded, "Not if you run for president, Frank."[17] Clearly, Keeney and Mooney dedicated themselves to Socialist ideals.

Their dedication did not end with mere rhetoric. Once in control of the Paint Creek and Cabin Creek strike, Keeney and Mooney led the miners to war. Keeney first went to Eskdale and appealed to Mayor G. W. Williams

....

15   Fred Barkey, "A History of the Socialist Party in West Virginia," 44. Other scholars who claim that Keeney and Mooney were not committed to their Socialist beliefs cite two quotes. The first comes from Mooney's autobiography, in which he claims that he couldn't "absorb Marx." The second comes from a statement to the press by Keeney during World War I, when he said it was the duty of the UMWA to "eliminate from their organization any group that is preaching their different 'isms.'" But Keeney and Mooney had a habit of pretending to be less radical when it suited their interests. In the same text in which he mentioned not understanding Marx, Mooney also claims that he had no involvement in the Armed March on Logan. Keeney also publicly condemned the march and privately organized it. The evidence seems to indicate that such statements against Socialism were not consistent with the actions of these rank-and-file leaders. See Corbin, *Life Work and Rebellion*, 240–41; Shogan, *Battle of Blair Mountain*, 224.

16   *The West Virginia Mine Workers Bulletin*, February 6, 1931, and May 16, 1931, the William Blizzard Collection, West Virginia Department of Archives and History, Charleston, WV (hereafter cited as the William Blizzard Collection).

17   John Herling, "A Union Santa Claus," *New Leader*, December 26, 1931.

for help. Williams, a Socialist, designated twenty-five special officers to help protect Eskdale and the striking miners from the mine guards. Then, with an organized and militaristic approach, Keeney and Mooney set about turning the striking miners into an armed force, giving them precise directions on when and where to strike. With the Socialist Party supplying guns and ammunition, Keeney and Mooney divided miners into groups of "minutemen"—men designated to attack mine guards and retaliate when attacked. A select group of eleven miners were chosen to carry out special attacks. Known as the "Dirty Eleven," this group was at the heart of the most violent incidents of the strike.[18]

The miners directed all violence towards the mine guards, never toward state militia or civilians. Before the battle at Mucklow in 1913, the miners leaked information to the townspeople that there would be an attack. Families left by train in the two days preceding the battle. Those who stayed behind hid underneath their houses. During the battle, and others like it, the miners attacked from the hillsides with rifles. One miner in each company of minutemen would have a pair of binoculars. This man would spy on the town and point out a mine guard to the miners so that fire could be concentrated on him. Then, the minuteman would search for other targets and the pattern would continue, usually until the miners ran out of ammunition.[19]

The miners often ran low on ammunition because of the frequent skirmishes and the amount of hunting necessary for food. During the three declarations of martial law in 1912 and 1913, the miners could not smuggle ammunition through Eskdale because of the state militia's presence. The militia had, after the first declaration of martial law, arrested Mayor Williams and disbanded the special officers he had assembled to protect the miners. To compensate, miners from Boomer in Fayette County traveled up Morris Creek and over the mountains to Paint Creek and smuggled supplies to the miners. The miners from Boomer, often pro-union Italian immigrants, left bullets, gunpowder, and dynamite at designated spots to be picked up later by minutemen scouts. The miners used the

18   James and Geraldine Jackson interview, *Bluefield Daily Telegraph*, August 15, 1912, and September 5, 1912; Mooney, *Struggle in the Coal Fields*, 29–30.

19   John T. Walton, interview by Michael J. Galgano, May 25, 1976, Oral History of Appalachia, OH-64–0143, Special Collections Division, William E. Morrow Library, Marshall University, Huntington, WV (hereafter cited as OHA).

dynamite to explode railroad tracks and prevent scabs from entering the region. Keeney himself was nearly gunned down one night while attempting to lay dynamite on the tracks.[20]

In 1913, Henry Hatfield, nephew of "Devil Anse" Hatfield of the Hatfield-McCoy feud, became the new governor of West Virginia. Realizing that the fight between the coal operators and the miners had only intensified in the past year, he ordered the two sides to reach an agreement or he would dictate a settlement himself. Despite Hatfield's threat, Cairns and Haggerty stood firm on the miners' demands while the coal operators firmly intended to squash the union. Hatfield then took action. He released the military prisoners held under martial law, gave the union thirty-six hours to end the strike, and dictated his own settlement.[21] The settlement, signed by union officials and the coal operators on May 1, 1913, became known as the Hatfield Contract. It granted the miners a nine-hour work day, which the miners didn't ask for because they were paid by the ton and not by the hour, a two-and-a-half-cent raise per ton, and allowed the miners to hire their own check-weighman. However, the union failed in its effort to gain recognition as the miners' bargaining agent and the mine guards remained. Local headlines announced the conclusion of the strike, and Governor Hatfield, President Cairns, and Thomas Haggerty were congratulated for their bold efforts and compromise.[22] Finally, the bloody conflict had ended. Apparently, someone neglected to tell this to Frank Keeney and Fred Mooney.

Keeney and Mooney not only embodied the rank-and-file element of the strike but the radical element as well. From the time Keeney and Mooney took over the strike, the struggle developed into a more revolutionary movement. The miners grew willing to fight and even kill for their rights and the livelihood of their families. After spending over a year in tents, Keeney and Mooney had no intention of agreeing to a dictated settlement that failed to meet the miners' demands.

20   *Bluefield Daily Telegraph*, September 5, 1912; Dave Tamplin, interview by Stephen W. Brown, April 2, 1973, OHA, OH-64–0040; James and Geraldine Jackson interview.

21   Joseph Platania, "Three Sides to the Story: Governor Hatfield and the Mine Wars," *The Goldenseal Book of the West Virginia Mine Wars*, Ken Sullivan, ed. (Charleston, WV: Pictorial Histories Publishing Company, 1991), 23–24.

22   Platania, "Three Sides to the Story," 23–24; *Huntington Herald-Dispatch*, May 3, 1913.

Governor Hatfield, Cairns, and Haggerty not only recognized and feared this radical upsurge sweeping through the coal camps; they blamed it on Socialist agitation. After the implementation of the Hatfield Contract, Governor Hatfield shut down two local Socialist newspapers, the *Socialist and Labor Star* of Huntington and the *Labor-Argus* of Charleston. Disregarding freedom of the press, he believed these newspapers were "inciting to riot and giving aid and comfort to the enemy."[23]

Cairns and Haggerty publicly supported the termination of these newspapers. The editor of the *Labor-Argus*, Charles Boswell, called Haggerty "a traitor and a Judas to the miners" because he had agreed to the Hatfield Contract. Haggerty retorted by blaming the *Labor-Argus* for many of the problems in the strike district and went on to say that the Hatfield Contract was accepted by "an exceedingly large delegation of miners from the entire strike zone."[24] Keeney and Mooney would soon prove Haggerty's claim incorrect. Quietly, almost nonchalantly, Keeney and Mooney led the miners back into the hills. Yet the strike zone remained quiet for nearly two months. Then, on the evening of July 7, gunfire exploded into the Ohley mining camp just a few miles from Eskdale. Throughout the rest of the night and the following two weeks, squads of minutemen emerged from the thickly forested hillsides at different points along Cabin Creek and peppered the towns with gunfire. Turmoil had returned to Cabin Creek, and it became evident to everyone involved that the union officials had no control over the miners.[25] In a public statement, Haggerty said, "I am reasonably certain that a 'dark horse' is responsible for these petty differences between operators and members of our organization recently."[26]

Cairns and Haggerty retaliated against this "dark horse" by threatening to revoke the UMWA membership of any strikers who refused to return to work. Yet the strikers remained in the hills and continued their guerrilla warfare until the end of July. Union officials also created the *Montgomery*

---

23 *Beckley Messenger*, May 13, 1913. State militia not only shut down the newspapers, but they also destroyed their printing equipment and the most recent addition of the papers before they could be distributed. Charles Boswell, the editor of the *Labor-Argus*, was also arrested. Boswell would later allow Keeney to write editorials in the paper when it restarted under the name "the *Argus-Star.*"

24 *Fayette Tribune*, June 5, 1913.

25 *Huntington Herald-Dispatch*, July 9 and 10, 1913.

26 *Fayette Tribune*, September 18, 1913.

Miners Herald, a pro-union newspaper that praised the local union officials, denounced Keeney and Mooney, and veered away from Socialist rhetoric. But the Socialist tide had already swept over the miners. In the newly founded District 29 in West Virginia (located in the Beckley area), the first elected officers were all recognized Socialists. Even the coal operators attempted to stem this tide by creating the Operators Protective Association of Southern West Virginia, which raised a defense fund of one million dollars to "oppose the growth of Socialism among their mines and employees."[27]

Significantly, Frank Keeney and Fred Mooney spearheaded this radical movement among the miners of southern West Virginia. The Cabin Creek and Paint Creek miners accepted the leadership of the rank and file over the union officials. By the end of July, the coal operators, unable to employ mine guards because of a Senate Investigative Committee sent to Cabin Creek by the federal government, capitulated to the miners' demands.[28] Keeney and Mooney had led the miners to victory. Here we find the heart of the violent, radical movement in southern West Virginia. Specifically directed by Keeney and Mooney, the miners took direct action to achieve their goals. Over the next three years, Keeney and Mooney sought to consolidate power within District 17. After proving that Cairns and Haggerty had secretly owned stock in the local coal companies, new elections were held. In 1917, the "dark horse" rose to power. Keeney was elected district president, while Mooney became the secretary-treasurer.[29]

Now in control of UMWA District 17, Keeney and Mooney could use the power of their new positions to steer the miners toward a more militant movement. In the first three months of his presidency, Keeney named Harold Houston the official attorney of District 17, conducted over one hundred local meetings, added over two thousand members to the union, and organized twelve new local districts. He also negotiated a new wage contract for District 17 that the *United Mine Workers Journal* called, "the best contract of the previous twenty years."[30]

27 *Fayette Tribune,* May 5, 1913, and September 25, 1913; *Montgomery Miners Herald,* September–October 1913; *Huntington Herald-Dispatch,* July 12–29, 1913.

28 *Huntington Herald-Dispatch,* July 16 and 30, 1913.

29 Mooney, *Struggle in the Coal Fields,* 41–50. Mooney gives a detailed narrative of the fall of Cairns and Haggerty from 1913 through 1916, as well as Keeney's and his own rise to power. Also see *The United Mine Workers Journal,* January 4, 1917.

30 *The United Mine Workers Journal,* March 15 and April 26, 1917.

However, portions of the state remained stubbornly antiunion. After the First World War, Keeney and Mooney began an aggressive campaign to organize Logan, Mingo, and McDowell counties. Soon thereafter, the Mine Wars erupted again, bloodier than ever. The Battle of Matewan, between Sid Hatfield, striking miners, and the Baldwin-Felts detectives, which left ten people dead, the Three Day Battle of the Tug, and the state militia's attack on the Lick Creek tent colony are the most well-known outbreaks of violence in 1920 and 1921 that embody the desperation and brutality of the struggle. Contemporaries blamed the violence on Bolshevism, moonshine, and the violent, savage nature of mountaineer coal miners. Such stereotypes and shallow conclusions still resonate today. In a 2004 article concerning the Scots-Irish of Appalachia, James Webb argued that the birth of the modern redneck came from Scots-Irish culture in southern Appalachia, that theirs is a "culture founded on guns" and prone to violence, and that they are "naturally rebellious, often impossible to control."[31] Keeney and Mooney both hailed from a Scots-Irish heritage, and their followers used guns and were nearly impossible to control. But the reasons for militant radicalism in the southern West Virginia coalfields go deeper than the cultural traits of the southern Appalachian people. Class ideology, economic disparity, and injustice drove Keeney and Mooney, and these leaders drove the union movement. From Charleston, or occasionally by sneaking into the strike zone when necessary, Keeney and Mooney privately directed the violence while publicly condemning it.

One of the best sources for information during this period comes from the Baldwin-Felts detectives themselves. Thomas Felts, head of the Baldwin-Felts Detective Agency in 1920 and 1921, hired a secret agent for each mine in Logan, Mingo, and McDowell counties. The agent posed as a worker and wrote weekly updates to Felts. These operatives attended union meetings and crawled under company houses and listened to conversations of the miners and their families.[32] Letters to Felts, sometimes anonymous or identified by a number such as Operative #9 or #16, demonstrate conclusively that Fred Mooney made regular secret trips into Matewan and McDowell counties. Mooney specifically directed violent activities

---

31 For the most detailed accounts of the violence during this period, as well as the union's organizational push into Logan, Mingo, and McDowell counties, see Lon Savage, *Thunder in the Mountains*. Also see James Webb, "Why You Need to Know the Scots-Irish," *Parade*, October 3, 2004, 5.

32 Anonymous interview with Henry Warden, July 18, 1983, the Felts Papers.

and organized new miners. Other letters reveal that the union leadership in Charleston sent funds and ammunition directly to Matewan's famous chief of police, Sid Hatfield. Before the Three Days Battle at Merrimac in May 1921, the UMWA sent funds directly to Hatfield. Before the Three Days Battle of the Tug, the union leadership arranged for ten thousand rounds of ammunition to be sent to Hatfield for use in the battle.[33]

While Mooney worked on McDowell and Mingo counties, Keeney directed his attention to Logan County with the help of another Hatfield. "Devil Anse" Hatfield, famous for his leading role in the Hatfield-McCoy feud, was a union sympathizer. More accurately, Hatfield hated Don Chafin, the sheriff of Logan County who was on the payroll of the coal operators. Hatfield also hated the coal companies themselves, who mined beneath the Mingo County land that his family once owned. To spite his enemies, Hatfield offered Keeney his help. The Hatfields lived near the strike zone, which put them in position to aid the union. During the night, Keeney went into the strike zone on horseback. Eventually, one of the Hatfields would meet and escort Keeney to Devil Anse's home. Strikers used light signals with lanterns to indicate whether or not Keeney's route was clear of mine guard patrols. Because of the frequency of the patrols, Keeney never came in and out the same way.[34]

Once at the Hatfield home, Keeney and Devil Anse sat on the front porch and drank moonshine together while Devil Anse supplied Keeney with information. Hatfield let Keeney know where the mine guards were putting their machine gun emplacements, how many men and how much material they had, and if any attacks were planned in the near future. Devil Anse also smuggled Keeney into Logan County so that Keeney could personally help organize miners and give instructions to them. Because of the number of death threats that Keeney received during this time, Devil Anse would send some of his "boys" to guard Keeney's family at his house on Charleston's west side. Geraldine, Keeney's daughter, recalled watching the Hatfield "boys" toting rifles and pistols as they patrolled by her bedroom window at night.[35]

33   Operative #9 to Felts, February 1, 1921; unsigned letters to Felts, August 9, 1920, June 29, 1921, and July 8, 1921; anonymous report on Sid Hatfield, August 1921, the Felts Papers.

34   James and Geraldine Jackson interview, C. B. Keeney, interview by author, June 28, 2000, Alum Creek, WV.

35   James and Geraldine Jackson interview. To protect his home, Keeney also gave

The measure of control that Keeney and Mooney exercised over the miners during the Mine Wars is best exemplified through the two armed marches of 1919 and 1921. In September 1919, rumors circulated that women and children had become victims of the rising violence in Logan County. In response, about five thousand armed miners assembled at Lens Creek, just south of Charleston, and prepared to march to Logan County. Keeney, at a union meeting in Fairmont, received a telegram from Governor John J. Cornwell asking him to hurry to Lens Creek and stop the marchers.[36]

Keeney went to Lens Creek but soon thereafter rushed to the capital to tell the governor that his attempt had failed. Cornwell asked him to try again. Frank Keeney returned to the scene and again "failed." Mooney called the governor and asked him to come to Lens Creek himself. The governor did so and, with Keeney behind him, addressed the crowd and promised to personally investigate the conditions in Logan County. The miners shot their guns into the air to salute the governor and dispersed.[37]

Governor Cornwell credited Keeney with playing a key role in stopping the 1919 march. However, other evidence suggests that Keeney himself organized the march. John L. Spivak, a New York journalist on assignment in Charleston, had spent several months with the union officials and accompanied Keeney and Mooney when they went to confront the miners. Spivak indicated that a confrontation between Keeney and miners seemed staged because at the end of the "heated" confrontation between Keeney and one of the "leaders" of the miners, Keeney turned back and grinned at the nearby crowd. Many of the miners grinned back. As they drove away, having failed to disperse the mob, Spivak told them how amazing it seemed that all those miners would just "spontaneously" arrive at an appointed place and at an appointed time. Sitting between them in the car, Spivak said, "There must be a lot of telepathy in these hills." Keeney and Mooney silently glanced at each other and then burst into laughter. Mooney patted him on the shoulder. "There sure is," he said.[38]

---

his wife, Elizabeth, a revolver and insisted that she keep it under her pillow at night when he was gone. Keeney's ventures into Logan County often lasted two or three days at a time.

36 Lane, *Civil War in West Virginia*, 104–07.

37 Lane, *Civil War in West Virginia*, 104–07.

38 John L. Spivak, *A Man in His Time* (New York: Horizon Press, 1967), 67–71.

Keeney and Mooney wanted to make a dramatic demonstration that would force the state government to act on behalf of the miners. The union leadership had direct control over the actions of these miners and had the power to disperse them at any time they wished. Spivak had noted that in the days preceding the march, Harold Houston spent a great deal of time at district headquarters. He also noted the presence of a conspicuous look-ing man with a peg leg who met privately with Keeney in his office several times within a week of the march. This conspicuous man was Lawrence "Peg Leg" Dwyer, a radical union organizer known for smuggling guns to the miners. Dwyer had been a close ally of Keeney since the days of the Paint Creek and Cabin Creek strike. The presence of Keeney's old radical allies at district headquarters just before the attempted march has obvious meaning. Keeney gave the orders while Dwyer and Houston distributed them among the miners. Then, for the sake of appearances, Keeney and Mooney headed for Fairmont, about 125 miles north of Charleston, just before the miners began to assemble. By making the march seem like a spontaneous event carried out by the miners themselves, the union lead-ers dramatized the situation in their favor. These miners were responding to injustice; if the government didn't act, war might ensue.[39]

Keeney's two "failures" to persuade the miners to go home are also of importance. It is interesting that Keeney twice seemed unable to stop five thousand miners from marching in 1919, yet with one speech in 1921, he was able to stop over ten thousand miners from continuing the march when they were within just a few miles of Blair Mountain, the border of Logan County. During the 1921 march, the two union leaders were sum-moned by Brigadier General H. H. Bandholz and told to call off the march or face intervention by the U.S. Army. The leaders then rushed to Madison and called a meeting with the marchers after which the miners began to turn back. The march continued on only after a shootout between miners and mine guards in Sharples after the Madison meeting.[40]

Thus, Keeney and Mooney recognized the most prudent time for the miners to heed their advice. The union leaders wanted to make the situ-ation appear out of their hands and, therefore, pretended they could not persuade the miners to disband without Cornwell's help. Nevertheless, the

39 Spivak, *A Man in His Time*, 67–71; James and Geraldine Jackson interview. For more information on Lawrence Dwyer, see Lee, *Bloodletting in Appalachia*, 199.

40 For the most detailed narrative of Keeney's 1921 Ballpark Speech, see Savage, *Thunder in the Mountains*, 86–89.

governor's promise to investigate the situation in the southern counties proved a shallow one. For even though Cornwell appointed a commission to investigate the counties, that proved to be the last action he took to rectify the situation.[41]

Some time later in McDowell County, Sid Hatfield and fellow union sympathizer Ed Chambers prepared to stand trial for their alleged involvement in a shootout in Mingo County. Harold Houston, the union's official attorney, prepared their defense. On their walk up the courthouse steps, Hatfield and Chambers met their deaths at the hands of Baldwin-Felts detectives. Riddled with bullets in front of their wives, Hatfield and Chambers instantly transformed from heroes into martyrs.[42] One week later, on August 7, 1921, five thousand miners met at the state capitol in Charleston. Mother Jones and the union leadership all spoke before the inflamed crowd. Keeney's most famous quote summarized the mood: "You have no recourse except to fight. The only way you can get your rights is with a high powered rifle!"[43]

The next day, Harold Houston sent a letter to the local union at Lens Creek. Houston assured the miners that guns were on their way and money was being pulled from the union's special "funeral fund" to aid in the coming march. Houston also notified the recipients of the letter to destroy it upon reading it. Fortunately, the letter was not destroyed and some years later was discovered in the attic of union leader, Bill Blizzard. Also resurfacing was Lawrence "Peg Leg" Dwyer. From Beckley, he secretly delivered an old machine gun and three thousand rounds of ammunition to the miners. As demonstrated before, when Houston and Dwyer were present, Keeney and Mooney were somewhere nearby.[44]

Keeney and Mooney decided to finish what they started in 1919. The union leaders became convinced that the state government, controlled by the money of the coal operators, would not help them. Perhaps if the miners could capture the attention of the entire nation and make Americans see their plight, public opinion would demand government intervention

41   Lane, *Civil War in West Virginia*, 108–109.

42   *Huntington Herald-Dispatch*, August 2, 1921.

43   Lee, *Bloodletting in Appalachia*, 96. Lee actually attended this meeting and gives a firsthand account of the proceedings.

44   Lee, *Bloodletting in Appalachia*, 96; letter from Harold Houston to Lens Creek local, August 8, 1921, William Blizzard Collection.

on behalf of the miners. In order to get the attention of the country, Keeney and Mooney needed an act bigger and more dramatic than in 1919. The miners would have to go all the way to Logan County, and Keeney knew they would be willing because union miners all over the state were in a fit of perpetual rage. The ill feelings harbored against the mine guards and coal operators over the past three decades had reached a climax. Now was the appropriate time. But who would direct the miners in the field? Keeney himself could not lead the march because it needed to appear as a spontaneous action led by the miners. The public knew Frank Keeney too well, and he needed to be in Charleston, ready to speak with reporters. He would condemn the violence in public, direct the violence in private, and tell the miners' story of oppression to anyone who would listen.[45] Mooney was also too well known to lead the march. Keeney needed someone known by the miners but not known to the general public. He needed someone he trusted. He needed Bill Blizzard.

In 1921 Bill Blizzard, from Cabin Creek, served as president of Sub-District No. 2. He and Keeney became good friends in the years leading up to the 1921 march. Keeney had known Blizzard's parents, who served as union organizers, since the Paint Creek and Cabin Creek strike. Young Blizzard had grown in prominence since that time, and by 1919 he had passed adolescence. Energetic, feisty, and hot-tempered, Blizzard and Keeney shared similar characteristics. From 1919 to 1921, Blizzard spent a great deal of time at union headquarters in Charleston. He had become well known by the miners of southern West Virginia and would emerge as one of the most prominent union leaders in the decades to come.[46]

Keeney approached Blizzard about the march. He wanted Blizzard to be in charge of the miners from Marmet to Blair. Keeney and Mooney would organize the affair, making sure the miners had supplies and that they assembled at the appropriate times and places. Blizzard would guide the

45 James and Geraldine Jackson interview, *New York Times*, August 25, August 26, and September 3, 1921. Keeney invited numerous out-of-state reporters to join him as he made his way to Madison to "stop" the march. While reporters listened, he spoke freely of the march, simultaneously condemning the violence and emphasizing the plight of the miners.

46 William Blizzard Jr., telephone interview by author, tape recording, Alum Creek, WV, June 15, 2000.

marchers along and make sure the march proceeded according to plan. In addition, he could send informants back to district headquarters as the marchers made progress. Blizzard agreed. The miners would depart Marmet on August 24.[47]

Before the miners could depart from Marmet, however, Mother Jones, sent by John L. Lewis, arrived and implored them to abandon their undertaking. This was a departure for Mother Jones, who had supported the violence of the Paint Creek and Cabin Creek strike. In this famous incident, she claimed to hold a telegram from President Warren G. Harding. The telegram promised that if the miners disbanded, he would personally look into the conflict. The telegram was a fraud and Keeney and Mooney knew it. Keeney told the miners to ignore the telegram. The miners loved Mother Jones, but they were loyal to Frank Keeney and Fred Mooney. The miners marched.[48]

The resulting Armed March on Logan and the Battle of Blair Mountain remains one of the largest domestic uprisings in American labor history. Fitting well into the rank and file's ideology, the battle lines were drawn heavily along class lines. Middle-class citizens and veterans rushed from Charleston and Huntington to join Don Chafin's antiunion army while unionists and radicals from other states traveled to West Virginia to join the march. Even along racial lines, class seemed to take precedence. The middle-class organization, the Bureau of Negro Welfare and Statistics, worked to discourage black miners from joining the march, but most of the black miners ignored the Bureau and marched on. Such allegiances based on class must have confirmed the fears of many Americans: that the West Virginia union leadership was indeed what former West Virginia governor John J. Cornwell called a "mysterious radical influence" that con-

47 James and Geraldine Jackson interview, Melvin Triolo, interview by John Hennen, July 27, 1989, Matewan Oral History Project, 660–094, Special Collections Division, William E. Morrow Library, Marshall University, Huntington, WV. Triolo, who worked under Blizzard for a number of years, believed that Keeney manipulated Blizzard into leading the marchers in the field so that Blizzard would be the "sacrificial lamb" if things went wrong.

48 *Huntington Herald-Dispatch*, August 24, 1921. Jones's most recent biographer, Elliot Gorn, explains Jones's actions by saying she "feared the miners were walking into a trap, that they could not win this fight, that marching against state and federal troops would be seen as treason." This seems a very reasonable explanation. See Gorn, *Mother Jones*, 273.

trolled the miners and was bent on overthrowing the government and establishing a Socialist commonwealth.[49]

There would, of course, be consequences for arousing such fear. Federal troops soon intervened, and the miners surrendered en masse before they could break through Don Chafin's defenses atop Blair Mountain. Keeney, Mooney, Blizzard, and 525 marchers were charged with murder, conspiracy to commit murder, accessory to murder, and treason. The jury found Blizzard not guilty. Keeney's trial was transferred twice and finally dismissed by the discouraged coal operators. Mooney was never tried. In 1924, because of his disapproval of the Armed March, and because of Keeney and Mooney's radicalism, UMWA President John L. Lewis forced Keeney and Mooney to resign from their union positions. Blizzard left the union temporarily but returned in 1931, and was eventually appointed to the presidency of District 17 by Lewis.[50]

The enduring legacy of the West Virginia Mine Wars lies partially in the fact that they were so intensely militant and violent over such a long period of time. The struggle in West Virginia began with a higher ante than many other labor struggles across the United States. The survival of the UMWA and the West Virginia Coal Operators depended upon the outcome. Yet, the heart of the militant radicalism of the West Virginia Mine Wars lies with the radical rank-and-file leadership. This leadership, beginning with the Paint Creek and Cabin Creek strike, wrestled power away from state union officials and pursued its own agenda. To achieve this agenda, union leaders Frank Keeney, Fred Mooney, and later Bill Blizzard masterminded nearly all of the direct action employed from the summer of 1912 to the summer of 1921. In the light of the aforementioned evidence, what began as a struggle with national labor implications developed into a uniquely West Virginian affair. The rank and file would not have had it any other way.

But these conclusions beg the question: why were the union leaders so set upon a militant course of action? Why were they so radical? The mine guard system and the company towns again surface as the easy ex-

---

49 Savage, *Thunder in the Mountains*, 114–118; Joe Trotter, "Black Migration to Southern West Virginia," *Transnational West Virginia*, 145; and Shogan, *The Battle of Blair Mountain*, 8.

50 Lee, *Bloodletting in Appalachia*, 104; Savage, *Thunder in the Mountains*, 165–166; and Charles B. Keeney, "A Union Man: The Biography of C. Frank Keeney" (master's thesis: Marshall University, 2000), 47–48.

planation. While that explanation cannot be discounted, one other factor must be considered. Aside from their coal-mining backgrounds, Keeney, Mooney, and Blizzard all shared one common characteristic—all three of them came from families who had their land taken from them in the previous generation by the coal companies.[51] The bitter residue left from this particular injustice undoubtedly helped sow the radical seeds that drove Keeney and Mooney to Socialism, to direct action, and to orchestrate some of the bloodiest acts in American labor history. Injustice and economic disparity lead groups to radicalism far more often than cultural ethnic traits. The experiences of the union leadership in West Virginia fed their radicalism while the notion that their radicalism originated from cultural traits was an invention imposed by outside industrialists and journalists. The "rednecks" of West Virginia, as defined by contemporary writers and industrialists, threatened the security of America while the "rednecks," as defined by the miners themselves, were an oppressed group who looked to radicalism for their social salvation.

Other native West Virginia families lent significant support to the union leadership during this period. As demonstrated earlier in this study, the Hatfield family, one of the oldest and most prominent West Virginia families, aided Keeney and Mooney in their efforts to achieve unionization through direct action. Additionally, the miners who followed Keeney and Mooney during the Mine Wars were mostly West Virginians. In 1913, native workers made up 46.4 percent of the total number of miners employed in West Virginia while imported workers made up 53.6 percent. But in the most violent areas of southern West Virginia, the proportions were very different. In 1913, white natives made up 85.6 percent of the miners in Kanawha County, where the Paint Creek and Cabin Creek strike occurred. By comparison, in each of the other five largest mining counties in 1913— Marion, Harrison, Fayette, McDowell, and Raleigh counties—less than 50 percent of the miners were native-born. These counties saw no industrial

---

51   The following sources elaborate on the taking of land by the coal companies and its significance to Keeney, Mooney, and Blizzard: Roscoe C. Keeney Jr., *2,597 Keeney Relatives* (Parsons, WV: McClain Printing Company, 1978), 6–10; Corbin, *Life, Work, and Rebellion in the Coal Fields*, 4–8; Mooney, *Struggle in the Coal Fields*, 1–8; Shae Ronald Davidson, "The Boys'll Listen to Me: The Labor Career of William Blizzard," unpublished master's thesis: Marshall University, 1998, 1–15; C. B. Keeney interview; Edmund Wilson, "Frank Keeney's Coal Diggers," *The New Republic*, July 8, 1931, 195–199.

violence during the same time. The tie between Frank Keeney and the Kanawha County miners is unmistakable. As late as 1931, when Keeney created his own union, the West Virginia Mine Workers, almost all of the union's twenty-four thousand members worked in Kanawha County. In 1922, the second phase of the Mine Wars, natives made up 54.1 percent of the state's miners. In the most violent county of the time, "Bloody Mingo," the number was 77.6 percent. While black migrants and immigrant workers, particularly Italians, certainly contributed to the union movement in West Virginia, these figures demonstrate that native West Virginians played a significantly larger role in participating in and dictating the militant direct action during the West Virginia Mine Wars.[52]

Frank Keeney once stated, "We are mountaineers, but above all we are working men who understand the feelings and sentiments of workers."[53] Classified as violent, uncivilized rednecks and dangerous radicals by many Americans, they were deemed a threat to the established power structure in post–World War I America. Indeed, they did present a threat. Keeney, Mooney, Houston, and Blizzard, of course, did not call for a Socialist revolution and the overthrow of the American government during the Armed March of 1921. Nonetheless, they were driven by a sort of Americanized Socialist ideology that sought to secure the miners the constitutional rights denied them by the coal operators and mine guard system while simultaneously restructuring the economic balance of power by nationalizing the industry, engaging in sustained collective bargaining, and returning wealth to citizens of a state that had lost control over their land and resources. In this sense, the term "redneck" dons a new meaning and may be more appropriately applied to the rank and file for both the heritage of injustice they endured and the political views they held.

These rank-and-file rednecks who ran District 17 during the Mine Wars grew apart as the years progressed, and their crucial role in shaping the labor movement in West Virginia faded. Harold Houston retired from his law practice and moved to Florida in the late 1930s. He died there within a few years. Fred Mooney worked with Keeney during the formation of the West Virginia Mine Workers in 1931. The two remained friends until

52 State Department of Mines, *Annual Reports*, 1913 and 1922. For details on the West Virginia Mine Workers, see C. Belmont Keeney, "The Last Mine War: Frank Keeney and the West Virginia Mine Workers Union, 1931–33," *The Mountain Messenger* (December 2000), 2–13.

53 *Argus-Star*, March 30, 1916.

Mooney shot himself in 1952. Some claim that he had tried, but failed, to kill his wife, and had committed suicide to cover up his crime; the man that Frank Keeney had called "crazy mean" died under circumstances as strange as his reputation. Lawrence "Peg Leg" Dwyer remained active in the union movement in both West Virginia and eastern Kentucky, but he lost contact with the District 17 officials after the 1930s.[54]

Bill Blizzard served as president of District 17 during the forties and fifties. Blizzard, like Keeney, had his own conflict with Lewis, though not in the form of a dual union. Blizzard punched Lewis's younger brother for allegedly reading his mail. John L. Lewis then summoned Blizzard to Illinois and told him he would not be fired. Instead, Lewis offered him a pension of four hundred dollars a month if Blizzard agreed to retire. He did agree to Lewis's terms but never received any pension from the UMWA. On his deathbed in 1958, Blizzard told his friends that if he could have lived his life over, he would never had supported John L. Lewis.[55]

Frank Keeney outlived them all. After his independent union, the West Virginia Mine Workers, disbanded in 1933, Keeney worked with the Progressive Miners of America until the late 1930s. After several failed business ventures, Keeney ended up as a parking lot attendant in downtown Charleston. He died in 1970 at the age of eighty-eight, believing himself and his comrades to be forgotten warriors in the state's labor movement. However, the radicalism and militarism of the rank and file had not been forgotten by many miners. To the great surprise of Keeney's family, dozens of elderly miners attended his funeral in Belle, West Virginia. Many of them shed tears and told stories about Keeney, Mooney, and Blizzard to his family members. One elderly man approached C. B. Keeney Jr., Frank Keeney's grandson and my father, and told him what a great leader Keeney had been and what his life had meant to the union in West Virginia. C. B. Keeney reflected on the man's comments and said, "You must've thought a lot of him." The old man smiled. "Son," he said, "we killed men for him." The old man then turned and hobbled away. He had a peg leg.[56]

54 James and Geraldine Jackson interview; Charles Payne interview, Oral History of Appalachia; Howard B. Lee, *Bloodletting in Appalachia*, 114–115, 199.

55 Melvin Triolo, interview by John Hennen, July 27, 1989, Matewan Oral History Project, 660–094, Special Collections Division, William E. Morrow Library, Marshall University, Huntington, WV.

56 *Charleston Gazette*, May 23, 1970; Kathleen Keeney and Donna K. Lowery interview, C. B. Keeney, interview by author, Alum Creek, WV, June 28, 2000.

THE OVERLOOKED SUCCESS:

A RECONSIDERATION OF THE U.S. MILITARY INTERVENTIONS IN MEXICO DURING THE WILSON PRESIDENCY

Mark Mulcahey

T HE EVENTS OF SEPTEMBER 11, 2001, however horrific in scale, were not the first instance in which the United States stood paralyzed in the wake of a terrorist attack against U.S. citizens on U.S. soil. While a near unanimity of the American populace initially entrusted President George W. Bush with either the capture or death of Osama bin Laden, they made similar demands of President Woodrow Wilson in the case of the outlaw/revolutionary leader Francisco "Pancho" Villa. The raid led by Pancho Villa on the town of Columbus, New Mexico, on March 9, 1916, transfixed Americans and came perilously close to ensnaring Mexico and the United States in a state of war. Villa attacked Columbus with the intention of fermenting a war between the United States and Mexico. Fearful of being enmeshed in a war with Mexico while attempting to avoid the conflict in Europe, President Wilson used military force with utmost precision in order to forestall such an occurrence.

President Wilson did not intend to use military force in Mexico in order to make the Mexican people more tractable to U.S. aims, but simply to restore security along the U.S.-Mexican border so as to safeguard border communities from guerilla attacks. Unlike his objectives at Versailles following World War I, Wilson did not possess an exalted purpose in ordering the military to intervene in Mexico during his tenure in office. Instead, Wilson ascertained the problem and prescribed a defined solution, thereby disentangling the United States from becoming embroiled in a grim predicament with a bordering country.

On January 19, 1917, Major General John J. Pershing, commander of the forces of the U.S. Punitive Expedition in Mexico, received an order from the headquarters of the Southern Department of the U.S. Army, directing him that it was: "the intention of the [U.S.] government to withdraw his command from Mexico at an early date."[1] The following day after getting this order, Pershing wrote a bitter letter to his father-in-law, U.S. Senator Francis E. Warren (R-WY). Pershing observed in this letter that "when the true history of this Expedition, especially the diplomatic side of it, is written it will not be a very inspiring chapter for school children or even grown-ups to contemplate."[2] Though willing to convey his frustrations to his father-in-law that after crossing the border into Mexico "with the intention of eating the Mexicans raw . . . [and then] turn[ing] back at the very first repulse and . . . sneaking home under cover like a whipped cur with his tail between his legs" to family and close friends, Pershing refrained from disclosing his dissatisfaction concerning the conduct of the expedition publicly.[3] The expedition's inability to capture Francisco "Pancho" Villa, initially the prime objective of the expedition, caused Pershing to reflect sullenly upon this shortcoming for the rest of his life.[4]

....

1   John J. Pershing, "Report of General John J. Pershing on the Mexican Punitive Expedition, July 1, 1916 to February 5, 1917," Records of the Adjutant General's Office, RG 94, National Archives and Records Service, G.P.O., Washington, DC, microfilm copy in Dartmouth College Library.

2   Pershing to Senator Warren, January 20, 1917, John J. Pershing Papers, Manuscript Division, Library of Congress, Washington, DC, Box 426.

3   The closest Pershing ever came to expressing publicly his displeasure regarding the Punitive Expedition was a brief statement in his memoirs describing that "the increasing disapproval of the Mexican Government doubtless caused the administration to conclude that it would be better to rest content that the outlaw bands had been severely punished and generally dispersed, and that the people of Northern Mexico had been taught a salutary lesson." Pershing to Warren, January 20, 1917, Pershing Papers, Box 426; John J. Pershing, *My Experience in the World War*, vol. 1 (New York: Frederick A. Stokes Co., 1931).

4   Pershing recorded observations in a 1934 memo book with the possible intention

Initially, there was minimal public dissatisfaction with the Punitive Expedition's failure to capture Pancho Villa, but the passage of time caused most of its participants, and U.S. historians, to regard the operation with mixed sentiments. The more pessimistic commentators state "that the Punitive Expedition was doomed to failure,"[5] "served little more than to escalate the diplomatic and military tensions between the two countries,"[6] and was "an improper application of military persuasive force."[7] The optimistic accounts commonly acknowledge the failure to capture Villa, but they argue that the expedition gave the U.S. Army "invaluable field experience with troops,"[8] "forged a General of the Armies and produced a cadre for two world wars."[9] A common theme present in most accounts of Pershing's attempt to capture Villa was President Woodrow Wilson's acquiescence to the demands of Venustiano Carranza, the *de facto* President of Mexico, causing the U.S. Army to be "hobbled" in its pursuit of Villa.[10]

Wilson did not believe it necessary for the U.S. military to occupy Mexico in order for that country to achieve stability. The guiding principle Wilson employed in formulating his Mexican policy was the conviction that the Mexican people were capable of republican self-government. Wilson re-

---

of writing another autobiography detailing his experiences before the First World War. On the pages for Tuesday, January 2 through Wednesday, January 3, Pershing wrote this passage: "Memo—Do not fail to emphasize the certainty of the capture of Villa if we had not been recalled toward the border. Look up every scrap of evidence to that effect and give Villa's statement made later confirming it if such statement can be located" (Pershing Papers, Box 460).

5   Carlo D'Este, *Patton: A Genius for War* (New York: HarperCollins, 1995), 177.

6   Joseph A. Stout Jr., *Border Conflict: Villistas, Carrancistas, and the Punitive Expedition, 1915–1920* (Fort Worth: Texas Christian University Press, 1999), 1.

7   Benjamin D. Foulois and Colonel C. V. Glines (USAF), *From the Wright Brothers to the Astronauts: The Memoirs of Major General Benjamin D. Foulois* (New York: McGraw-Hill, 1968), 133.

8   Herbert Malloy Mason Jr., *The Great Pursuit* (New York: Random House, 1970), 231.

9   Haldeen Braddy, *Pershing's Mission in Mexico* (El Paso: Texas Western Press, 1966), 66.

10   Colonel Frank Tompkins, *Chasing Villa: The Story Behind the Story of Pershing's Expedition into Mexico* (Harrisburg, PA: The Military Service Publishing Co., 1934), 219.

sisted the temptation to intervene directly in Mexican affairs, preferring instead to allow Mexico to experience the growing pains of developing an enduring non-authoritarian government. Wilson's perspective on Mexican affairs gained few supporters in either the United States or Mexico and drew ire from both sides of the border. Wilson's Mexican policy was not without its flaws, but its positive aspects diminished significantly because of the inability of Americans to regard the Mexicans as being anything more than illiterate peons who required an iron fist to temper their innate savagery. This myopic view of Mexico by Americans caused most Mexicans, even those who desired the same outcome for Mexico as did Wilson, to view the possibility of U.S. intervention, however benign, with malevolence.[11]

A subtle, but pertinent aspect to Wilson's use of force was the need to establish legitimacy. Its importance rests in the reality recognized by Wilson, that military interventions frequently need to garner domestic and international support. The lack of initial support and understanding for Wilson's policy of military intervention against Mexico remains relevant today.

Wilson Inherits the Mexican Problem

On February 22, 1913, ten days before Wilson's inauguration, Francisco I. Madero and Jose M. Pino Suarez, the deposed president and vice president of Mexico respectively, were shot and killed during a prison transfer in Mexico City. The Mexican federal government, now led by General Victoriano Huerta, declared that both Madero and Suarez had died in a failed attempt by Maderistas to release both men.[12] Rumors immediately circulated in both Mexico and the United States that the deaths of Madero and Suarez were nothing more than the standard practice of *ley fuega*.[13]

11 For the purposes of this paper, the term "intervention" will denote the willful attempt by one country to interfere in the affairs of another country for the purpose of subjugation.

12 U.S. Department of State, *Papers Relating to the Foreign Relations of the United States, 1913*, "Mr. de la Barra to the Mexican Embassy" (Washington, DC: G.P.O., 1920), 732. Future references to this source will be condensed to *"FRUS*, [year], '[heading],' (p[p].) "x."

13 The English translation of *ley fuega* is "fugitive law;" however, it served also as a

After being informed of the assassinations of Madero and Suarez, president-elect Wilson remarked simply that "it's too bad."[14]

Once sworn into office, however, Wilson shed his reticence. On March 12, 1913, Wilson commented that one of his administration's "chief objects" was to improve U.S. relations with Latin American countries. Without mentioning Huerta or Mexico directly, Wilson declared that the U.S. sought improved relations with countries having "thoughtful leaders of republican government" who recognized "that just government rests always upon the consent of the governed, and that there can be no freedom without order based on law and . . . the public conscience and approval."[15] Wilson had been president for just over a week, and within that time-span, he voiced a course of action defining U.S.-Mexican relations until World War I.

After Madero's assassination, Venustiano Carranza and Pancho Villa formed a counterrevolutionary faction known as the Constitutionalists. Despite the fact that the predominant European nations extended diplomatic recognition to the Huerta government, President Wilson withheld U.S. recognition. Wilson intended to "teach Mexicans the proper methods of self-government."[16] It did not take long for Wilson, the former college

---

euphemistic expression in Mexico referring to the death of a person "while attempting to escape from policy custody." The best English language description of the varying accounts concerning the assassinations of Madero and Suarez and whether or not Huerta was complicit in their deaths is in Michael C. Meyer, *Huerta: A Political Portrait* (Lincoln: University of Nebraska Press), 70–82.

14   "News Shocks Wilson, but President-Elect Declines to Comment on Mexico," *Washington Post*, February 24, 1913, 1.

15   Arthur S. Link, ed., *The Papers of Woodrow Wilson*, vol. 27 (Princeton, NJ: Princeton University Press, 1978), 172. Any further reference to this multi-volume collection will consist of an abbreviated reference to the title, followed by volume and page number(s) (*PWW*, vol. 27, 172).

16   Robert E. Quirk offers a more descriptive assessment of Wilson's mood with regards to Huerta's usurpation of power. Wilson planned to lead "the Mexicans . . . by the nose into Zion." This "Zion" was according to Calhoun "a political paradise bounded on one side by the ideals of the eighteenth century philosophers, on the other by stern Calvinistic piety" (Robert E. Quirk, *An Affair of Honor: Woodrow Wilson and the Occupation of Vera Cruz* [Lexington: University of Kentucky Press, 1962], 2). Calhoun, *Power and Principle*, 39.

professor, to discover that Carranza and Villa were not amenable pupils to instruct.

Carl von Clausewitz's Hidden Influence on Woodrow Wilson

Whatever his reluctance to rely upon military power, Woodrow Wilson acknowledged that a nation's leader sometimes had to resort to force in order to attain national objectives. When the United States became a world power at the beginning of the twentieth century, Wilson observed that the president of the United States could no longer be "a mere domestic officer."[17] The president, according to Wilson, "must stand always at the front of our affairs" and utilize the absolute power of the office to control U.S. foreign policy.[18]

Too often Wilson is disparaged as being vague and hesitant in areas in which he possessed little to no experience prior to becoming president.[19] On the contrary, Wilson formulated a policy for the discriminatory, but significant, use of military force so as to prevent the escalation of minor conflicts from developing into full-scale war. The contemporary application of limited military force by the United States against an antagonist must be acknowledged as being modeled after the U.S. military interventions in Mexico during the Wilson administration.

The possibility of Woodrow Wilson developing his own strategic model regarding the use of military force seems surprising, given that he paid minimal attention to military history and theory. Wilson's most sympathetic biographer, Arthur S. Link, contended that Wilson had "little understanding of the role that force plays in the relations of great powers."[20] But Wilson both scrutinized and admired the leading European statesmen and political philosophers of his time. It is reasonable to hypothesize that he adopted some of their ideas concerning military strategy, tempt-

17 Woodrow Wilson, *Constitutional Government in the United States* (New York: Columbia University Press, 1908), 78.

18 Wilson, *Constitutional Government*, 77–79.

19 George F. Kennan, *The Decision to Intervene* (Princeton, NJ: Princeton University Press, 1958), 12.

20 Link also incorrectly surmised that Wilson had "a near contempt for *Realpolitik*, and the men who made it" (Arthur S. Link, *Wilson: The New Freedom* [Princeton, NJ: Princeton University Press, 1954], 77). This suggestion is befuddling since Wilson greatly respected Otto von Bismarck.

ing one to explore what influence English political leaders and theorists had on Wilson's planning of military matters. This is a barren avenue to investigate, however, as Wilson's high opinion for England's statesmen and political commentators remained confined to exulting the primacy of England's parliamentary system.[21] While Woodrow Wilson praised England's statesmen and its parliamentary government, he did so within the confines of domestic affairs.[22]

Wilson did not allot a significant amount of time and space to foreign and military matters in his writings, but when he did do so, he viewed Germany as the most impressive example. In his writings and speeches concerning Germany's diplomatic and martial prowess, Wilson was particularly impressed by Otto von Bismarck. It was Bismarck's "keenness of insight, clearness of judgment, and promptness of decision" that resulted both in Germany reaching unprecedented heights and in Bismarck becoming the unrivaled statesman of Europe.[23]

Wilson's admiration for Bismarck rebuts critics who belittled Wilson for being a moralist in both foreign policy and the use of military force. Wilson accepted that unscrupulous behavior in foreign policy was inevitable and must be excused when it occurred in the course of safeguarding one's country from external threats; Wilson thus rationalized Bismarck's transgressions committed in the operation of *Realpolitik*. During his presi-

21 Wilson's repeated allusion to England's Parliament in his academic writings attempted to illustrate the conspicuous deficiencies in Congress. While Wilson quoted Gladstone in stating that the "choicest" of men served in the House of Commons, he contrasted Congress as populated by men of lesser distinction who, by "the deadening mechanism of committee government," transformed Congress into such a powerful branch of government that "it had come to exceed its authority as defined by the Constitution" (*PWW*, vol. I, 352). See also Baker, *Woodrow Wilson, Life and Letters: Youth-Princeton, 1856–1910*, 91; Woodrow Wilson, *Congressional Government: A Study in American Politics* (Cleveland: Meridian Publishing, 1956), 54.

22 In his essay "Prince Bismarck" published in the *Nassau Literary Magazine* in November 1877, Wilson readily conceded that the "talents so necessary to the English statesman as a leader of Parliament" did not correspond to the faculties required of a German statesman, particularly when empowered by his Kaiser to "negotiat[e] treaties and organiz[e] armies" (Henry Wilkinson Bragdon, *Woodrow Wilson: The Academic Years* [Cambridge, MA: Belknap Press, 1967], 54; *PWW*, vol. I, 311).

23 *PWW*, vol. I, 307, 311–312.

dency, necessity compelled Wilson to express "an occasional contempt to strict duty" in order to achieve a laudable purpose.[24] Wilson employed the same moral rhetoric regarding his foreign policy goals that he used to propel his domestic agenda, but the realist tactics he utilized to accomplish such aims followed the Bismarck model.

Although Wilson neither wrote nor spoke about the minutiae of military issues, he maintained ironclad views concerning the application of military force to resolve interstate crises. Once more, Wilson tailored his ideology in imitation of the German model. The origins of Wilson's principles can be traced in his authorship of *The State*. In writing *The State*, Wilson tried to provide a comparative history of the forms of government and administrative procedures as practiced by the United States and the leading industrialized nations of Europe.[25] Wilson's description of the German emperor's authority to use military force foretold Wilson's own military interventions as president. Wilson described in *The State* that the emperor's executive authority depended on his "control[ling] the foreign affairs of the Empire and command[ing] its vast military forces."[26] According to the German Constitution, the emperor could use the military within the imperial states only with the active consent of the *Bundesrath*; however, in foreign affairs, the emperor acted as he saw fit.

When he became president, Woodrow Wilson had already settled on both a strategic model to emulate (Bismarck) and an operative context ("the emperor"). Without necessarily being cognizant of the fact, Wilson's strategic thought can be traced back to the writings of Carl von Clausewitz, predominantly his seminal work *On War*. Clausewitz was a major-general in the Prussian Army during the Napoleonic era. Clausewitz's simple definition of war as "an act of force to compel [an] enemy to do [their opponent's] will" would attract the attention of Wilson's "consummate leader."[27] Clausewitz's dictum, that "the political object . . . will thus de-

---

24   *PWW*, vol. I, 327.

25   Wilson's ambitions for *The State* did not exceed its being used as a textbook in political-science college courses; in a moment of self-deprecation, Ray Stannard Baker recorded that Wilson's reference to *The State* as being no more than a "dull fact book." Woodrow Wilson, *The State: Elements of Historical and Practical Politics* (Boston: D.C. Heath, 1895), xxxiv–xxxv; Baker, *Woodrow Wilson, Life and Letters: Youth-Princeton*, 275.

26   Wilson, *The State*, 253.

27   Carl von Clausewitz, *On War*, trans. Michael Howard and Peter Paret (Princeton,

termine both the military objective to be reached and the amount of effort" required, can be perceived in Wilson's directive for U.S. military forces to seize the Mexican port city of Vera Cruz in 1914.

War, according to Clausewitz, had evolved into "a paradoxical trinity—composed of primordial violence, hatred, and enmity . . . the play of chance . . . [and] reason."[28] Clausewitz affirmed that the first part of the trinity represents the degree of support provided by a nation's populace during wartime; "chance," the second part, to reiterate, symbolizes the nation's military. The third component, "reason," as Clausewitz explained it, necessitates that war must no longer remain within the sole purview of the uniformed commander but must also include the political leader as a participant since political objectives define and limit the military aims and the means employed. The U.S. military interventions against Mexico during Wilson's presidency exhibited the infusion of reason by providing parameters to both strategic and operational planning.

It cannot be proven that President Wilson had even heard of Carl von Clausewitz, much less read his works. Wilson's unfamiliarity of Clausewitz notwithstanding, his admiration for Bismarck and the German methodology in foreign affairs exposed Wilson to individuals who had read and fully absorbed the lessons imparted by Clausewitz. B. H. Liddell Hart credited the spread of Clausewitzian theory to the triumphant Prussian military campaigns during the Seven Weeks War (1866) and the Franco-Prussian War (1870–1871). Liddell Hart specifically cited Bismarck and General Helmuth von Moltke, chief of the General Staff of the Prussian Army for both wars, as the rare individuals who read and "appreciated Clausewitz's qualifying remarks."[29] Given his military education and

NJ: Princeton University Press, 1976), 83.

28 Clausewitz, *On War*, 101.

29 B. H. Liddell Hart, *The Revolution in Warfare* (New Haven, CT: Yale University Press, 1947), 68; This observation remains a topic of historical debate for a number of reasons. A notable example is the fact that Bismarck admitted never to have read *On War*. In 1889, Bismarck confessed to "have never read Clausewitz and . . . [knew] little more about him than that he was a meritorious general." It is my assertion that Bismarck's tenacity and political acumen, coupled with his working relationship with Moltke, allowed him to discern Clausewitz's theories. Christopher Bassford disagrees with Liddell Hart's views with regards to the popularity of Clausewitz after the Prussian military victories over Austria and France. Bassford's objections remain moot since he conceded that "there is no internal or external evidence" regarding the increased

experience, Moltke was the more dominant of the two in understanding Clausewitz's military concepts, but it is unlikely that Wilson overlooked Bismarck's unwillingness to cede the primacy of the political purpose to the military objective.[30]

The conflict between military and political considerations remained problematic for Wilson. His outlook on this matter, which proved no different from Bismarck's, followed Clausewitz's recommendation. In a May 17, 1915, political speech given in New York City, President Wilson stated that the appropriate function of the U.S. military was to concern themselves solely to "the mission of America . . . [and] support her policy whatever it is" without attempting to influence the formulation of the policy.[31] Wilson also insisted that "those who represent America sometimes seem perhaps to forget her programs, but the people never forget them." This aside served as a subtle reminder to military personnel who bristled under the restraints placed upon them by their civilian superiors. What further aggravated the relationship between Wilson and his military commanders was his lack of military service and disinterest in military affairs prior to becoming president. Even those officers who established amicable relations with Wilson treated him condescendingly because of his inexperience in martial matters. Brigadier General Hugh L. Scott, who became army chief of staff in 1914, regarded the election of then-Governor Wilson to the presidency in 1912 with trepidation, especially when he considered Wilson's "profound ignorance of persons and things military."[32] Scott,

exposure to Clausewitz following Prussia's military successes. See also Christopher Bassford, *Clausewitz in English: The Reception of Clausewitz in Britain and America, 1815–1945* (Oxford: Oxford University Press, 1994), 35–36; Beatrice Heuser, *Reading Clausewitz* (London: Pimlico, 2002), 59; Peter Paret, "Military Power" *The Journal of Military History* 53:3 (July 1989): 252; Otto Pflanze, *Bismarck and the Development of Germany: The Period of Unification, 1815–1871* (Princeton, NJ: Princeton University Press, 1990), 47 on.

30   During the Franco-Prussian War, Bismarck objected to not being informed of military operations and Moltke's attempt to exclude him from planning future operations. After receiving a direct order from the Kaiser, Moltke rectified his intentional slighting of Bismarck. See Michael Howard, *The Franco-Prussian War: the German invasion of France, 1870–1871* (New York: MacMillan, 1961), 325–326; and Pflanze, *Bismarck and the Development of Germany*, 474–475.

31   *PWW*, vol. 33, 211.

32   Hugh L. Scott, *Some Memories of a Soldier* (New York: The Century Co., 1928),

who maintained a cordial rapport with Wilson, thought the president-elect required an intensive tutorial in military matters so as to avoid making significant blunders.[33] Scott's optimistic estimate of Wilson remained a minority position: the majority of senior officers looked upon their new commander-in-chief with suspicion and contempt.[34]

Wilson's antipathetic relationship with his military commanders was but one shortcoming that afflicted him. William Allen White, an early Wilson biographer, commented that Wilson was an intellectual snob. Wilson's apparent "respect for his intellectual processes begot a certain impatience with duller wits . . . This intellectual attitude contributed many impediments . . . and possibly obscured the clarity of his intentions abroad."[35] The main impediment that Wilson created for himself was that he considered his major advisors, principally Secretary of State William Jennings Bryan and Secretary of War Lindley M. Garrison, to be his intel-

---

468–469.

33 Scott congratulated himself for influencing Wilson's selection of the secretary of war and retention of General Leonard Wood as army chief of staff (Scott, *Some Memories of a Soldier*, 469–471).

34 In Jack C. Lane's biography of General Leonard Wood, he recorded Wood, who was a personal friend of Theodore Roosevelt, referring to Wilson as a "spineless rabbit." Wilson biographer Arthur Link noted that Wilson considered Rear Admiral Bradley A. Fiske, aide for operations, the highest ranking U.S. naval officer in 1913 and the chief military advisor to the secretary of the navy (the creation of the office of chief of naval operations did not occur until 1915), grossly insubordinate; General John J. Pershing was another personal friend of Theodore Roosevelt. In 1903, Roosevelt promoted Pershing from the rank of captain to brigadier general. Pershing, a professed Republican and son-in-law to U.S. Senator Francis E. Warren (R-WY), considered his future prospects while in the service of a Democratic president as "peculiarly dim." E. David Cronon, ed., *The Cabinet Diaries of Josephus Daniels, 1913–1921* (Lincoln: University of Nebraska Press, 1963), 67–68; Jack C. Lane, *Armed Progressive: General Leonard Wood* (San Rafael, CA: Presidio Press, 1978), 174–175; Link, *Wilson: The New Freedom*, 77–78; Frederick Palmer, *John J. Pershing, General of the Armies* (Harrisburg, PA: The Military Service Publishing Co., 1948), 75; See also Frank E. Vandiver, *Black Jack: The Life and Times of John J. Pershing*, vol. 1 (College Station: Texas A&M University Press, 1977), 326–328, 588.

35 William Allen White, *Woodrow Wilson: The Man, His Times, and His Task* (Boston: Houghton Mifflin Co., 1924), 306.

lectual inferiors.[36] This resulted in both U.S. military and foreign policy being created in a vacuum.

Wilson used military power against foreign states seven times, a number unmatched, so far, by any of his successors.[37] Wilson resorted to force only after first attempting to persuade recalcitrant countries to change their atavistic tendencies by their own accord. Wilson rationalized the use of military force against such countries because the United States exemplified "the life of Christian brotherhood and love."[38] Wilson formulated a distinct American foreign policy modeled after John Winthrop's "city upon a hill." While Winthrop sought to establish a godly society for England to emulate, Wilson possessed a more ambitious goal with the United States serving as the moral exemplar for the rest of the world. Wilson did not shy away from forcefully proselytizing American morality abroad with a righteous bayonet.[39]

The Aggravating Success: Occupying Vera Cruz

During his first two years in office, President Wilson consistently refused to recognize the military dictatorship of General Victoriano Huerta. He abstained, however, from the impulse to use military force to unseat Huerta;

36 David F. Houston, Wilson's secretary of agriculture, confirmed that Woodrow Wilson "was contemptuous of ignorant men . . . and sometimes showed it" (Ray Stannard Baker Papers, Manuscript Division, Library of Congress, Washington, DC, Reel 77).

37 The seven instances consist of the U.S. military's occupation of Vera Cruz, Mexico, in 1914; the Punitive Expedition led by General John J. Pershing against Francisco "Pancho" Villa's guerillas in Northern Mexico from 1916 through 1917; the occupation of both the Dominican Republic (1913–1915) and Haiti by U.S. marines to provide political stability; joining the Allied fight against the Central Powers in 1917; and the invasion of Siberia and Northern Russia in 1918 so as to recreate an Eastern Front against Germany and guard against the Japanese expanding its empire farther into Russia.

38 Calhoun, Power and Principle, 18.

39 Wilson expressed this juxtaposition in a May 15, 1916, speech before the National Press Club in Washington, DC. Wilson observed, "If I cannot retain my moral influence over a man except by occasionally knocking him down, if that is the only basis upon which he will respect me, then for the sake of his soul I have got to occasionally knock him down" (PWW, vol. 37, 48).

instead, Wilson sought to secure a peaceful solution through diplomatic negotiation in August 1913.[40] In September 1913, Huerta intimated to the American delegation that he intended to resign and hold a free election by October. When the time arrived for Huerta to fulfill his promise, he reneged. Though "frustrated and angered with Huerta's double cross," Wilson refrained from using military might to displace him.[41] Instead, Wilson waited for an opportunity that would indisputably allow him to intervene militarily in Mexico.[42]

Wilson did not have to wait long before a pretext for U.S. military action against Mexico presented itself. On April 9, 1914, unarmed sailors from the USS *Dolphin,* a gunboat anchored off the port city of Tampico, ventured ashore to purchase supplies. When the detachment wandered into a restricted area of the city, Mexican marines apprehended the sailors at Tampico's docks and, at gunpoint, forced them to disembark from a whaleboat flying the American flag. The Mexican military governor of Tampico, General Morelos Zarazoga, ordered the immediate release of

---

40   President Wilson entrusted this diplomatic mission to John Lind, a former governor of Minnesota and a political ally of William Jennings Bryan, his first secretary of state (1913–1915). The terms offered to Huerta by the American delegation called for him to resign from office and hold free elections, with Huerta disqualifying himself as a candidate.

41   Calhoun, *Power and Principle,* 41–42. Calhoun specifies that while Huerta's deception outraged Wilson, Wilson did not have a moral imperative to order a military remedy. In immediate response to Huerta's actions, Wilson authored a draft of a joint resolution specifying the use of military force to execute the terms of the Lind delegation and a speech he intended to give before Congress to gain their approval of the resolution. Wilson tabled this speech after learning he would face opposition to his use of force from Congress, an overwhelming majority of European nations, and from the counterrevolutionaries in Mexico.

42   While waiting for this opportunity, Wilson aimed to provide indirect assistance to the Constitutionalists. He did this in February 1914 by selectively lifting the arms embargo against Mexico, an embargo ordered by President Taft in 1912, so as to allow the Constitutionalists to buy weapons and ammunition from the United States and other countries. The embargo remained in place against the Huerta regime. To enforce the embargo, Wilson ordered the United States Navy to deploy ships from the Atlantic Fleet to the Gulf of Mexico to intercept any vessels carrying arms and ammunition to Huerta's military forces.

the sailors and offered a personal apology to Admiral Henry T. Mayo, commander of the U.S. naval forces in the Gulf of Mexico, in order to avoid an international incident with the United States.[43] Admiral Mayo rejected General Zarazoga's apology and demanded a formal apology from the Mexican government. Mayo also insisted that the Mexican military forces present in Tampico "hoist the American flag in a prominent position on shore and salute it with 21 guns."[44] Huerta refused to offer a formal apology to the United States, and General Zarazoga—believing his personal apology to be sufficient—likewise refused to give a twenty-one-gun salute to the American flag.[45] Wilson availed himself of the opportunity to take military action against the Huerta regime. On April 22, 1914, Congress granted Wilson's request to use military force against the Huerta government so as "to obtain . . . the fullest recognition of the rights and dignity of the United States."[46]

Wilson accepted the opportunity to move against Huerta militarily, however dubious the reason.[47] Wilson himself privately admitted to

43   A Mexican policeman in Vera Cruz temporarily detained a mail orderly from the USS *Minnesota* on April 10, 1914, after the orderly got into an argument with a post office clerk.

44   Quirk, *An Affair of Honor*, 26.

45   Josephus Daniels, Wilson's secretary of the navy, remarked that Huerta's behavior throughout the Tampico Affair was a "studied insult" to the United States (R. S. Baker Papers, Reel 73).

46   Woodrow Wilson, "Wilson's Special Message on the Tampico Affair," ed. Albert Shaw, *The Messages and Papers of Woodrow Wilson*, vol. 1 (New York: The Review of Reviews Corp., 1924), 62. One day before Wilson gained Congress's approval to employ military force, U.S. marines went ashore in the Mexican port city of Vera Cruz in order to seize the city's custom house to prevent the delivery of arms and ammunition from a German cargo ship. The marines were executing standard orders issued by Wilson to Admiral Frank Fletcher, the commanding officer of the naval squadron located in Vera Cruz coastal waters.

47   Perhaps the most stinging criticism concerning the rationale for the U.S. military intervention against Mexico was voiced by Smedley D. Butler. Butler, a major in the Marine Corps, participated in the amphibious assault on Vera Cruz, April 22, 1914. Reflecting upon the operation in a letter to his father, Thomas S. Butler, who also happened to be a U.S. Congressman (R-PA), Butler congratulated him for voting against Wilson's request to militarily intervene in Mexico. Major Butler received the Medal

the irrelevance of the temporary detention of U.S. military personnel by Mexican military and police forces.[48] Nonetheless, he possessed the political shrewdness to manipulate a trifling occurrence into a validation for the military encroachment of another country's sovereignty.

U.S. military operations against Mexican garrison forces at Vera Cruz commenced April 21, 1914, when warships shelled the city and a landing party composed of 787 marines and sailors went ashore at 1100 hours to establish a beachhead.[49] The landing party encountered no initial resistance since General Gustavo Maas, the military commander of Vera Cruz, withdrew his forces as soon as the warships began bombarding the city. Although the majority of Mexican military regulars retreated from Vera Cruz, the U.S. landing party came under fire by 1230 hours. Mexican irregulars, a ragged composition of Vera Cruz policemen, remnants of Maas' regulars, midshipmen from the Mexican Naval Academy, recently freed prisoners, and a significant number of Vera Cruz civilians led the attack. By nightfall, U.S. forces had repelled Mexican resistance and secured the landing site for the second assault force.

---

of Honor for his actions during the Vera Cruz operation. Butler attempted to turn down the decoration, but he was forced to accept the medal and received direct orders compelling him to wear it. See Anne Cipriano Venzon, ed., *General Smedley Darlington Butler: The Letters of a Leatherneck, 1898–1931* (New York: Praeger Publishers, 1992), 146–147, 164; and Lowell Thomas, *Old Gimlet Eye* (New York: Farrar and Rineheart, 1933), 180.

48   Reprint of an April 16, 1914, *New York World* article, "Wilson Tells Long Series of Affronts that Caused Action to Curb Huerta," *PWW*, vol. 29, 440–441.

49   Josephus Daniels, Wilson's secretary of the navy, detailed in his biography of Wilson that the invasion of Vera Cruz occurred one day before Wilson's request to Congress to use military force out of necessity. On April 20, 1914, the *Ypiranga*, a German steamer with cargo of arms and ammunition to be delivered to Huerta loyalists, attempted to break the U.S. blockade at Vera Cruz. Wilson instructed Secretary Daniels to impart the following orders to Admiral Frank Fletcher, commander of the Fourth Division of the Atlantic Fleet based at Vera Cruz: "Seize the custom house. Do not permit war supplies to be delivered to Huerta government or to any other party." Josephus Daniels, *The Life of Woodrow Wilson, 1856–1924* (Chicago: John C. Winston Co., 1924), 182–183; Jack Sweetman, *The Landing at Vera Cruz: 1914* (Annapolis, MD: Naval Institute Press, 1968), 61.

On April 22, at approximately 0400 hours, the main assault force of three thousand sailors and marines landed at Vera Cruz. Though badly outmanned, Mexican irregulars forced U.S. personnel to engage in house-to-house fighting. Their courage notwithstanding, Mexican irregulars were overwhelmed within seven hours' time by the better equipped and better trained U.S. military personnel. U.S. casualties totaled 17 killed and 63 wounded; the estimated amount of Mexican casualties included 126 killed and 195 wounded.[50]

Admiral Frank Fletcher established his headquarters in Vera Cruz on April 23 and immediately ordered a flag-raising ceremony. Witnessing the ceremony, Marine Colonel John A. Lejeune commented, "[T]here was scarcely a dry eye among the Americans."[51] Lejeune contrasted the flag-raising ceremony in Vera Cruz to Huerta's refusal to apologize for the USS *Dolphin* incident by noting the restoration of U.S. honor after marines and sailors "forcibly seized [Huerta's] principal maritime city and had ourselves wiped out the indignity which had been put upon our country."[52] The marines and sailors under Admiral Fletcher's command fulfilled their mission's objective: the seizure of Vera Cruz. While Lejeune looked at this accomplishment as canceling out the USS *Dolphin* affair, a significant portion of both the U.S. public and military remained unsatisfied, demanding greater retribution. President Wilson aimed to prevent the capture and occupation of Vera Cruz from spiraling into a U.S.-Mexican war.

An impartial observer of the U.S. military's occupation of Vera Cruz might construe it as an act of war. While Wilson sought to militarily intervene in the interests of the Constitutionalists by blocking the supply of munitions intended for Huerta's forces, the group strongly opposed to Huerta nonetheless condemned the U.S. raid on Vera Cruz.[53] After Vera Cruz had been captured, Constitutionalist leader Venustiano

---

50   Sweetman, *The Landing at Vera Cruz*, 123.

51   Major General John A. Lejeune, *The Reminiscences of a Marine* (Philadelphia: Dorrance & Co., 1930), 211.

52   Lejeune, *Reminiscences of a Marine*, 211.

53   In a speech before Congress on April 20, 1914, Wilson requested congressional sanction for military intervention in Mexico and avowed that the United States would not be in a conflict against the Mexican people, but would "be fighting only General Huerta and those who adhere to him . . . [O]ur object would be only to restore to the people of the distracted republic the opportunity to set up again their own laws and their own government" (*PWW*, vol. 29, 473).

Carranza told President Wilson that the U.S. invasion was a "violation of the rights that constitute [Mexico's] existence as a free and independent sovereign entity."[54] In order to preserve national honor, Carranza said the Constitutionalist government would have to declare war against the United States.[55] In press conferences both before and after the Vera Cruz invasion, Wilson consistently refused to declare such an operation as being a war-like act.[56]

Since sailors and marines have never been trained for extensive occupational duty, it was inevitable that the U.S. Army would become the occupying force in Vera Cruz. The force selected for this duty was the U.S. Fifth Infantry Brigade, Second Division, Brigadier General Frederick Funston commanding.[57] After the official transfer of command from Admiral Fletcher to General Funston on April 30, 1914, Funston became the military governor of Vera Cruz. Prior to taking command of the occupational forces, Funston received precise orders regarding his operational authority. Lindley M. Garrison, Wilson's secretary of war, instructed Funston that his command was restricted "to the occupation of [Vera Cruz] . . . and that you under no circumstances extend those limits . . . and that you do not initiate any activities or bring about by your initiative any situations which might tend to increase the tension of the situation or embarrass your government in its present relations with Mexico."[58]

54   *PWW*, vol. 29, 485.

55   *PWW*, vol. 29, 485.

56   The dates of the press conferences were April 20 and 23, 1914 (*PWW*, vol. 29, 468–471, 488–493).

57   The Fifth Infantry Brigade was supposed to have taken part in the Vera Cruz assault, but by the time it mobilized, Vera Cruz had been captured (John S. D. Eisenhower, *Intervention: The United States and the Mexican Revolution* [New York: W. W. Norton & Co., 1993], 123).

58   It was not without irony that Garrison transmitted this order to Funston. As early as August 1914, Garrison advocated the reinforcement of "the Vera Cruz garrison and certainly send them sufficient land equipment to move to the interior if needed." Joseph P. Tumulty, President Wilson's personal secretary, recorded in his memoirs that Garrison later "demanded radical action in the way of intervention . . . insisting that we intervene and put an end to the pusillanimous rule of Carranza and 'clean up' Mexico" following Villa's raid on Columbus, New Mexico (Joseph P. Tumulty, *Woodrow Wilson as I Know Him* [New York: Doubleday, 1921], 154). *PWW*, vol. 29, 510;

Funston, who did not particularly like occupational duty, considered combat to be the primary role of a soldier.[59] He wanted to march on Mexico City and unseat Huerta from power. During his first month commanding the occupational force, Funston repeatedly requested permission from Secretary Garrison to march on Mexico City, stating in one communiqué that Garrison had to "merely give the order and leave the rest to me."[60] Garrison more than sympathized with Funston but could not accede to his request.[61]

Wilson never abandoned his goal of helping the Mexican people to attain a freely elected government; he foreswore any intention for a military conquest of Mexico. Wilson deemed that the use of military force be limited to compelling Huerta's abdication. U.S. military officers viewed the concept of limits being placed on their fighting capability as alien. Any mission seeking to restore a constitutional form of government, they insisted, required the defeat of the Mexican military forces and the occupation of the entire country.[62] Following the Columbus raid, *The Army-Navy*

PWW, vol. 30, 361.

59 Funston's martial attitude was not a pretense; Funston fought Filipino insurrectionists following the Spanish-American War, receiving the Medal of Honor for acts of heroism during the Battle of Calumpit. Funston personally led the operation that captured Emilio Aguinaldo, the leader of the Filipino insurrection, in 1901.

60 Quirk, *An Affair of Honor*, 126.

61 To Funston's credit, he stopped making further requests seeking permission to conduct an offensive campaign. His effectiveness as the military governor of Vera Cruz received not only the commendations of President Wilson, but also from the majority of Vera Cruz's populace. Funston's capability as the military governor of Vera Cruz provided him no relief. William Allen White, a friend of Funston from when they both attended the University of Kansas, recalled in his autobiography that Funston described the U.S. withdrawal from Vera Cruz with "dazzling, wrathful profanity." Funston confided to White his frustration in "going meekly out of a dirty stinking greaser hole—withdrawing my command under fire!" Quirk, *An Affair of Honor*, 154–155; *PWW*, vol. 31, 375–376; William Allen White, *The Autobiography of William Allen White* (New York: MacMillan, 1946), 502.

62 The idea of the complete annihilation of one's military opponents and occupation of enemy territory in order to achieve victory was subscribed to by U.S. officers since the Civil War. See also Russell Weigley, *The American Way of War: A History of United States Military Strategy and Policy* (Bloomington: Indian University Press, 1973),

Journal lamented the occupation of Vera Cruz as no more than a "great expenditure of money and . . . lives," and a missed "psychological moment when Mexican lawlessness might have been curbed once and for all."[63] Despite the reservations of his military commanders, Wilson ordered that American military presence be contained within the port city, enabling the United States to negotiate from a position of strength. The fact that the majority of Mexicans viewed the U.S. military occupation of Vera Cruz as overly aggressive weakened Wilson's diplomatic advantage. Carranza denounced the U.S. military presence in Mexico and refused to enter into negotiations mediated by Argentina, Brazil, and Chile. Huerta was driven from power in July 1914 when surrounded by Constitutionalist forces. The U.S. military withdrew from Vera Cruz in November 1914.

The U.S. military intervention in Vera Cruz was a missed opportunity for senior military commanders. Distrustful of their new commander-in-chief, U.S. military leaders did not comprehend Wilson's motives or policy objectives. The commanders' obstinate attitude in this matter resulted in a refusal to modify their tactics. The inflexibility of his military commanders caused Wilson to be more severe in his dealings with them, further widening the gulf between him and his generals. This vicious cycle inhibited the success of future interventions during President Wilson's tenure.[64]

The Alienation of Pancho Villa

Huerta's abdication from power on July 15, 1914, provided a short-term respite to the problematic relations between Mexico and the United States. The seeds for future discord rested in the contentious relationship between

---

xxi–xxii; and Calhoun, *Power and Principle*, 42–45.

63 "The Fruits of our Folly," *The Army-Navy Journal, 1915–1916*, vol. 53 (March 18, 1916), 932.

64 This mutual suspicion between Wilson and his generals manifested itself again during the Punitive Expedition against Villa. Once again, Wilson placed limits on the use of force so the conflict would not escalate and involve the Carranza government. General John J. Pershing compared the hunt for Villa and his forces to that of "a man looking for a needle in a haystack with an armed guard standing over the stack forbidding you to look in the hay." Reflecting back on the failed expedition, Pershing bitterly recalled that Villa would have been caught "had it not been for interference" from politicians in Washington. See Calhoun, *Power and Principle*, 51, 57, 65.

Venustiano Carranza and Pancho Villa.[65] Villa, the one-time bandit, enlisted with the Maderistas in 1910 after both an unsatisfactory experience as a conscript in Huerta's forces and a conference with Abraham Gonzalez, an influential Maderista in the province of Chihuahua. George C. Carothers, the U.S. State Department's representative attached to Carranza's camp, informed Secretary of State William Jennings Bryan on June 18, 1914, that it "was impossible to prevent [a] breach between Villa and Carranza."[66] U.S. Consul Thomas D. Edwards (Ciudad Juárez) transmitted to Secretary Bryan a more optimistic assessment; Consul Edwards believed that "the differences . . . between the two men . . . will not in the least retard the campaign against [the] Huerta Government."[67] Consul Edwards's hopes for improved relations between Villa and Carranza soon fizzled. By the end of June 1914, Villa complained through U.S. diplomatic agents to President Wilson that Carranza continued to deny his division the supplies needed to advance upon Mexico City.[68] Unfortunately for Villa, President Wilson was not willing to intercede on behalf of anyone in the competition to suc-

---

65 The third most important Constitutionalist opposed to Huerta, after Carranza and Villa, was Emiliano Zapata. While Villa and Carranza forged an alliance of necessity against Huerta, Zapata refused to enter into such a relationship with Carranza, whom Zapata held in disdain. Zapata and Villa regarded each other with mutual admiration. Nevertheless, their geographic distance from one another, with Villa in Northern Mexico and Zapata in Southern Mexico, prevented them from meeting and forming an alliance against Huerta, and later against Carranza, until December 1914. Zapata's popularity and influence remained confined within his home region of Morelos. During the Punitive Expedition, Zapata concentrated his forces in Morelos against Carranza's forces. Zapata was assassinated on April 10, 1919, by Carranza loyalists. See Mason, *The Great Pursuit*, 216.

66 *FRUS, 1914,* 538–539, 542. Villa had resigned the command of his division to Carranza on June 13, 1914, in a dispute regarding the transfer of Villa's division to a general held in low regard by Villa. Carranza accepted Villa's resignation but later rescinded it when every general in Villa's division signed a letter of protest demanding Villa's restoration to command.

67 *FRUS, 1914,* 541.

68 *PWW*, vol. 30, 220–221. Villa entrusted Lazaro de la Garza to transmit this message to Felix A. Sommerfeld, Villa's principal financial agent in the United States. Sommerfeld would then carry this message to General Hugh L. Scott, who would then convey the message to President Wilson.

ceed Huerta. Wilson intended to "watch with the greatest interest and concern the course . . . pursued by the leaders of the Constitutionalist cause in effecting a transfer of power at Mexico City."[69]

Pancho Villa failed to win control of Mexico for many reasons: Carranza enjoyed overwhelming financial support from landowners and wealthy merchants, gained the support of nationalists from every strata of Mexican society as a result of his consistent objection to U.S. military presence at Vera Cruz, and minimized potential internal threats by choosing commanders personally loyal to him.[70] Initially, Villa enjoyed the esteem of a significant number of high-ranking U.S. diplomats and military officers.[71] He squandered this advantage, however, when his supporters began exacting revenge against those they deemed responsible for Carranza's ascension to power.

The stereotypical portrayal of Pancho Villa conjures up an image of a Mexican *bandito* upon horseback, adorned with a sombrero and crisscrossing bandoliers. In the case of Villa, the legend does not exactly correspond to fact. Edith O'Shaughnessy's superficial description of Villa as a thuggish bandit grew in popularity.[72] O'Shaughnessy's assessment of Villa fails to

69   *PWW*, vol. 30, 220–221.

70   Stout, *Border Conflict*, 11–13.

71   General Hugh L. Scott was sympathetic to Villa, even doubting that the raid on Columbus, New Mexico, was done with either Villa's knowledge or approval. Scott's estimation of Villa was that "he was a great sinner but had been greatly sinned against" (Scott, *Some Memories of a Soldier*, 518). By July 1914, "George C. Carrothers [sic] friendship for Gen. Villa [rendered] unavailable in dealing with the situation in connection with General Carranza" (*PWW*, vol. 30, 347). Even Villa's future antagonist General John J. Pershing admired Villa. In an October 1914 letter to General Scott, Pershing assessed that Villa was "a strong man and may be the man of the hour"; Villa "impressed" Pershing "as being very strong and very sincere" (Clarence C. Clendenen, *The United States and Pancho Villa: A Study in Unconventional Diplomacy* [Ithaca, New York: Cornell University Press, 1961], 131–132). Villa reciprocated Pershing's respect. When a house-fire killed Pershing's wife and three daughters in August 1915, Villa sent Pershing, who was assigned to border duty in El Paso, Texas, a note of condolence (Vandiver, *Black Jack*, vol. 2, 598).

72   Edith O'Shaughnessy was the wife of Nelson O'Shaughnessy, U.S. *charge d'affaires* at the U.S. embassy in Mexico City during Huerta's tenure as dictator. O'Shaughnessy, who quietly supported Huerta, acknowledged the fact that Villa's brutality was primarily based upon rumor. See Edith O'Shaughnessy, *A Diplomat's Wife in Mexico* (New

note that Villa's acts differed little from the tactics employed by Huerta. She also failed to note Villa's commitment to reform and his willingness "to do right when directed by those he respected" as observed by General Hugh L. Scott.[73]

Villa was willing to abide for a time by the rules of war, as best practiced by Mexican revolutionaries. When Villa and Zapata combined their forces and marched against Carranza's men in Mexico City in December 1914, Carranza fled and established a provisional government in Vera Cruz. The inhabitants of Mexico City feared the potential horrors that Villa's and Zapata's supporters would inflict. Allene Tupper Wilkes, a U.S. national living in Mexico City commented:

> All kinds of rumors were current and most of them were listened to and believed. Then one morning of unbelievable smiling sky and warming sunshine something happened, just what is still a matter of dispute, some say an automobile tire exploded. Whether it was that or the firing of a gun, soon other shots were fired and the city was in a panic. Mexico shivered and was afraid.[74]

Wilkes's fears proved to be unfounded. The joint entry of both Villa's and Zapata's forces, close to thirty thousand in number, was orderly and conducted under an official review consisting of Villa, Zapata, Mexican officials who did not flee with Carranza, and the entire diplomatic corps.[75]

York: Harper & Brothers, 1916), 90.

73   In a conversation with Villa, General Scott observed that "civilized people" viewed Villa as being a feral animal since he executed unarmed prisoners (Scott, *Some Memories of a Soldier*, 501–503). O'Shaughnessy herself admitted, "The hero in any Mexican drama is never more than a few months removed from being the villain. The actors alone change; never the horrid plot of blood, treachery, and devastation" (O'Shaughnessy, *A Diplomat's Wife in Mexico*, 112).

74   Allene Tupper Wilkes, "The Gentle Zapatistas," *Harper's Weekly* 60 (January 6, 1915): 56.

75   An official State Department report commented "that conditions in [Mexico City] have never been better than since the Zapatista forces began doing police duty" (*FRUS, 1914*, 628).

The triumphant entry of Villa and his forces into Mexico City marked the apex of his success. Carranza reorganized his forces and defeated Villa's army in every meaningful engagement in 1915. Though President Wilson cared little for Carranza personally, referring to him as "the stiff-necked First Chief," Wilson began to accept the prospect that Carranza would defeat Villa.[76] Secretary Bryan passed to Wilson a report on April 20, 1915, detailing the inevitability of Villa's military defeat and the necessity to recognize Carranza. Without specifically mentioning Carranza by name, Wilson attempted to encourage Carranza to quickly defeat Villa's forces. In an announcement on June 2, 1915, he declared that the United States would lend its "active moral support to some man or group of men, if such could be found, who could rally the suffering people of Mexico to their support in an effort to ignore, if they could not unite, the warring factions of the country, return to the constitution of the Republic so long in abeyance, and set up a government at Mexico City which the great powers of the world can recognize and deal with, a government with whom the program of the revolution will be a business and not merely a platform."[77]

Villa recognized the political tactics employed by Wilson, principally his tacit encouragement for Carranza.[78] Villa replied to Wilson's pronouncement nine days later by disparaging the idea of Carranza's having established a legitimate civil government. True Constitutionalists, Villa declared, would refuse in "submitting to foreign suggestions [so that they] might obtain the sympathy of a powerful nation."[79] Villa communicated a veiled threat to Wilson with the implication that he would resort to forceful action should the U.S. attempt to interfere in the internal political affairs of Mexico.

....

76 *PWW*, vol. 34, 385.

77 *FRUS, 1915*, 695. This message was transmitted to the Brazilian Minister in Mexico City who would then issue this message to Mexican authorities in a public statement on behalf of the U.S. government.

78 In a June 2, 1915, letter to Secretary Bryan, President Wilson commented that he was "entirely open to anything that events may open to us, even the recognition of Carranza should he develop the necessary influence and begin to bring real order out of chaos" (*PWW*, vol. 33, 308).

79 *FRUS, 1915*, 701–703.

Despite his warnings, Villa lacked the necessary power to supplant Carranza and prove that he was a viable aspirant for U.S. support. On October 19, 1915, Secretary of State Robert Lansing announced that the U.S. government formally recognized the "Government of Mexico, of which Venustiano Carranza is the Chief Executive."[80] Following the U.S. recognition of Carranza, Carrancistas received permission to cross over into the United States in order to use railways in New Mexico and Arizona in their campaign against Villa at Agua Prieta. General Scott, resentful that the Wilson administration decided to recognize Carranza, a "man who rewarded [the United States] with kicks on every occasion,"[81] over Villa, remarked that this decision to elevate Carranza would "undoubtedly embitter Villa very much and there is no telling what his savage mind will do."[82] Villa and his supporters were driven into the mountains of Northern Mexico by November 1915. Villistas only ventured outside their safe confines to cross into the United States in an attempt to steal supplies. U.S. border troops were not permitted to pursue the trespassing Villistas across into Mexico. At the onset of 1916, Villa and his supporters held the U.S. government culpable for Carranza's elevation to power.

The Punitive Expedition is Predestined to Fail

Following the U.S. government's formal recognition of the Carranza government, the Cusi Mining Company, located in the state of Chihuahua, reopened its mines. The company employed a significant number of U.S. citizens, primarily as engineers and technicians. Prior to the reopening of the mines, a majority of the U.S. employees departed Mexico and were living in El Paso, Texas, while waiting for hostilities between Villistas and Carrancistas to abate. With Villa and his followers in hiding by November 1915, Cusi Mining convinced its U.S. employees it was safe to resume mining operations. Cusi Mining's assurances evaporated on January 10, 1916, when a Villista force of approximately six hundred men stopped and boarded a passenger train carrying U.S. employees of Cusi Mining at the cattle loading station near Santa Ysabel. The Villistas robbed all the

---

80   *FRUS, 1915*, 735–736, 771. The countries of Brazil, Chile, Argentina, Bolivia, Uruguay, and Guatemala entered into this arrangement.

81   Scott, *Some Memories of a Soldier*, 517.

82   Letter from General Hugh L. Scott to Colonel Herbert J. Slocum, Hugh Lenox Scott Papers, Manuscript Division, Library of Congress, Washington, DC, Box 20.

Mexican passengers and summarily executed every U.S. passenger, murdering sixteen in total.[83]

President Wilson resisted public pressure to use military force to punish Villa and his supporters because he did not want to destabilize Carranza's tenuous political control by elevating Villa to a national hero once U.S. military forces crossed the border into Mexico. Wilson instructed Secretary Lansing to emphasize to Carranza the importance of his government's "ability . . . to perform its international obligations," namely to ensure the safety of foreign nationals working in Mexico. Carranza could restore the people's confidence in his government by taking "prompt and vigorous efforts on the part of Mexican military authorities to capture and punish" those responsible for the Santa Ysabel massacre.[84] On January 19, 1916, six days after Lansing's stern counsel to Carranza, Carranza responded that Villa and Pablo Lopez, the latter reported to have led the Santa Ysabel massacre, were outlaws, subject to immediate execution by any Mexican citizen.[85] Although the U.S. government grew perturbed at what they perceived to be Carranza's reluctance to expend his full resources in capturing Villa, they believed this at least prevented U.S. military intervention into Mexico.[86]

Stymied in his intent to have the United States intervene militarily following Santa Ysabel, Villa organized an even more daring plan: an in-

83 The only U.S. survivor, Thomas B. Holmes, quickly ran off the train and feigned death after being shot at by Villistas. His version of events has been considered the standard account of the Santa Ysabel massacre.

84 FRUS, 1916, 656.

85 FRUS, 1916, 465.

86 Secretary of War Lindley M. Garrison was a notable exception. Garrison believed Wilson's "national defence programme" to have been deficient and was not hesitant in making his objections known to Wilson. In a more subtle attempt, Garrison included a report to Lansing about the tense circumstances along the U.S.-Mexican border following Santa Ysabel. Quoting from a January 17, 1916, letter written by General Pershing to General Funston, Garrison stated, "There is little confidence in Carranza among Americans coming out of Mexico and many Mexicans are of the same mind. Practically all Americans think him powerless to establish anything like a stable government." Garrison's continued intransigence compelled Wilson to force Garrison's resignation on February 10, 1916. FRUS, Papers, 1916, 662–663; David H. Houston, Eight Years in Wilson's Cabinet, 1913 to 1920, vol. 1 (New York: Doubleday, Page & Co., 1926), 164–179; PWW, vol. 36, 162–165.

cursion into U.S. territory which would compel the United States to re-spond militarily.[87] This raid occurred on the morning of March 9, 1916, at Columbus, New Mexico. Villistas, totaling approximately five hundred in strength, attacked Columbus and the 13th U.S. Cavalry garrisoned in the southwest part of town. The attack lasted two hours. According to various reports, Villistas continually screamed, *"Viva Villa! Viva Mexico! Muerte a los gringos!"*, burned the town's buildings, and fired at civilians and soldiers alike.[88] Elements of the 13th Cavalry, under the command of Major Frank Tompkins, immediately pursued the Villistas fifteen miles into Mexico. General Funston defended this breech of Mexican sovereignty by argu-ing that "Villa might immediately have returned to attack" with a reserve force.[89] The Columbus raid resulted in fifteen U.S. deaths and the death of approximately seventy-five Villistas. Villa achieved his strategic objec-tive by compelling the United States to take action.

On March 10, 1916, the White House issued a press release outlining the administration's plans:

> An adequate force will be sent at once in pursuit of Villa with the single object of capturing him and putting a stop to his forays. This can and will be done in entirely friendly aid of the constituted authorities in Mexico and with scrupulous respect for the sovereignty of that Republic.[90]

87   General Hugh L. Scott's doubts concerning Villa's level of involvement proved to be Pollyannaish. Villa's plans, some of which were dated as early as January 6, 1916, were discovered in Columbus, New Mexico, immediately following the raid. See Tompkins, *Chasing Villa*, 41–42; and Haldeen Braddy, *Pancho Villa at Columbus: The Raid of 1916* (El Paso: Texas Western College Press, 1965), 15–16.

88   James Hopper, "What Happened in Columbus," *Collier's Magazine* 57 (April 15, 1916): 11.

89   Stout, *Border Conflict*, 37; Tompkins, *Chasing Villa*, 57.

90   The initial order transmitted to the U.S. Army, Southern Department, on March 10, 1916, detailed "that an armed force be sent into Mexico with the sole object of capturing Villa"; General Pershing received his orders the following day "designat[ing him] to command [an] expedition into Mexico to capture Villa and his bandits." *PWW*, vol. 36, 287, *FRUS, 1916*, 483, "Records of the War Department; Office of the Adjutant General, Pershing's Report of October 7, 1916, Regarding the Punitive Expedition, and Appendices to Pershing's Final Report of the Punitive Expedition," Record Group 94, National Archives Building, Washington, DC.

This release caused two significant difficulties: it assumed the support of the Carranza government and created a false mission objective. Carranza was unwilling to cooperate with the United States. On the same day the White House issued the aforementioned press release, Secretary Lansing received a cable from El Paso, stating "that Carranza authorities will resent American troops entering Mexico." Mexican papers printed a statement from Carranza on March 12, 1916, in which he said that his government would view any U.S. military expedition against Villa and his supporters as a violation of Mexican sovereignty and an act of war.[91] The White House's press release was intended to demonstrate the Wilson administration's resolve in avenging the Columbus raid to the U.S. public. It was neither intended to define the mission objective to the expedition assigned with neutralizing Villa's forces nor to cause a state of anxiety among Carrancistas. Nevertheless, these problems should not have proven too difficult for U.S. military personnel entrusted with reducing Villa's effectiveness.

General Hugh L. Scott, U.S. Army Chief of Staff, ordered the following orders be sent to General Frederick Funston, commanding general, Southern Department:

> You will promptly organize an adequate military force of troops under the command of Brigadier General J.J. Pershing and will direct him to proceed promptly across the border in pursuit of the Mexican band which attacked the town of Columbus and the troops there on the morning of the 9th instant. These troops will be withdrawn to American territory as soon as the de facto Government of Mexico is able to relieve them of this work. In any event the work of these troops will be regarded as finished as soon as Villa's band or bands are known to be broken up.[92]

These orders neither required Pancho Villa's specific apprehension nor demanded the occupation of Mexican territory. It can not be argued that the first order sent to General Pershing on March 11, 1916, authorized him "to command [an] expedition into Mexico to capture Villa and his bandits" two days after the attack on Columbus, but the conflicting objectives expressed in both orders resulted in confusion as to the Punitive

---

91   *FRUS, 1916,* 484, 487.

92   *PWW,* vol. 36, 285–286.

Expedition's mission.[93] President Wilson, castigated previously for his Mexican foreign policy resulting in the deaths of American citizens and military personnel on both sides of the border, committed the U.S. military to a mission in which the objective would be the elimination of threats to the security of the United States and its citizenry. The capture of Pancho Villa, though desirous, was not necessary for the Punitive Expedition to succeed. This was never made clear to either Pershing's expeditionary force or the American people.

President Wilson and his senior military commanders, with a few notable exceptions, differed as to how the elimination of potential border raids by Mexican irregulars could be attained. The prevailing thought shared by most U.S. military commanders was that the optimum strategy in preventing future border raids was to overcome "all organized Mexican forces found in the field . . . [eliminate] guerillas, and occup[y] . . . municipalities for the restoration of law and order and the resurrection of civil government."[94] These objectives, formulated by the U.S. Army War College Division three days prior to Villa's Columbus raid, dictated that it would take a force of 557,280 U.S. military personnel no less than three years to fulfill these objectives.[95] This plan dictated that "it is neither sound nor logical to attempt a partial occupation of Mexico without being prepared to look squarely in the face of the problem and to carry forward the vigorous operations of our war plans without vacillation or confusion of council."[96]

President Wilson made no response to this plan submitted by the War College Division. His silent rejection was deafening. War with Mexico held no allure for Wilson, particularly with the increased probability of the United States entering World War I as a belligerent. Wilson's policy

93   John J. Pershing, "Pershing's Report of October 7, 1916, Regarding the Punitive Expedition, and Appendices to Pershing's Final Report of the Punitive Expedition," Records of the Adjutant General's Office, RG 94, National Archives and Records Service, G.P.O., Washington, DC, microfilm copy in Dartmouth College Library.

94   Office of the Chief of Staff, War College Division, "The Military Strength for Armed Intervention in Mexico," Correspondence of the War College Division and Related General Staff Offices, 1903–1919, RG 165, National Archives and Records Administration, College Park, MD (NARA II), File 6474, Reel 83.

95   Office of the Chief of Staff, "The Military Strength for Armed Intervention in Mexico."

96   Office of the Chief of Staff, "The Military Strength for Armed Intervention in Mexico."

toward Mexico not only went against his generals, but also against his own cabinet members who considered Mexicans "a lot of treacherous bandits" who could only be made to behave "with a big stick."[97] Wilson maintained his belief that the Mexican people possessed the capability of republican self-government and that a massive military intervention by the United States following the Columbus raid could have no final outcome other than war between the United States and Mexico.[98]

The size and strength of the Punitive Expedition, which eventually totaled ten thousand soldiers, alarmed Carranza. Its four hundred-mile penetration into Mexico also troubled him. These factors resulted in mounting political pressure being brought upon Carranza to compel a withdrawal of U.S. soldiers from Mexico, by force if needed. Upon learning that the crossing of Pershing's force could possibly meet opposition from a Carrancista garrison, Wilson wanted to withdraw Pershing's orders to cross into Mexico. Wilson relented after being persuaded that this action would be tantamount to political suicide.[99] These difficulties encountered by General Pershing and the Punitive Expedition did not yet include Villa's elusiveness and tactical adroitness. Pershing's forces enjoyed early triumphs in routing Villistas at Guerrero, Agua Caliente, and Ojos Azules and in skirmishes resulting in the deaths of Villa's top lieutenants. These early successes temporarily restored American dignity.[100] The victories attained during the early days

---

97   Diary entry for May 8, 1914, 74, Edward Mandell House Papers, Yale University Library, New Haven, CT, vol. 4, reel 2.

98   Brigadier General Tasker H. Bliss, the assistant chief of staff of the U.S. Army, had a bleaker assessment than did Wilson. Bliss believed "that the invasion of Mexico by the United States, for any reason whatsoever, will be regarded by the Mexicans as an act of war and we must therefore be prepared for all of the reasonably assumable consequences of that act" (Letter from Bliss to General Scott, March 13, 1916, Scott Papers, Box 22).

99   House Diary, Entry for March 17, 1916, House Papers. Reel 2.

100   "American residents of the state of Chihuahua, Mexico, have assured General Pershing that the American troops have restored respect on the part of the natives for United States soldiers to a degree not existing for five years . . . After the Ojo Azules fight, however, signs of the growing respect on the part of the natives became more manifest. American non-combatants living in the vicinity were treated with a courtesy which astonished them and the like of which they had not experienced for years" (Unsigned article in *The Army-Navy Journal, 1915–1916*, vol. 53 [May 27, 1916], 1251).

of the Punitive Expedition unraveled when U.S. forces engaged in hostile encounters with Carrancistas at Parral and Carrizal.

The first clash between U.S. forces and Carrancistas at Parral on April 12, 1916, brought an end to the active pursuit of Villa. Although only two U.S. soldiers were killed in the Parral encounter, Wilson wanted to take measures to decrease the probability of war between the United States and Mexico. As a result of Wilson's reticence for war, Pershing commented that the Parral clash "brought the whole matter into the sphere of diplomacy, and it was soon deemed advisable to withdraw for the time being."[101] Vexed with the restrictions placed on him by the Wilson administration following the "unprovoked and outrageous attack" by the Carrancistas at Parral, Pershing's dissatisfaction increased following a second hostile encounter between U.S. soldiers of the 10th Cavalry and Carrancistas at Carrizal on June 21, 1916. The fight at Carrizal resulted in an alarming number of U.S. casualties, ten dead, twelve wounded, and twenty-three taken prisoner by Carrancistas. General Funston himself reacted with alarm at the "terrible blunder" at Carrizal.[102] The aftermath of Carrizal relegated Pershing to conducting training exercises and inspections since Funston transmitted orders to Pershing forbidding him from sending out patrols from the encampments at El Valle and Colonia Dublan. For the remaining months of the Punitive Expedition, Pershing battled boredom and the Mexican climate while failing in his attempts to persuade General Scott to permit him to renew the pursuit of Villa.[103] While Pershing could not help "but feel the embarrassment of sitting here while Villa is cavorting about only a few miles south of [his] positions," the Wilson administration wanted to avoid any further U.S. military activity that might arouse Mexican indignation after Carrizal.[104]

---

101   "Report of General John J. Pershing on the Mexican Punitive Expedition, July 1, 1916 to February 5, 1917," RG 94.

102   Dispatch from Funston to Pershing, June 22, 1916, "Punitive Expedition to Mexico, 1916–1917, HQ General Correspondence, 1916–1917," Records of the Punitive Expedition to Mexico, 1916–1917, RG 395, National Archives Building, Washington, DC.

103   Letters from Pershing to Scott, August 8, 1916, September 23, 1916, October 21, 1916, and November 16, 1916, Pershing Papers, Box 372.

104   Letter from Pershing to Senator Warren, December 4, 1916, Pershing Papers, Box 426.

Evaluating Woodrow Wilson's Mexican Policy

Although the Punitive Expedition proved to be a success with the passage of time, with Villa's forces scattered and his lieutenants killed by both U.S. and Carrancista forces, the U.S. military's immediate misinterpretation of its mission caused the Punitive Expedition to be considered a failure by contemporary observers since Pancho Villa was not caged by General Pershing. If the Punitive Expedition need be only judged a failure by immediate, short-term gratification objectives rather than attaining long-term goals; Wilson achieved his long-term goals of averting war with Mexico and allowing Mexico to develop a stable form of government. The capture of Pancho Villa would have been satisfying for those whose shortsightedness caused them to value vengeance over enduring peace and security.

John Milton Cooper views Wilson's foreign policy "as an example to be shunned" since the American people's need "to be either hoodwinked or inflamed into pursuing the right course" has become obsolete.[105] If domestic and international support for a military intervention is absent, an administration will be unable to institute its domestic agenda, and may eventually suffer at the ballot box. The lack of international support for unilateral, armed intervention can have even greater, long-lasting significance. Should one country decide to employ military might against another country without establishing a moral imperative, it will not only breed distrust, fear, and hatred in the aggrieved country, but it will also arouse contempt from those countries that empathize with the aggrieved country. Such a result counteracts the objective sought by President Wilson, the establishment of peace and trust among a community of nations.

---

105   John Milton Cooper Jr., *The Warrior and The Priest: Woodrow Wilson and Theodore Roosevelt* (Cambridge, MA: Harvard University Press, 1983), 360–361.

NO MORE CUBAS:

THE LESSONS OF COUNTERINSURGENCY, 1961-1963

David Lauderback

T HE TRADITIONAL FOCUS of the United States' foreign and economic policy on Europe and Asia has led policymakers to treat Latin America on a largely ad hoc basis. While the United States in the twentieth century made certain the security of the Panama Canal, Washington routinely dismissed the region in favor of more pressing economic and security concerns across the oceans east and west. Yet, despite the marginal status of Latin America, the United States has prized political stability in the region to ensure economic opportunity and to deny the occasional potential security threat. When the United States has acted, it generally has done so abruptly to satisfy immediate security and economic considerations with little attention to the specific context or the long-term consequences. The success of the Cuban revolution and the threat of further spread of the Communist contagion brought the region, once again, into sharp relief. The new administration of John F. Kennedy sought to solve the recurring problem of political instability once and for all. The United States offered advanced military training designed to enable the nations of Latin America to preserve their own internal security. Thus saved, Washington could once again focus on the pressing battle against communism in Europe and the Far East. Kennedy marshaled stirring rhetoric to get the job done.

Kennedy sought from the very beginning of his administration to change the tenor and tone of U.S. policy toward Latin America. With his inaugural address, President Kennedy made a promise to the people of Latin America: "We offer a special pledge . . . to convert our good words into good deeds . . . in a new alliance for progress."[1] With massive economic aid and broad infrastructure improvements, Latin America was to become a petri dish for a new policy designed to combat the spread of communism in the world's underdeveloped regions. The grandeur and scope of the project tapped into a deep well of American idealism and helped to foster a missionary zeal for programs such as the Peace Corps, which was designed to carry out the good works of this new Alliance for Progress.[2] When President Kennedy launched the Alliance in his March 13 speech at a White House reception for Latin American diplomats, he announced that "the genius of our scientists" had left the hemisphere poised "to strike off the remaining bonds of poverty and ignorance." To succeed "at this moment of maximum opportunity," however, the Americas had to be prepared to battle "the alien forces which once again seek to impose the despotisms of the old world on the people of the new."[3]

President Kennedy believed Cuba represented a new and dangerous Soviet effort to provoke instability in the underdeveloped nations of the world. Nikita Khrushchev declared to the Soviet leadership only days before Kennedy took office that the future of communist expansion lay in helping the colonial peoples of the world in "wars of national liberation."[4] Eisenhower had properly chalked this up to Soviet bluster and in-

---

1 John F. Kennedy, Inaugural Address, January 20, 1961, http://www.umb/jfkli-brary/j012061.

2 See Elizabeth Cobbs Hoffman, *All You Need Is Love: The Peace Corps and the Spirit of the 1960s* (Cambridge, MA: Harvard University Press, 1998).

3 John F. Kennedy, Address, March 13, 1961, "White House Reception for Latin American Diplomats, Members of Congress, and Their Wives," RG 59 Records of the Department of State, Task Force on Latin America, Subject and Country Files, 1961, Box 2, FN The President, 1, National Archives and Records Administration II, College Park, MD [hereafter "NARA II"].

4 See Stephen G. Rabe, *The Most Dangerous Area of the World: John F. Kennedy Confronts Communist Revolution in Latin America* (Chapel Hill: University of North Carolina Press, 2000), 20–2; and Michael McClintock, *Instruments of Statecraft: U.S. Guerrilla Warfare, Counter-Insurgency, and Counterterrorism, 1940–1990* (New York: Pantheon, 1992), 162–3.

tra-Communist wrangling.[5] Kennedy, however, viewed this as a personal challenge by the Soviet premier and a real threat to world peace.[6] That is why Kennedy found the ideas of Walt W. Rostow so inviting. Rostow boldly joined a chorus of economists and academics during the late 1950s when he authored his "Non-Communist Manifesto," arguing that the conditions for Western-style economic development could be stimulated in the so-called underdeveloped areas of the world with infusions of capital and, especially, expertise.[7] Rostow, though, feared that during the tender and liminal "take-off" stage, when a middle class and democratic capitalism were fighting to take root, outside forces could disrupt or even stymie the time-elapsed growth process. Hence, he argued that maintaining internal security remained the paramount priority of those nations.[8] For Kennedy, Rostow's ideas gave him the considered rationale for the Alliance for Progress and the tools, in the persons of what would be called the United States Special Forces, to insert himself, forcefully, into Latin America and thereby prevent Cuban subversion. And since the Latin American military already perceived communism as the greatest threat to order in their societies, they readily agreed with the president and his advisor and sought U.S. aid and training.[9]

5   Michael Beschloss, *The Crisis Years: Kennedy and Khrushchev, 1960–1963* (New York: HarperCollins, 1991), 60–1.

6   John Giglio, *The Presidency of John F. Kennedy* (Lawrence: The University of Kansas Press, 1991), 46–7.

7   Walt W. Rostow, *The Stages of Economic Growth: A Non-Communist Manifesto* (Cambridge, MA: Cambridge University Press, 1960). See principally Raul Prebisch, *The Economic Development of Latin America and Its Principal Problems* (New York: United Nations, 1950); Gunner Myrdal, *Economic Development and Underdeveloped Regions* (London: Gerald Duckworth, 1957); Daniel Lerner, *The Passing of Traditional Society: Modernizing the Middle East* (New York: Free Press, 1958); and Max Millikan and Walt W. Rostow, *A Proposal: Key to an Effective Foreign Policy* (New York: Harper, 1957).

8   Walt W. Rostow, "Guerrilla Warfare in Underdeveloped Areas," *Marine Corps Gazette*, vol. 46, no. 1 (January 1962), 46–9.

9   Brian Loveman, *For La Patria: Politics and the Armed Forces in Latin America* (Wilmington, DE: Scholarly Resources, 1999), 160–62; Edwin Lieuwen, *Arms and Politics in Latin America*, rev. ed. (New York: Praeger, 1961), 282–95. For a more optimistic assessment, see John J. Johnson, *The Military and Society in Latin America* (Stanford, CA: Stanford University Press, 1964), 244–67.

Much has been made, then and now, of Kennedy's desire to successfully counter the Soviet Union in world affairs.[10] In many respects, his
insistence to "get tough" with the Russians served as the driving force
behind his foreign policy. The example of Munich 1938, used so often to
justify American policy initiatives during the Cold War, also motivated
the young president. Any hint of appeasement of the forces of aggression, he concurred, would only threaten world stability and lead to war.
Mao's successful revolution in China in 1949 proved more relevant to the
new president. As a junior congressman from Massachusetts, Kennedy
had observed firsthand the domestic political fallout for the Democratic
Party—and a Democratic president—when the world's most populous
nation "fell" to communism. Kennedy had learned in his first days as a
politician the ravages that domestic anti-communism could wreak on his
party and on the careers of American politicians. communism had to be
contained abroad, he believed, to prevent its insidious spread. And, to keep
his position at the head of his party, the president had to contain communism abroad. Hence, Kennedy initially viewed Cuba as a litmus test, not
only of his will to serve as president, but also of his political future. By the
end of his brief tenure, however, the region no longer held the president's
interest, nor did Latin America represent the threat it had initially seemed
to pose.

Readying for War

The new Kennedy Administration lost little time in wedding counterinsurgency training to the foundation of the new Latin American policy of
the United States. On January 30, 1961, just ten days after taking office,
the president's national security advisor, McGeorge Bundy, argued that
"the most urgent need is for a review of basic military policy."[11] Bundy
raised what would become the beginnings of Kennedy's "flexible response" posture when he specifically targeted the need to develop "limited war forces" as opposed to the previous emphasis on maintaining

----

10 See Rabe, *Most Dangerous Area*, for a recent account of Kennedy and Latin
America.

11 McGeorge Bundy (NSA) to President Kennedy, memorandum, January 30, 1961,
"Policies Previously Approved in NSC Which Need Review," NSF, NSF Meetings, Box
313, FN #470, 1, John F. Kennedy Presidential Library, Boston [hereafter "Kennedy
Presidential Library"].

"strategic" defense capabilities. In that vein, "the President requested" at the February 1, 1961, meeting of the National Security Council "that the Secretary of Defense . . . examine means for placing more emphasis on the development of counterguerilla forces."[12] Secretary of Defense Robert McNamara responded to the National Security Council's "Action Memorandum" Number 2[13] on February 23, informing Kennedy that his department had initiated efforts to formulate "a doctrine for improved counterinsurgency operations."[14]

Cuba's ability to project its revolution into the nations of Latin America represented the primary threat to U.S. national security in the hemisphere for the new president and his staff. Back on August 1, 1960, specialists in the state department warned that "no sooner had the Revolutionary Government of Cuba taken power than it launched a program for exporting its revolution to other countries in the Hemisphere." Castro's regime, the Policy Planning Council warned, relied on Ché Guevara's "handbook, *La Guerra de Guerrillas* [for] organizing, supporting, and encouraging a number of revolutionary leaders and movements" in the region with the sole intent to "undermine and violently overthrow existing national governments."[15] Arthur Schlesinger concurred. Reporting to Kennedy on

12 NSC, minutes, "Military Budgets and National Security Policy," in 475th NSC Meeting, February 1, 1961, "Record of Actions," National Security Files, NSC Meetings, Box 313, FN #470, 4, Kennedy Presidential Library.

13 McGeorge Bundy (Spec. Asst. NSA) to the President, National Security Memorandum No. 2, February 3, 1961, "Development of Counter-Guerilla Forces," NSF, NSAM, Box 328, FN NSAM 2, 1, Kennedy Presidential Library. Bundy instituted the "action memoranda" in a deliberate attempt to replace what he viewed as the institutional lethargy of the Eisenhower administration. The new national security advisor abhorred the lengthy process that produced the detailed reports of the National Security Council and sought to, in the spirit of the new administration, impose an activist, "can-do" mentality. Ironically, his action memoranda often produced bureaucratic bottlenecks that required later memoranda to clear up.

14 Robert McNamara (Sec. of Def.) to McGeorge Bundy (Spec. Asst. NSA), memorandum, February 23, 1961, "Development of Counter-Guerilla Forces," NSF, NSAM, Box 328, FN NSAM 2, 1, Kennedy Presidential Library.

15 Frank J. Devine (American Republics) to Walt W. Rostow (Chair, PPC), memorandum, May 1, 1961, "Contributions for Your Paper on the Rationale," Tab C, Department of State, draft paper, 1 August 1960, "Responsibility of Cuban Government for Increased International Tensions in the Hemisphere," NSF, Country, Box 35a, Cuba,

March 10 after his visit to South America, the president's advisor argued forcefully that "obviously communism is aiming to conquer Latin America by penetration and not invasion."[16]

The Bay of Pigs debacle on April 17, 1961, forced the United States to rapidly accelerate the drive to provide Latin Americans with the skills to defend themselves from Cuban-communist subversion.[17] The National Security Council met on April 22, 1961 to reevaluate U.S. policy. In response to those "discussions," McNamara directed the secretary of the army, Elvis Stahr, to provide, post haste, a "plan . . . for stepping up Latin American attendance in counter-guerrilla training activities, notably those at Fort Bragg and Fort Gulick" in the Panama Canal Zone.[18] The army reported back that the United States needed to expand counterinsurgency training because "most Latin American MAAGs [Military Assistance and Advisory Groups] and missions who advise local governments do not have personnel qualified in counterinsurgency, counter-intelligence, civic action, and psychological warfare."[19] Even more alarming, Secretary Stahr's

General, State Dept. "Rationale," 5/61, 47–8, Kennedy Presidential Library.

16   Arthur Schlesinger (Spec. Asst.) to McGeorge Bundy (Spec. Asst. NSA), memorandum, March 11, 1961, enclosure, Arthur Schlesinger (Spec. Asst.) to President Kennedy, memorandum, March 10, 1961, NSF, Reg. Sec. Box 211–6, LA-General, 3/8–3/16/61, 13, Kennedy Presidential Library.

17   Peter Wyden, *Bay of Pigs: The Untold Story* (New York: Touchstone, 1979); Trumbell Higgins, *The Perfect Failure: Kennedy, Eisenhower, and the CIA at the Bay of Pigs* (New York: Norton, 1987); Richard E. Welch, *Response to Revolution: The United States and the Cuban Revolution, 1959–1961* (Chapel Hill: University of North Carolina Press, 1985), 64–100; Giglio, *John F. Kennedy*, 48–63; Thomas G. Paterson, *Contesting Castro: The United States and the Triumph of the Cuban Revolution* (New York: Oxford University Press, 1994); Jorge I. Dominguez, *Cuba: Order and Revolution* (Cambridge, MA: Belknap Press, 1978).

18   Robert McNamara (secretary of defense) to Elvis Stahr (secretary of the Army), memorandum, April 22, 1961, RG 407 Records of the Adjutant General's Office, 1917, Classified Central General Admin. Files, 1955–1962, 1961 Cases, Box 436, FN AG 353, I. 1–6–61, 1, NARA II.

19   Elvis Stahr (Sec. of the Army) to Robert McNamara (Secretary of Defense), memorandum, April 27, 1961, "Plan to Step Up Latin American Attendance in Counter-Guerrilla Training Activities," Inclusion 4, "Plan to Step Up Latin America Attendance in Counter-Guerrilla Training Activities," RG 407 Records of the Adjutant General's

report went on to say, few "officials" outside of the Latin American military appreciate the threat of communist subversion or "for internal reasons ignore the importance of counterinsurgency, civic action, intelligence/security, and psychological operations."[20] The Joint Chiefs of Staff quickly concurred and authorized the expansion of counterintelligence training beyond the USARCARIB School at Ft. Gulick to include the U.S. Army Intelligence School, the Inter-American Defense Board, the Foreign Area Specialist School, and all service schools and colleges that trained MAAGs, missions, and attachés. [21] Ideally, expanded U.S. military training would enable "local governments" throughout the region to "gradually develop their own capability for counterguerrilla training."[22] "The prime mission" of the facilities at Ft. Bragg and Ft. Gulick, Secretary Stahr continued, was "to develop cadres, capable of conducting similar courses in their own countries."[23]

Internal security training, it seemed, offered the best defense against Cuban subversion in the hemisphere. Brigadier General Edward Lansdale argued that "it would be more purposeful to concentrate" on developing the counterinsurgency strength of specific "countries with currently critical or potentially critical situations," e.g., Vietnam and Colombia.[24]

Office, 1917–, Classified Central General Admin. Files, 1955–1962, 1961 Cases, Box 436, FN AG 353, I. 1–6–61, 2, NARA II.

20   Stahr, "Plan to Step Up Latin American Attendance," 3.

21   "Intelligence," Annex B in "Plan to Step Up Latin America Attendance in Counter-Guerrilla Training Activities," Inclusion 4, in Elvis Stahr (Sec. of the Army) to Robert McNamara (Secretary of Defense), memorandum, April 27, 1961, "Plan to Step Up Latin American Attendance in Counter-Guerrilla Training Activities," RG 407 Records of the Adjutant General's Office, 1917–, Classified Central General Admin. Files, 1955–1962, 1961 Cases, Box 436, FN AG 353, 1–1–6–61, 1–2, NARA II.

22   Elvis Stahr (Sec. of the Army) to Robert McNamara (Sec. of Defense), memorandum, April 27, 1961, "Plan to Step Up Latin American Attendance in Counter-Guerrilla Training Activities," RG 407 Records of the Adjutant General's Office, 1917–, Classified Central General Admin. Files, 1955–1962, 1961 Cases, Box 436, FN AG 353, 1–1–6–61, 1, NARA II.

23   "Plan to Step Up Latin America Attendance," Inclusion 4, 1–2.

24   Brig. Gen. Edward Lansdale (Spec. Asst. Spec. Ops.) to Roswell Gilpatric (Dep. Sec. of Def), memorandum, June 19, 1961, "Counter-Guerrilla Training," NSF, Meetings and Memoranda, Box 326–7, FN Staff Memos, Rostow, Guerrilla Warfare,

The president himself told Congress in mid-June that the growing threat of communist subversion in Latin America, and elsewhere in the Third World, mandated a "complete reevaluation of the role of military assistance."[25] Consequently, the State Department's Policy Planning Council focused on internal security in the region as the most salutary curative in a series of detailed papers issued in June 1961. Rostow now headed the State Department's primary policy group, and while debating the use of the term "internal security" and suggesting that perhaps "internal stability, public safety, or constitutional order" might be "more psychologically palatable," Rostow emphasized that "the object is to find a phrase which would embody the positive concepts of deterrence of guerrilla warfare, and of counter-guerrilla operations, and project the thought that, if the right actions are taken during the deterrence stage, a country will be better able to cope with guerrilla rebellion if it occurs."[26] For Rostow, one of the foremost architects of economic development policy in the Kennedy administration, counterinsurgency training became essential to preserving the stability of emerging democracies. And Rostow intended that the U.S. military would provide the requisite instruction.

The Joint Chiefs advised the president that the U.S. Army planned to launch its new training program on July 31, 1961, at Ft. Gulick in the Canal Zone.[27] Secretary Stahr initially promoted the USARCARIB School at Ft. Gulick, "rather than Fort Bragg," as the best first choice for counterinsurgency training because of its Spanish-language instruction.[28] The Associated Press reported that the army planned to establish a "special

---

6/14/61–6/30/61, 2, Kennedy Presidential Library.

25 U.S. House, *Message from the President of the United States Transmitting the Final Report on the Operations of the Mutual Security Program*, House Doc. 432, 87th Cong., 2nd Sess., June 12, 1961, 33.

26 Department of State, Policy Planning Council, PPC 61–2, June 13, 1961, "Counter Guerilla Operations," National Security Files, Meetings and Memoranda, Box 3267, FN Staff Memos, Rostow, Guerilla Warfare, 6/1–6/13/61, Kennedy Presidential Library.

27 "Training of Police and Armed Forces of Latin America (U)," Appendix to General L. L. Lemnitzer (Chairman, Joint Chiefs of Staff) to President, memorandum, JCSM 341–61, May 19, 1961, "Training of Police and Armed Forces of Latin America (U)," POF, CO, Box 121A, FN Latin America, Security, 1960–63, 3, Kennedy Presidential Library.

28 See n. 22.

guerrilla and anti-guerrilla warfare school" in the Panama Canal Zone that summer for "Latin American nations which ask [for] such training."[29] In an article that touted the new course as the key to U.S. efforts to "Nip New Castros," the *Wall Street Journal,* in early August, extolled the "little-publicized training program" that was "quietly indoctrinating key officers in the varied skills required to crush Red insurgent movements." The *Journal* reported that the instruction, in keeping with the doctrines of economic development, stressed civic action. As one Guatemalan captain put it, "'we want to further these poor classes which constitute precisely the seed-bed for communist demagoguery that is trying to destroy us' (the military)."[30]

The USARCARIB School began providing counterinsurgency training to Latin American military as far back as 1944. The United States had used its control of territory in the Canal Zone to train U.S. military for many years prior to World War II. During the war, British commandos brought their experience from Burma and south Asia to Panama and helped train the U.S. Army's new Mobile Force. Elements of the Nicaraguan National Guard[31] were the first to receive jungle warfare training in Panama, and fifty officers from the Colombian War College also received "two week instruction with the Mobile force."[32] Following the war, the United States continued to send troops, in particular, squads from U.S. Ranger battalions, to the Jungle Training Center at Ft. Sherman, located across the river from Ft. Gulick. But it was not until 1959 that the USARCARIB School led the first cadre of Latin American students through the course at Ft. Sherman. Informally, instructors from the school took a small detachment from the Panamanian National Guard, led by a young, up-and-com-

29   "U.S. to Set Up Guerrilla War School in C.Z.," *Star Herald*, April 6, 1961, p. 1, c. 6, Ramsay Papers, John Amos Library, Ridgeway Hall, Ft. Benning, GA [hereafter "John Amos Library"].

30   Louis Kraar, "U.S. Teaches Latins Anti-Guerrilla Tactics to Nip New Castros," *Wall Street Journal,* [nd] August 1961, p. 1, col. 8, Ramsay Papers, John Amos Library.

31   Office of the Staff Secretary, Caribbean Defense Command, "Training in the Caribbean Defense Command, 1941–1946," 1948, Historical Manuscript File, 8–2.8 AC, 48–9, Center for Military History, Washington, DC [hereafter "CMH"].

32   Historical Section, Panama Canal Department, "Training of Latin American Military Personnel in the Panama Canal Department," in Preliminary Historical Study, Panama Canal Department—Training, vol. 2, Department Schools, HMF 8–2.9 AM 57, CMH.

ing officer by the name of Manuel Noriega, on a counterguerilla course fashioned after the instruction given to prospective U.S. Army Rangers.[33] During the summer of 1959, "Panamanian National Guardsmen . . . trained in the USARCARIB Jungle Warfare Training Center, quelled the riots in Panama."[34]

The USARCARIB School took advantage of the White House's unprecedented interest in counterinsurgency to launch a major campaign to make itself the primary institution for Latin American training. In early 1961, the new commandant, Colonel Edgar Schroeder, installed a branch at the school to reflect the new emphasis on counterguerilla training. The new Department of Internal Security included "sections" that targeted "Counterinsurgency Operations," "Military Intelligence," "Military Police," "Research and Analysis," and "Medical." In 1961, "in recognition of the increasing communist threat in Latin America, those courses which were most directly related to national internal defense capabilities were grouped into one department." By 1962, the school had declared in its catalog: "Every course taught has definite application in the counterinsurgency field." And the school assured prospective students that the new "Department provides instruction in every aspect of counterinsurgency operations, be it military, paramilitary, political, sociological, or psychological."[35] At the Inter-American Army Conference held at Ft. Amador July 10–14, 1961, the new head of counter-resistance training at the USARCARIB School, Lt. Col. Felipe Vías, informed the assembled generals that the new course "devotes 60 hours to Civic Action"[36] and instructed members of the Latin American military in the importance of "stimulation of economic growth

....

33   Lt. Col. Russell Ramsay, Ret., Oral History, March 18, 1998, John Amos Library.

34   "Training of Police and Armed Forces of Latin America (U)," Appendix to General L. L. Lemnitzer (Chairman, Joint Chiefs of Staff) to President, memorandum, JCSM 341–61, May 19, 1961, "Training of Police and Armed Forces of Latin America (U)," POF, CO, Box 121A, FN Latin America, Security, 1960–63, 1, Kennedy Presidential Library.

35   USARCARIB School, *The U.S. Army Caribbean School: "One for All and All for One"* (USARCARIB School: Ft. Gulick, CZ, 1962), 5, John Amos Library.

36   Lt. Col. Felipe Vías, "Counter Resistance Training," in USARCARIB, *Final Report: Inter-American Army Conference, 1961* (Ft. Amador, CZ: USARCARIB, 1961), 87–91, RG 218 Records of the U.S. Joint Chiefs of Staff, Central Decimal File, 1961, Box 168, FN CCS 9125–5410 Central America (July 17, 1961), 87, NARA II.

by civic action."[37] The colonel added that the "Military Police Section will cover public relations, physical security, and tactical and psychological factors necessary to quell a disturbance in the early period without unnecessary bloodshed." The school added a shorter and smaller Senior Officers course that concentrated on communist tactics, "propaganda techniques, infiltration tactics, front groups," and the role of civic action as "an instrument for fostering . . . active [civilian] participation and support of counter-resistance operations."[38]

The rest of the United States' national security apparatus did not react as promptly as the USARCARIB School. On September 5, 1961, President Kennedy had to direct his administration to intensify the training of Latin American military by the United States in National Security Action Memorandum 88 (NSAM 88). The president asked for an update on U.S. efforts to "train the Armed Forces of Latin America in controlling mobs, guerrillas, etc." Given that the "military occupy an extremely important strategic position in Latin America," Kennedy wanted to know "what steps we are taking to increase the intimacy between our armed forces and the military of Latin America." The president concluded that perhaps the FBI could be used to assist in the instruction process.[39] Acting Secretary of State Chester Bowles cautioned at the end of September 1961 that given the "strategic position the military hold in most under-developed countries . . . we can do much to include in our training programs for foreign military personnel a better appreciation of their role as builders, as well as defenders, of the emerging democratic societies."[40]

As the year wound down, the president continued to push the Defense Department to formulate a specific overall policy for U.S. counterinsurgency training of the Latin American armed forces. The Joint Chiefs of Staff responded to NSAM 88 on November 30, 1961, with a detailed proposal

37 USARCARIB School, *The U.S. Army Caribbean School: History and Operations* (USARCARIB School: Ft. Gulick, CZ, 1962), 5–6, John Amos Library.

38 Vías, "Counter Resistance Training," 90.

39 President to Robert McNamara (Sec. of Def.), NSAM 88, September 5, 1961, "Training for Latin American Armed Forces," in *Foreign Relations of the United States, 1961–1963*, vol. 12, *American Republics* (Washington: GPO, 1996), 180 [item 80].

40 Chester Bowles (Acting Sec. of State) to President Kennedy, letter, September 30, 1961, NSF, NSAM, Box 331–2, FN NSAM 88, 1.

for new "military actions for Latin America."[41] JCSM 832–61 called for "congressional action" to reduce the limitations on internal security training and spending, and a reorientation from "hemispheric defense only to internal security, anti-submarine warfare, counterinsurgency, and civic action." The memorandum also pushed "all US Government representatives in Latin America . . . to stress that the military is an instrument responsive to democratic government and should act in support of the constitutional principles of that government."[42] While the president acknowledged the general principles of JCSM 832–61, he also made it clear on December 5, 1961, in NSAM 118 that he wanted the Department of State and especially the Department of Defense to provide greater clarity and specificity in their intentions and efforts.[43] In mid-December, McGeorge Bundy further admonished the secretary of state and secretary of defense that "the President is concerned that we may be missing an opportunity this year to develop methods for supporting whatever contribution military forces can make to economic and social development in less-developed countries." Bundy added that "while recognizing that civic action is not universally applicable . . . we must coordinate civic action with other programs directed at the same goals."[44]

President Kennedy grew increasingly impatient with the limited improvements made in Latin American internal security forces as he entered his second year in office. On January 11, 1962, the president issued a stern note to Robert McNamara, writing that, "I am not satisfied

41 L. L. Lemnitzer (Chair, JCS) to President Kennedy, memorandum, JCSM 832–61, November 30, 1961, "Military Actions for Latin America (U)," in *Foreign Relations, 1961–1963*, vol. 12, *American Republics*, 197–8 [item 89].

42 L. L. Lemnitzer (Chair, JCS) to President Kennedy, memorandum, JCSM 832–61, November 30, 1961, "Military Actions for Latin America (U)," Appendix A, "Military Actions for Latin America," in *Foreign Relations, 1961–1963*, vol. 12, *American Republics*, 199 [item 89].

43 McGeorge Bundy (Spec. Asst. NSA) to Secretary of State and Secretary of Defense, memorandum, NSAM 118, December 5, 1961, "Participation of U.S. Armed Forces in the Attainment of Common Objectives in Latin America," NSF, NSAM, Box 333, FN NSAM 118, 1, Kennedy Presidential Library.

44 McGeorge Bundy (Spec. Asst. NSA) to Secretary of State and Defense, NSAM 119, December 18, 1961, "Participation of U.S. Armed Forces in the Attainment of Common Objectives in Latin America," NSF, NSAM, Box 333, FN NSAM 119, 1, Kennedy Presidential Library.

that the Department of Defense, and in particular the Army, is according the necessary degree of attention and effort to the threat of communist-directed subversive insurgency and guerrilla warfare, although it is clear that these constitute a major form of politico-military conflict for which we must carefully prepare."[45] Kennedy chastised the army's effort at some length and specifically directed the Joint Chiefs to add a general officer to direct counterinsurgency training efforts, and that all MAAG officers receive training at Ft. Bragg.[46] Two days later, in JCS Memorandum 30–62, the chairman of the Joint Chiefs, General L. L. Lemnitzer, sent the update the president had requested in early December. The charts the general provided the president, however, listed activities then underway—much of which had already been reported to the president—and did not address Kennedy's concerns about a unified counterinsurgency training mechanism, both within and outside the United States.[47]

The Special Group Takes Charge

President Kennedy decided on January 18, 1962, to establish the Special Group Counter Insurgency (CI) to oversee the development of United States counterinsurgency training and capacity.[48] President Eisenhower had formed the Special Group as a body in 1954 to supervise U.S. activities in Guatemala.[49] Called the Special Group 5412, so named after

---

45   President Kennedy to Robert McNamara (Sec. of Def.), memorandum, January 11, 1962, RG 330 Records of the Office of the Secretary of Defense, Office of the Assistant Secretary of Defense (International Security Affairs), Box 56, FN 370.64 January–July, 1962, 1, NARA II.

46   Kennedy to McNamara., January 11, 1962, 2.

47   L. L. Lemnitzer (Chair, JCS) to Robert McNamara (Sec. of Def.), memorandum, JCSM 30–62, January 13, 1962, "Participation of US and Latin American Armed Forces in the Attainment of Common Objectives in Latin America (U)," NSF, NSAM, Box 333, FN NSAM 118-JCS Proposal, Tab B, Annex A, 3/62, 2, Kennedy Presidential Library.

48   Barber and Ronning, *Internal Security*, 97. See McClintock, *Instruments of Statecraft*, 166–70; and Rabe, *Most Dangerous Area*, 128, for discussion of the formation of the Special Group and its role in Latin American policy.

49   On U.S. intervention in Guatemala, see Nick Cullather, *Secret History: The CIA's Classified Account of Its Operations in Guatemala, 1952–1954*, with afterword by Piero

the National Security Council action that authorized its formation, it continued to serve Eisenhower throughout the 1950s on clandestine internal security matters abroad.[50] Kennedy appointed Major General Maxwell Taylor to lead this small but very influential group when he took office. Taylor had reportedly left his post as Army chief of staff under Eisenhower in part because the president did not share the general's convictions about counterinsurgency forces and also because Taylor openly challenged the defense posture of the United States under Eisenhower.[51] But Taylor did fit the new president's mold.[52] While McGeorge Bundy drafted the initial memorandum calling for a reformulation of the Special Group,[53] details emerged out of an evaluation of the Bay of Pigs disaster conducted by Richard Bissell.[54]

The Special Group (CI) carried significant weight within the Kennedy administration. The Group was initially comprised of Taylor as the chair, along with Deputy Secretary of Defense Roswell Gilpatric, the Undersecretary

Gliejeses (Stanford, CA: Stanford University Press, 1999); Richard Immerman, *The CIA in Guatemala: The Foreign Policy of Intervention* (Austin: The University of Texas Press, 1982); Stephen Schlesinger and Stephen Kinzer, *Bitter Fruit: The Untold Story of the American Coup in Guatemala* (New York: Anchor Books, 1982); Piero Gleijeses, *Shattered Hope: The Guatemala Revolution and the United States, 1944–1954* (Princeton, NJ: Princeton University Press, 1991); and Ronald Schneider, *Communism in Guatemala* (New York: Octagon, 1979).

50   National Security Council, paper, NSC 5412, March [12,] 1954, "National Security Council Directive on Covert Operations," WHO, NSA, Box 10, FN NSC 5412, Eisenhower Presidential Library. See also McClintock, *Instruments of Statecraft*, 166.

51   On Taylor, Eisenhower, and counterinsurgency, see McClintock, *Instruments of Statecraft*, 512, n. 19. For the general's views on the military in general, see Maxwell Taylor, *The Uncertain Trumpet* (New York: Harper, 1960).

52   Barber and Ronning, *Internal Security*, 94.

53   Maxwell Taylor (Chair, Special Group 5412) to President Kennedy, memorandum, January 2, 1962, "Establishment of the Special Group (Counter-Insurgency)," enclosure, McGeorge Bundy (Spec. Asst. NSA) to Special Group 5412, memorandum, Draft NSAM, "Establishment of Special Group (Counter-Insurgency)," NSF, NSAM, Box 333, FN NSAM 124, 1–3. Kennedy Presidential Library.

54   Robert W. Komer (Spec. Asst. Intelligence) to McGeorge Bundy (Spec. Asst. NSA), letter, January 31, 1962, NSF, NSAM, Box 333, FN NSAM 124, 1, Kennedy Presidential Library.

of State for Political Affairs U. Alexis Johnson, Chairman of the Joint Chiefs of Staff General Lemnitzer, the new CIA director John McCone, National Security Advisor McGeorge Bundy, and the administrator of the Agency for International Development (AID), Fowler Hamilton.[55] Robert Kennedy rounded out the initial complement and proved to be perhaps the most important member of the Special Group (CI). The attorney general shared—or at least openly supported—his brother's conviction of the necessity of confronting communism in this manner and fought to instill the president's sense of urgency into his administration. Robert Kennedy also reported directly to the president immediately following each weekly meeting.[56] The members that constituted the Special Group (CI), as well as the importance the president attached to the group's purpose, assured its influence.

Developing a uniform standard for counterinsurgency training quickly became the primary responsibility for the Special Group (CI). As early as August 1961, the Policy Planning Council advised General Taylor that the United States needed to institutionalize a "comprehensive course in counter-guerrilla operations."[57] Eight months later, in NSAM 131, the national security advisor issued a directive to the secretaries of state and defense, the attorney general, the chairman of the Joint Chiefs, and the heads of the CIA, AID, and USIA, requiring training for "officer grade personnel . . . who may have a role to play in counterinsurgency programs as well as in the entire range of problems involved in the modernization of developing countries."[58] The Special Group (CI) developed the criteria contained in NSAM 131, which stressed that "personnel of all grades will be required to study the history of subversive insurgency movements, past and present, in order to familiarize themselves with . . . communist tactics

55 President Kennedy to NSC, memorandum, NSAM 124, "Establishment of the Special Group (Counter-Insurgency)," NSF, NSAM, Box 333, FN NSAM 124, 1, Kennedy Presidential Library; and in McClintock, *Instruments of Statecraft*, 167.

56 See Roswell Gilpatric's comments in McClintock, *Instruments of Statecraft*, 167.

57 George McGhee (PPS) to Gen. Maxwell Taylor, memorandum, August 7, 1961, "US Counter-Guerrilla Operational and Training Capabilities," NSF, NSAM, Box 331–2, FN NSAM 88, 1, Kennedy Presidential Library.

58 McGeorge Bundy (Spec. Asst. NSA) to Special Group (CI), memorandum, NSAM 131, March 13, 1962, "Training Objectives for Counter-Insurgency," RG 330 Records of the Office of the Secretary of Defense, Office of the Assistant Secretary of Defense (International Security Affairs), Box 32, FN 353, January–March, 1962, 2, NARA II.

and techniques."[59] Kennedy and his advisors were concerned that there was "an unfulfilled need to offer instruction on the entire range of problems" that would confront "middle and senior grade officers (both military and civilian) who are about to occupy important posts in underdeveloped countries." The president directed—"as a matter of urgency"—the newly formed and highly secret Special Group (CI) to "explore ways of organizing school . . . on the national level" to provide comprehensive instruction "for guiding underdeveloped countries through the modernization barrier and for countering subversive insurgency."[60]

A broad array of agencies and departments quickly responded to the president, touting their own counterinsurgency training efforts. Roswell Gilpatric, the deputy secretary of defense, informed the National Security Council in late February 1962 that the department had established a Defense Intelligence School "designed for advanced (or post graduate) intelligence staff officer and attaché training and generally will be based on (1) the postgraduate course on intelligence presently being offered at the Naval Intelligence School, and (2) the courses presently being offered at the Army Strategic Intelligence School."[61] By May, the reports had begun to roll in. The National War College reported that it offered a course on counterinsurgency training in May 1962.[62] The CIA offered its first two-week counterinsurgency course on May 28, 1962, noting that "officers preparing to command, staff and country-team positions should find this course particularly useful to identify the problems encountered in spe-

59   William P. Bundy (Dep. Asst. Sec. Def.) to Secretary of Defense, March 22, 1962, "Training Objectives for Counter-Insurgency," RG 330 Records of the Office of the Secretary of Defense, Office of the Assistant Secretary of Defense (International Security Affairs), Box 32, FN 353, January–March, 1962, 1, NARA II.

60   Bundy, NSAM 131, 2.

61   Roswell Gilpatric (Dep. Sec of State to NSC, memorandum, February 27, 1962, "Establishment of a Defense School," RG 330 Records of the Office of the Secretary of Defense, Office of the Assistant Secretary of Defense (International Security Affairs), Box 49, FN 352 January–March, 1962,1, NARA II.

62   Col. Goodman to Dir. of Personnel, OSD, memorandum, May 12, 1962, "Nomination to Counterinsurgency Course at National War College," RG 330 Records of the Office of the Secretary of Defense, Office of the Assistant Secretary of Defense (International Security Affairs), Box 51, FN 353 April–May, 1962, 1; NARA II.

cific countries and to plan courses of action."[63] The CIA offered a second counterinsurgency course in mid-September.[64] The assistant secretary of defense for international security affairs requested in early May 1962 a variety of experts to participate in an "Interdepartmental Course in counterinsurgency."[65] The secretary of agriculture, Orville Freeman,[66] and the secretary of labor, Arthur Goldberg, offered their departments' "cooperation in connection with this most important mission."[67] Finally, in December 1962, the Joint Chiefs submitted to Robert McNamara a "proposal to provide a counterinsurgency orientation for senior executives of the major North American corporations operating in Latin America."[68]

Not surprisingly, the various branches of the U.S. Armed Services weighed in to promote their specialized training. The army reported in May 1962 that "a number of foreign students attend relatively long courses at the Infantry School and at the Command and General Staff College, parts of which are devoted to counterinsurgency problems, counter-guer-

----

63   Lt. Gen. Marshall A. Carter (Acting Director, CIA) to Robert S. McNamara (Sec. of Def.), letter, May 11, 1962, RG 330 Records of the Office of the Secretary of Defense, Office of the Assistant Secretary of Defense (International Security Affairs), Box 49, FN 352 April–June, 1962, 1–3, NARA II.

64   Carter to McNamara, letter, May 11, 1962, 1.

65   William Bundy (ASD/ISA) to JCS, memorandum, May 9, 1962, "Interdepartmental Course on Under-development and Counterinsurgency," RG 330 Records of the Office of the Secretary of Defense, Office of the Assistant Secretary of Defense (International Security Affairs), Box 49, FN 352 April–June, 1962, 1–3, NARA II.

66   Orville L. Freeman (Sec. of Agriculture) to Gen. Maxwell D. Taylor (Chair, Special Group, CI), letter, February 14, 1962, RG 330 Records of the Office of the Secretary of Defense, Office of the Assistant Secretary of Defense (International Security Affairs), Box 56, FN 370.64 January–July, 1962, 1–2, NARA II.

67   Arthur J. Goldberg (Secretary of Labor) to Gen. Maxwell D. Taylor (Chair, Special Group, CI), letter, January 31, 1962, RG 330 Records of the Office of the Secretary of Defense, Office of the Assistant Secretary of Defense (International Security Affairs), Box 56, FN 370.64 January–July, 1962, 1–2, NARA II.

68   JCS to Secretary of Defense, memorandum, December 22, 1962, "Counterinsurgency Orientation (U)," RG 330 Records of the Office of the Secretary of Defense, Office of the Assistant Secretary of Defense (International Security Affairs), Box 55, FN 370.64 November–December 1962, 1, NARA II.

rilla techniques and tactics."[69] While the air force acknowledged that it needed to "increase its COIN [counterinsurgency] forces to a level that will be capable of properly fulfilling requirements," [70] the service did point out that it possessed "facilities . . . to train foreign personnel in the use of the C-130A, B, and E aircraft as well as the C 118 and C 119 aircraft," useful for short airstrips and low-altitude airdrops. [71] The assistant secretary of the navy reported in mid-May 1962 that the navy had incorporated counterinsurgency training into everything from OCS, pilot, and submarine training as well as "supply corps school, hospital administration school and dental officer indoctrination courses."[72] The Naval War College wanted students to understand the "political, economic, social and military conditions in which the selected insurgency occurred together with strategy tactics, and techniques used by the communists and by those who sought to counter the insurgency,"[73] while Navy SEALs received training not only

....

69   Col. Thomas A. Kenan to Walt Rostow (Chair, PPC), memorandum, May 24, 1962, "Report Required by NSAM 131," RG 330 Records of the Office of the Secretary of Defense, Office of the Assistant Secretary of Defense (International Security Affairs), Box 51, FN 353 April–May, 1962, 1, NARA II.

70   Eugene M. Zuchert (Sec. of the Air Force) to Secretary of Defense, memorandum, May 9, 1962, "(U) Expansion of USAF Counterinsurgency (COIN) Capability," RG 330 Records of the Office of the Secretary of Defense, Office of the Assistant Secretary of Defense (International Security Affairs), Box 56, FN 370.64 January–July, 1962, 1–2, NARA II.

71   Kenan to Rostow, "Report Required by NSAM 131," 2.

72   Fred Korth (Asst. Sec. of the Navy) to Secretary of Defense, memorandum, May 12, 1962, "Training Objectives for Counterinsurgency (U)," enclosure, "Navy and Marine Corps Counterinsurgency Education and Training Program," Tab 1, "Naval War College Pilot Course in Counterinsurgency," Appendix 1, "Navy Three-Level Program for Counterinsurgency Indoctrination," RG 330 Records of the Office of the Secretary of Defense, Office of the Assistant Secretary of Defense (International Security Affairs), Box 51, FN 353 April–May, 1962, 1, NARA II.

73   Fred Korth (Asst. Sec. of the Navy) to Secretary of Defense, memorandum, May 12, 1962, "Training Objectives for Counterinsurgency (U)," Enclosure, "Navy and Marine Corps Counterinsurgency Education and Training Program," Tab 1, "Naval War College Pilot Course in Counterinsurgency," Appendix 1, "Navy Three-Level Program for Counterinsurgency Indoctrination," RG 330 Records of the Office of the Secretary of Defense, Office of the Assistant Secretary of Defense (International

in "underwater demolition" but also in "ranger training," "airborne train-ing," and "jungle operations."[74]

The Kennedy administration relied on the U.S. Army Special Forces and the AID to spearhead counterinsurgency operations and economic development. Certainly, the army's Green Berets were the poster children of Kennedy's counterinsurgency push.[75] By May 1962, the army had of-fered counterinsurgency courses at the Special Warfare Center, the prima-ry Special Forces base at Ft. Bragg, to military from Europe, the Near and Far East, and the Western Hemisphere.[76] Five more courses took place in the last half of 1962.[77] In addition, the army operated training facilities at "Fort Gulick in the Panama Canal Zone, in [Bishiwaka] Okinawa and at Oberammergau in Germany" for foreign military personnel. The latter two facilities did not open until fiscal year 1962.[78] The West German camp had trained fifteen Greek cadres by May 1962,[79] while the Bishiwaka base

---

Security Affairs), Box 51, FN 353 Apr.-May, 1962, 2–3, NARA II.

74 Fred Korth (Asst. Sec. of the Navy) to Secretary of Defense, memorandum, May 12, 1962, "Training Objectives for Counterinsurgency (U)," enclosure, "Navy and Marine Corps Counterinsurgency Education and Training Program," Appendix 1, "Navy Three-Level Program for Counterinsurgency Indoctrination," RG 330 Records of the Office of the Secretary of Defense, Office of the Assistant Secretary of Defense (International Security Affairs), Box 51, FN 353 April–May, 1962, 5. NARA II.

75 A. M. Rosenthal, "Guerrilla Base Gets U.S. Priority: Elite Officers Trained in Special Okinawa School," *New York Times*, September 10, 1961, p. A1, col. 4.

76 Col. Thomas A. Kenan to Dir. Policy Planning Staff, memorandum, May 24, 1962, "Report Required by NSAM 131," Tab B, "Number of Courses Provided to Foreign Nationals at the U.S. Army Special Warfare School, Fort Bragg, N.C. by Fiscal Year," RG 330 Records of the Office of the Secretary of Defense, Office of the Assistant Secretary of Defense (International Security Affairs), Box 51, FN 353 April–May, 1962, 1–5, NARA II.

77 John E. Moore (Director of Personnel, OSD), administrative memorandum, June 26, 1962, "Counterinsurgency and Special Warfare Course," RG 330 Records of the Office of the Secretary of Defense, Office of the Assistant Secretary of Defense (International Security Affairs), Box 49, FN 352 April–June, 1962, 1, NARA II.

78 Kenan to Rostow, "Report Required by NSAM 131," 2.

79 Col. Thomas A. Kenan to Dir. Policy Planning Staff, memorandum, May 24, 1962, "Report Required by NSAM 131," Tab E, "Number of Counter-Insurgency Courses Provided Foreign Nationals at Oberammergau by Fiscal Year," RG 330 Records of

held over three hundred courses for Asian nationals,[80] primarily for those soldiers from Taiwan, South Korea, Thailand, and South Vietnam.[81] The AID, the foremost non-military agency established to direct the modernization projects of the United States, reported to the Special Group (CI) in July 1962, touting its broad range of "counterinsurgency activities,"[82] that included six "courses for Agency personnel"[83] and two for "foreign nationals."[84] Not surprisingly, AID emphasized "economic and social development programs through the Alliance for Progress" in Latin America. In the same vein, the agency described the range of civic action activities around the world as part of their "specific counterinsurgency programs."[85] In the region, AID wrote that "programs are underway in Honduras, Paraguay, Bolivia, Peru, Ecuador, and Chile. Guatemala and Brazil have had programs for a number of years with the need for U.S. assistance."[86]

the Office of the Secretary of Defense, Office of the Assistant Secretary of Defense (International Security Affairs), Box 51, FN 353 April–May, 1962, 1, NARA II.

80   Col. Thomas A. Kenan to Dir. Policy Planning Staff, memorandum, May 24, 1962, "Report Required by NSAM 131," Tab D, "Number of Counter-Insurgency Courses Provided Foreign Nationals at Okinawa by Fiscal Year," RG 330 Records of the Office of the Secretary of Defense, Office of the Assistant Secretary of Defense (International Security Affairs), Box 51, FN 353 April–May, 1962, 1, NARA II.

81   Col. Thomas A. Kenan to Dir. Policy Planning Staff, memorandum, May 24, 1962, "Report Required by NSAM 131," Tab A, "Number of Counter-Insurgency Courses Provided Foreign Nationals in the CONUS and Overseas by Fiscal Year," RG 330 Records of the Office of the Secretary of Defense, Office of the Assistant Secretary of Defense (International Security Affairs), Box 51, FN 353 April–May, 1962, 3, NARA II.

82   Frank M. Coffin (Dep. Admin. for Ops., AID) to Special Group (CI), memorandum, July 18, 1962, "A.I.D. Supported Counterinsurgency Activities," RG 330 Records of the Office of the Secretary of Defense, Office of the Assistant Secretary of Defense (International Security Affairs), Box 56, FN 370.64 January–July, 1962, 1, NARA II.

83   Dennis Brennan (PRCA/AID) to Special Group (CI), memorandum, June 20, 1960, "Agency for International Development Response to NSAM 131," RG 330 Records of the Office of the Secretary of Defense, Office of the Assistant Secretary of Defense (International Security Affairs), Box 51, FN 353 June–August, 1962, 2, NARA II.

84   Brennan to Special Group (CI), "AID Response to NSAM 131," 5.

85   Coffin to Special Group (CI), July 18, 1962, "A.I.D. Supported Counterinsurgency Activities," 2.

86   Coffin to Special Group (CI), July 18, 1962, "A.I.D. Supported Counterinsurgency

Navigating Congress

Congressional opposition to internal security training of Latin American military, however, continued to limit the Kennedy administration's efforts to counter communist subversion in the hemisphere. The State Department placed the blame squarely in the hands of Senator Wayne Morse, the Democratic senator from Oregon. Staffers correctly argued that Senator Morse sought to inhibit internal security training by requiring the president himself to make the determination of need.[87] Morse had a well-earned reputation as an opponent of internal security aid and training to Latin America. He chaired the Subcommittee for the American Republics on the Senate Foreign Relations Committee, and, as such, he possessed considerable institutional power over legislation, especially with regard to military and economic aid packages. Morse did not hesitate to make use of his authority, and during his tenure he routinely frustrated Defense and State Department staffers with his pointed attacks on their efforts to secure funding for various programs.[88]

Morse opposed military aid to Latin America on principle and as a matter of policy. He preferred a "deemphasis on military assistance."[89] Morse did not believe that the United States should fund dictators, and he felt that military aid and training—especially for internal security—only strengthened the repressive control of the "tight little oligarchies" that so plagued the region.[90] Like many in Congress, Morse also feared that giving mili-

---

Activities," 3.

87   J. O. Bell (DC/For. Asst.) to Dean Rusk (Sec. of State), memorandum, June 26, 1961, "Proposed Presidential Determination under Section 105 (b)(4) of the MSA of 1954 [sic], as amended, permitting the use of funds to furnish military assistance to Panama, Costa Rica, Nicaragua, El Salvador, Honduras, Guatemala, and Haiti," in *Foreign Relations, 1961–1963*, vol. 12, *American Republics*, 177 [item 77].

88   Arthur Robert Smith, *The Tiger in the Senate: The Biography of Wayne Morse* (Garden City, NY: Doubleday, 1962); Mason Drukman, *Wayne Morse: A Political Biography* (Portland: Oregon Historical Society Press, 1997).

89   Senate Committee on Foreign Relations, Sub-Committee on the American Republics, *South America: Argentina, Brazil, Bolivia, Chile, Colombia, and Venezuela*, Wayne Morse Study Mission to South America, 86th Cong., 2nd sess., February 20, 1960 (Washington, DC: GPO, 1960), 7.

90   Senate Committee on Foreign Relations, *South America*, Wayne Morse Study

tary hardware to Latin America would lead to an arms race that would "invite chaos" and intra-regional warfare. Most important, Congress felt that the emphasis on military assistance took money and effort away from economic development.[91] Morse laid the groundwork for Jimmy Carter when he opposed military aid to dictators and argued that the United States should reward democratic or democratizing governments with economic aid, and exclude aid to authoritarian ones.[92] Morse did believe in economic development. He fought with Eisenhower to increase economic assistance for just that reason.[93] But, he did not accept President Kennedy's insistence that internal security training must become a concomitant part of the process.

The Kennedy administration worked hard to convince Congress to dispense with the restrictions on internal security training to Latin America. The Defense Department, amidst strenuous efforts to reorient its hemispheric defense posture, had argued in May 1961 that the United States must "in our military programs, give first priority to measures designed to meet the threat to internal security."[94] In order to secure the necessary funding, the Department of Defense wanted the administration to "seek the repeal of the Morse Amendment" to foreign aid, which limited foreign aid to internal security purposes. The president's supporters in Congress did manage to modify the language somewhat in the 1961 funding to include some "new concepts."[95] The law spoke generally about the United

Mission, 2.

91   J. Lloyd Mecham, *The United States and Inter-American Security, 1889–1960* (Austin: The University of Texas Press, 1961), 339–40.

92   Senate Committee on Foreign Relations, *South America*, Wayne Morse Study Mission, 7–8.

93   Burton I. Kaufman, *Trade and Aid: Eisenhower's Foreign Economic Policy, 1953–1961* (Baltimore: The Johns Hopkins University Press, 1982), 133–52.

94   Haydn Williams (Dep. Asst. for International Security Affairs) to Adolph Berle (Chair, Task Force on Immediate Problems in Latin America), letter, June 28, 1961, Enclosure, Paper, May 19, 1961, "U.S. Policy for the Security of Latin America in the Sixties," in *Foreign Relations, 1961–1963*, vol. 12, *American Republics*, 176 [item 76].

95   Department of State, AID, *Latin American Internal Security Programs Under Mutual Security Act 1960, Foreign Assistance Acts 1961–1965*, Parts I–IV, RG 59 General Records of the Department of State, Central Foreign Policy File, 1964–66, Box 2413 FN POL 23

States' responsibility to provide military training and assistance that would permit "friendly countries . . . to deter or, if necessary, defeat communist or communist-supported aggression . . . to maintain internal security, and creat[e] an environment of security and stability in the developing countries."[96] On June 26, 1961, the State Department sought authorization for internal security training for the nations of Central America and Haiti for just those reasons.[97] But Congress balked and kept the "long-standing congressional prohibition on aid to Latin America for internal security purposes" in Section 511(b) of the 1961 Foreign Assistance Act.[98] Section 511(b) prohibited internal security aid "unless the president determines otherwise."[99] Congress did not forbid internal security assistance; it adopted the Morse Amendment to force the president to officially commit the United States to internal security training in Latin America. In Executive Order 10893, President Eisenhower sought to side-step Congress by authorizing the secretary of state to make the decision.[100] So Morse revised the 1961 Mutual Security Act and added section 105(b-4), which now required that the president *promptly [report] such determination to the Senate Committee on Foreign Relations and to the Speaker of the House of Representatives.*"[101] In late September 1961, Chester Bowles, acting for Secretary of State Dean

----

LA 9/11/65, 10, NARA II.

96 In Department of State, AID, *Latin American Internal Security Programs*, Parts I–IV, 11.

97 Bell to Rusk, June 26, 1961, "Proposed Presidential Determination," 176–7 [item 77].

98 Department of State, AID, *Latin American Internal Security Programs*, 11.

99 Chester Bowles (Acting Secretary of State) to President Kennedy, memorandum, September 29, 1961, "Determination Under Sections 511 (b) and 614 (a) of the Foreign Assistance Act of 1961, as Amended, Permitting the Use of Funds in Order to Furnish Military Assistance to Panama, Costa Rica, Nicaragua, El Salvador, Honduras, and Guatemala," in *Foreign Relations, 1961–1963,* vol. 12, *American Republics,* 187–90 [item 85].

100 Dwight D. Eisenhower to Secretary of State (Merchant), memorandum, January 5, 1960, "Determinations under Sections 105 (b)(4) and 451 (a) of the Mutual Security Act of 1954, as Amended, Permitting the Furnishing of Military Assistance to Colombia," White House Central File, Confidential. Subject, Box 42, FN Mutual Security Assistance [1961] (1), 1, Eisenhower Presidential Library.

101 Department of State, AID, *Latin American Internal Security Programs*, 11.

Rusk, revised the request for internal security training in Central America according to the new dictates of the 1961 act.[102]

Senator Morse continued throughout 1962 to stymie Kennedy administration efforts to remove the restrictions on internal security aid and training. In March 1962, Undersecretary of State George Ball went through legislative channels to ask Senator Morse to raise the ceiling on Military Assistance Program (MAP) spending for internal security training and aid. Instead, the senator responded that he felt the limit should be lowered.[103] General W. A. Enemark, the chief of Western Hemisphere Affairs for the office of the assistant secretary of defense for International Security Affairs, testified before Congress in June of 1962 and argued that, in order for the Alliance for Progress to succeed, the "security forces in Latin America . . . must have the effective force required to cope with subversion."[104] Congress refused to modify the restrictions any further, so Kennedy responded by once again delegating authority to the secretary of state.[105] Senator Morse in a letter to the secretary of state in August 1962 put his concerns bluntly when he countered that "for many years I have been appalled at the apparent lack of concern of the Department of Defense in providing political orientation and training to foreign military personnel brought to the United States for training." He went on to stress that he and the members of his subcommittee felt very strongly that "officials in the executive branch" did not seem to comprehend the "implications and

102   See n. 99.

103   Edwin M. Martin (Asst. Sec. of State, ARA) and Carl Marcy (COS, Senate For. Rels. Comm.), Department of State, memorandum of conversation, March 30, 1962, "Military Assistance Program for Latin America," RG 59 Records of the Department of State, Central Decimal File, 1960–1963, Box 1516, FN 720.5/2–962, 1, NARA II.

104   U.S. House, *Foreign Affairs Committee, Hearings, Foreign Assistance Act 1962*, 87th Cong., 1st Sess., 268, cited in Department of State, AID, *Latin American Internal Security Programs under Mutual Security Act 1960, Foreign Assistance Acts 1961–1965*, Parts I–IV, RG 59 General Records of the Department of State, Central Foreign Policy File, 1964–66, Box 2413 FN POL 23 LA 9/11/65, 15, NARA II.

105   Hollis B. Chenery (Dir., Program Review and Coord. Staff, AID) to Gen. W. B. Palmer (Dir. Military Assistance, ASD/ISA), letter, July 9, 1962, RG 330 Records of the Office of the Secretary of Defense, Office of the Assistant Secretary of Defense (International Security Affairs), Box 51, FN 353 June–August, 1962, 1, NARA II.

dangers of our military assistance programs to Latin America."[106] It would not be until 1965, with the war in Vietnam underway, that Congress would agree to lift the restrictions on MAP training and aid for internal security.

Action Plan for Subversion

The growing threat to Southeast Asia, and not Latin America, pushed President Kennedy despite congressional opposition to demand a standardized means of responding to continuing communist subversion. Ideally, the president wanted the Special Group (CI) to assess threat levels and direct the United States' response. To do that, the United States still needed an operating guide for assessing, developing, and ensuring internal security within the underdeveloped world. Spurred by the directives of the president and prodded by the Special Group (CI), every aspect of the executive branch—and not just the armed services—rushed to offer a counterinsurgency program. The Special Group (CI) drew upon that concerted effort to provide the president with the requisite manual as the summer of 1962 waned: NSAM 182 "US Overseas Internal Defense Policy."[107] Now, President Kennedy had the mechanism (the Special Group [CI]) and the guidance (NSAM 182) to combat La Guerra de Guerrillas.

Specifically, NSAM 182 sought the "defeat of . . . communist inspired, supported, or directed subversion or insurgency . . . which are inimical to U.S. national security interests in all countries of the free world, primarily those that are underdeveloped."[108] The new manual for combating subversion drew attention to the success of insurgents in Algeria, French Indochina, and Cuba, and thus emphasized the reality of the communist threat and the historical example each of these movements represented

106   William P. Bundy (Act. Asst. Sec. of Def.) to Secretary of the Army, memorandum, August 19, 1962, "Role of the U.S. in Providing Military Assistance to Latin American Countries," enclosure, Wayne Morse to Dean Rusk (Secretary of State), letter, August 3, 1962, RG FN Latin America, OSA 092.3 Latin America FW 8–9–62, 1–3, NARA II.

107   McGeorge Bundy (Spec. Asst. NSA) to Special Group (CI), memorandum, NSAM 182, August 13, 1962, "Counterinsurgency Doctrine," Tab A, "U.S. Overseas Internal Defense Policy," NSF, NSAM, Box 338–9, FN NSAM 182, 1–31, Kennedy Presidential Library.

108   Bundy to Special Group (CI), NSAM 182, "Counterinsurgency Doctrine," Tab A, "U.S. Overseas Internal Defense Policy," 1.

to future insurgent groups.[109] The Special Group (CI) argued that communist subversion followed clearly defined stages, from "building a power base," to limited tactical armed action, to strategic resistance against established regimes. Since each stage had its own purpose designed to take advantage of the vulnerability of developing nations, the United States had to perforce deny to communism the efforts of the people of underdeveloped nations.[110]

The Special Group (CI) continued to promote economic development as the clearest method to permanently forestall communist expansion in the underdeveloped world.[111] Civic action programs served the crucial dual purpose in this phase of the battle; they built up fragile developing infrastructures while securing the will of a developing nation's people for economic development.[112] The Special Group (CI) also did not ignore psychological warfare. Instead, psychological warfare served as a tactic, like counterinsurgency, that could be applied to negate subversive action and promote acceptance of economic and social changes fostered to promote economic modernization. Accordingly, Kennedy added the director of the United States Information Agency to the Special Group (CI) in NSAM 180.[113] The president wanted an effective propaganda mechanism to counter the blandishments of worldwide communism.

The Special Group (CI) bore the responsibility of identifying the existing threat levels and applying the commensurate action by the broad range of U.S. assets available. NSAM 182 called for the AID to bear the lion's share of the responsibility for stimulating economic development in threatened nations. Promoting and providing internal security fell to

---

109   Bundy to Special Group (CI), NSAM 182, "Counterinsurgency Doctrine," Tab A, "U.S. Overseas Internal Defense Policy," 2–3.

110   Bundy to Special Group (CI), NSAM 182, "Counterinsurgency Doctrine," Tab A, "U.S. Overseas Internal Defense Policy," 8–10.

111   Bundy to Special Group (CI), NSAM 182, "Counterinsurgency Doctrine," Tab A, "U.S. Overseas Internal Defense Policy," 6–8.

112   Bundy to Special Group (CI), NSAM 182, "Counterinsurgency Doctrine," Tab A, "U.S. Overseas Internal Defense Policy," 13–19.

113   McGeorge Bundy (Spec. Asst. NSA) to NSC, memorandum, NSAM 180, August 13, 1962, "Membership of the Special Group (CI)," RG 330 Records of the Office of the Secretary of Defense, Office of the Assistant Secretary of Defense (International Security Affairs), Box 55, FN 370.64 August–Oct., 1962, 1, NARA II.

the Department of Defense, whose responsibilities included providing equipment, advisors, and training to members of the police, paramilitary, and military.[114] Deputy Secretary of State U. Alexis Johnson, the new executive secretary of the Special Group (CI), sought to give the preeminent role to the State Department, particularly that of the ambassador, in assessing and implementing what he essentially viewed as political policy.[115] General Taylor disagreed and made sure to insert an important addendum to NSAM 182 that directed the Department of Defense to "support the CIA in clandestine operations" as well as to "execute assigned [deleted word] operations . . . which require . . . military experience of a kind and level peculiar to the Armed Services."[116] When the Special Group (CI) decided to intercede, they brought the full range of U.S. government agencies and departments to bear, putting into play the mechanisms they had worked to establish in the preceding months.

Periodic threats to established military regimes gave the Special Group (CI) the opportunity to put NSAM 182 into action. Persistent coup attempts in Guatemala called for a delicate balancing act by the Special Group in the Fall of 1962.[117] In what Undersecretary of State George Ball hailed as "one of the most carefully prepared and reviewed of all the Internal

----

114 McGeorge Bundy (Spec. Asst. NSA) to Special Group (CI), memorandum, NSAM 182, August 13, 1962, "Counterinsurgency Doctrine," Tab A, "U.S. Overseas Internal Defense Policy," Annex C, "Model Outline of Country Internal Defense Plan," NSF, NSAM, Box 338–9, FN NSAM 182, 1–2, Kennedy Presidential Library.

115 U. Alexis Johnson (Special Group [CI]) to Secretary of State, memorandum, August 8, 1962, "U.S. Overseas Internal Defense Policy," RG 59 Records of the Department of State, Executive Secretariat, Records of the Special Group (Counter Insurgency), 1962–1966, Box 1, FN Special Group (CI) 8/1/62–10/31/62, 1, NARA II.

116 McGeorge Bundy (Spec. Asst. NSA) to Special Group (CI), memorandum, NSAM 182, August 13, 1962, "Counterinsurgency Doctrine," Tab A, "U.S. Overseas Internal Defense Policy," Annex A, "Supplementary Role of the Department of Defense," NSF, NSAM, Box 338–9, FN NSAM 182, 1, Kennedy Presidential Library.

117 Charles Maechling (U/S Office Sec. Spec. Group [CI]) to Special Group (CI), memorandum, November 28, 1962, "Guatemala Country Internal Defense Plan," attachment, "Country Internal Defense Plan for Guatemala," RG 59 Records of the Department of State, Executive Secretariat, Records of the Special Group (Counter Insurgency), 1962–1966, Box 1, FN Special Group (CI) 8/1/62–10/31/62, 1–30, NARA II.

Defense Plans,"[118] the Special Group sought to promote a greater "understanding by Guatemalans of the objectives of the Alianza para el Progreso" while maintaining good relations with a nation that "has followed a strong anti-communist line" since 1954.[119] Unfortunately, competing elements within the Guatemalan military, the Central American nation's primary— and very effective—internal security force, proved the primary obstacle to that desired progress. The Guatemalan Air Force believed new jet aircraft would enhance their internal security mission, as they would enable them to bomb the Guatemalan Army and thereby "maintain the government." George Ball echoed the staff of the American Republics desk, as well as the general sentiment of the Joint Chiefs, when he opposed this plan.[120] Still, continued political instability threatened to engage the rural populace and university students, where communist influence, albeit definitely limited, appeared to be growing. The Special Group (CI) believed that the answer lay in the expansion and, it was hoped, professionalism of the civil-police authorities and in a concerted civic-action program by all internal security forces.[121]

In 1962, however, Southeast Asia swiftly replaced Latin America as the region of primary concern for the Kennedy administration. When he reformulated the Special Group (CI) in January, President Kennedy directed the group's efforts toward "Laos, South Viet-Nam, [and] Thailand."[122] And for the remainder of 1962, Laos occupied much of the group's at-

---

118   George Ball (U/S) to Jeffery C. Kitchen (G/PM), memorandum, November 29, 1962, "Agenda for Special Group (CI) Meeting, November 19, 1962," RG 59 Records of the Department of State, Executive Secretariat, Records of the Special Group (Counter Insurgency), 1962–1966, Box 1, FN Special Group (CI) 8/1/62–10/31/62, 1, NARA II.
119   Maechling to Special Group (CI), November 28, 1962, "Guatemala Country Internal Defense Plan," attachment, "Country Internal Defense Plan for Guatemala," 1.
120   See n. 118.
121   Maechling to Special Group (CI), November 28, 1962, "Guatemala Country Internal Defense Plan," attachment, "Country Internal Defense Plan for Guatemala," 15–24.
122   President Kennedy to Special Group (CI), memorandum, NSAM 124 Annex, January 18, 1962, "Annex to National Security Action memorandum No. 124," RG 330 Records of the Office of the Secretary of Defense, Office of the Assistant Secretary of Defense (International Security Affairs), Box 56, FN 370.64 January–July, 1962, 1, NARA II.

tention. By the time the Special Group (CI) completed NSAM 182, the level of administration attention toward Southeast Asia had increased. In mid-June 1962, the president accepted General Taylor's recommendation[123] and widened the scope of the Special Group's purview in NSAM 165 when he added several countries: Cambodia, Cameroon, Burma, Iran, Ecuador, Colombia, Venezuela, and Guatemala.[124] In October of 1962, the group's general concern for Southeast Asia led to a concerted effort in Indonesia.[125] The members offered to the president a detailed "plan of action" that included an analysis of the economic history of the nation and how its current "balance of payments" status affected its capacity to meet its foreign obligations, primarily to the Netherlands.[126] To assist this young nation, and to forestall the communist advance in the region, the Special Group (CI) recommended the intercession of substantial foreign aid along with military and paramilitary training.[127] They wanted to send in the Peace Corps.[128]

....

123   Maj. Gen. Maxwell Taylor (Chair, Special Group [CI]) to McGeorge Bundy (Spec. Asst. NSA), memorandum, June 14, 1962, "Assignment of Additional Responsibility to the Special Group (CI)," NSF, NSAM, Box 336–7, FN NSAM 165, 1, Kennedy Presidential Library.

124   McGeorge Bundy (Spec. Asst. NSA) to Special Group (CI), memorandum, NSAM 165, June 16, 1962, "Assignment of Additional Responsibility to the Special Group (CI)," NSF, NSAM, Box 336–7, FN NSAM 165, 1, Kennedy Presidential Library.

125   George W. Ball (Undersecretary of State) to the President, memorandum, October 10, 1962, "Plan of Action for Indonesia," RG 59 Records of the Department of State, Executive Secretariat, Records of the Special Group (Counter Insurgency), 1962–1966, Box 1, FN Special Group (CI) 8/1/62–10/31/62, 1–3, NARA II.

126   George W. Ball (Undersecretary of State) to the President, memorandum, October 10, 1962, "Plan of Action for Indonesia," RG 59 Records of the Department of State, Executive Secretariat, Records of the Special Group (Counter Insurgency), 1962–1966, Box 1, FN Special Group (CI) 8/1/62–10/31/62, enclosures 1–3, NARA II.

127   George W. Ball (Undersecretary of State) to the President, memorandum, October 10, 1962, "Plan of Action for Indonesia," RG 59 Records of the Department of State, Executive Secretariat, Records of the Special Group (Counter Insurgency), 1962–1966, Box 1, FN Special Group (CI) 8/1/62–10/31/62, Enclosure 9 and 11, NARA II.

128   George W. Ball (Undersecretary of State) to the President, memorandum, October 10, 1962, "Plan of Action for Indonesia," RG 59 Records of the Department of State, Executive Secretariat, Records of the Special Group (Counter Insurgency),

By 1963, the Special Group no longer viewed Latin America with the same urgency. Of course, the group remained sensitive to changing circumstances, such as a Cuban-sponsored insurgency in Venezuela.[129] Despite the secretary of the army's initial enthusiasm for the training offered at Ft. Gulick, by the end of 1961, the USARCARIB School had simply become one of many training options available to the U.S. armed forces, and not the preferred mode of instruction. And when on July 1, 1963, the Kennedy administration renamed the facility at Ft. Gulick the U.S. Army School of the Americas, the change came as part of a promotional campaign designed to enhance the flagging school in the eyes of the Latin American military.[130] By August 1963, only Honduras remained on the list of countries for which a quarterly internal defense report was required, since the Special Group (CI) had implemented Internal Defense Plans for the other five Latin American nations—Guatemala, Colombia, Venezuela, Bolivia, and Ecuador.[131] By year's end, the Bureau of Inter-American Affairs reported to the Special Group (CI) in December 1963 that "terrorism . . . is present in Latin America on a significant scale only in Venezuela."[132] The Bureau reported with confidence that the "Betancourt government is successfully keeping urban terrorism and rural insurgency within manageable limits while improving its internal security capabilities."[133]

1962–1966, Box 1, FN Special Group (CI) 8/1/62–10/31/62, enclosure 12, NARA II.

129   Sterling J. Cotrell (ARA) to Special Group (CI), memorandum, December 17, 1963, "Terrorism in the Latin American Countries on the Critical Insurgency List," RG 59 Records of the Department of State, Executive Secretariat, Records of the Special Group (Counter Insurgency), 1962–1966, Box 3, FN Special Group (CI) 10/17–12/19/63, 2, NARA II.

130   JCS, General Order No. 8, July 1, 1963, "Redesignation of Unit," in Col. Harry D. Temple (USARSO), to Commandant, USARSA, letter, September, 13 1963, Distinctive Insignia Request, File 228.01, HRC 352 Schools—U.S. Army School of the Americas, 1–2, CMH.

131   James W. Dingman (Exec. Sec., Spec. Group [CI]), memorandum, August 12, 1963, "Minutes of the Meeting of the Special Group (CI)," RG 59 Records of the Department of State, Executive Secretariat, Records of the Special Group (Counter Insurgency), 1962–1966, Box 2, FN Special Group (CI) 8/8/63–10/31/63, 2, NARA II.

132   Dingman, August 12, 1963, "Minutes," 1.

133   Dingman, August 12, 1963, "Minutes," 3.

The Most Dangerous Area in the World

President Kennedy wanted systems in place to enable the United States to respond to the subversive challenges posed by international communism in the underdeveloped world. President Kennedy assumed office convinced that the United States needed to fundamentally alter its defense posture. "Massive retaliation" had to give way to "flexible response" in order to contain the growing Soviet threat to the third world. Rising expectations left the peoples of the underdeveloped nations ripe for communist subversion. He saw in the rise of dissident insurgencies around the globe a pattern of attack directed by Moscow for so-called wars of national liberation.[134] The perceived successful co-optation of those movements by international communism, and the threat of Cuban subversion in the Western Hemisphere, convinced the Kennedy administration that the U.S. had to reorient its defense posture. A different era and a different type of conflict required a different response—counterinsurgency.

Kennedy pushed and prodded his administration to develop guidelines and protocols for the United States. Bureaucratic impediments continually frustrated the young president. Kennedy struggled to swiftly implement his new programs and found himself repeating his instructions year after year. The Joint Chiefs agreed with the need for a systemic overhaul and embarked on a thorough reorientation toward rapid deployment and response, with counterinsurgency the preferred preventative. The U.S. armed services, however, seemed bent on developing its new capabilities on its own schedule. The president countered with the Special Group (CI) and infused it with purpose and power. The United States now boasted a variety of agencies and a plethora of avenues through which Kennedy could assert his authority around the world.[135]

Kennedy kept up the public face on his Latin American policy in mid-February 1963 when he declared, "Latin America is the most critical area in the world today."[136] But his advisors had concurred the previous November that Cuba posed no immediate threat and nascent insurgencies

---

134 See Rabe, *Most Dangerous Area*, 20–2; Beschloss, *Crisis Years*, 60–1; Giglio, *John F. Kennedy*, 46–7; and McClintock, *Instruments of Statecraft*, 162–3.

135 See McClintock, *Instruments of Statecraft*, 161–257; and Barber and Ronning, *Internal Security*, 91–140.

136 Press conference reported in *New York Times*, February 13, 1963, p. 1, col. 4.

in the region stemmed from historical dilemmas and not subversion.[137] Latin America held great significance for the president during his first year in office, and the construction of Soviet missile bases in Cuba bid fair to consume the world in nuclear war in the fall of 1962. But Southeast Asia increasingly occupied the attention—and concern—of President Kennedy and his staff. Communist subversion in Laos and growing tensions in Thailand, Indonesia, and elsewhere in the region, combined with the successful violent opposition to the Diem regime in South Vietnam, led Kennedy to concentrate on developing internal security capabilities in these underdeveloped nations. While the administration turned to the growing trouble in Southeast Asia, Kennedy left the Latin American military to deal with subversion in their countries on their own.

The Latin American military, in turn, eagerly embraced counterinsurgency training. Policymakers for successive U.S. administrations correctly identified the military of Latin America as the most important power brokers in their society and concentrated on them accordingly. By the time Harry Truman signed the Military Assistance Act into law in 1949, the United States had superceded Europe as the primary source of military expertise in the hemisphere. Confronted with what they perceived as a pervasive venality that ran rampant in national and regional politics, by the eve of the Cuban Revolution the Latin American military had led for decades with the entrenched conviction that only they were fit to protect the fatherland.

Now equipped with the latest counterinsurgency doctrine and equipment, many of the region's military launched waves of violently repressive military dictatorships in the two decades after Kennedy launched his Alliance for Progress. While critics of internal security assistance for Latin American military decried the persistent use of such training for domestic political repression, the United States cared more about stability than democracy during the Cold War.[138]

---

137   John H. McCone (Dir. CIA) to President Kennedy, memorandum, SNIE 85-4-62, November 9, 1962, "Castro's Subversive Capabilities in Latin America," in *Foreign Relations, 1961–1963*, vol. 12, *American Republics*, 234-5 [item 102].

138   Barber and Ronning, *Internal Security and Military Power*, itemize regime changes in Appendix A, "Illegal and Unscheduled Changes of Heads of State," Part I, "By Country" [I–I5]. For the role of the U.S. military, see J. Lloyd Mecham, *The United States and Inter-American Security* (Austin: University of Texas Press, 1961); Raymond

Estep, *U.S. Military Aid to Latin America* (Maxwell AFB, AL: Air University, 1966); Samuel P. Huntington, *The Soldier and State: The Theory and Politics of Civil-Military Relations* (New York: Vantage, 1964); John Child, *Unequal Alliance: The Inter-American Military System, 1938–1978* (Boulder, CO: Westview, 1980); and Max Boot, *The Savage Wars of Peace: Small Wars and the Rise of American Power* (New York: Basic Books, 2002). Sonny B. Davis, *Brotherhood of Arms: Brazil-U.S. Military Relations, 1945–1977* (Niwot, CO: University Press of Colorado, 1996), 154; Loveman, *La Patria*, 101–38; Lieuwen, *Arms and Politics*, 24–8; and John J. Johnson, *The Military and Society in Latin America* (Stanford, CA: Stanford University Press, 1964), 93–133, trace the development of the institutional fervor of the Latin American military during the early Cold War. For the catalytic role of the Cuban Revolution, see Brian Loveman and Thomas M. Davies Jr., eds., *The Politics of Antipolitics: The Military in Latin America*, 2nd rev. ed. (Lincoln: University of Nebraska Press, 1989), 89–93, 163–5. See "The Military Speaks for Itself," in Loveman and Davies, eds., *Politics of Antipolitics*, 193–306, for a thorough sampling of the collective antipolitical mindset. See David F. Schmitz, *Thank God They're on Our Side: The United States and Right-Wing Dictatorships, 1921–1965* (Chapel Hill: University of North Carolina Press, 1999), for a global look at the predilection for authoritarian dictatorships. Frederick Nunn, *The Time of the Generals: Latin American Professional Militarism in World Perspective* (Lincoln: University of Nebraska Press, 1992); Edward Lieuwen, *Generals vs. Presidents: Neo-Militarism in Latin America* (New York: Praeger, 1964); Begnt Abrahamsson, *Military Professionalization and Political Power* (Beverly Hills: Sage, 1972); Victor Alba, *El militarismo* (Mexico: UNAM, 1960); Jan Knippers Black, *Sentinels of Empire: The United States and Latin American Militarism* (Westport, CT: Greenwood Press, 1986); Roderick Camp, *Generals in the Palacio: The Military in Modern Mexico* (New York: Oxford University Press, 1992); and Karen Remmer, *The Chilean Military under Authoritarian Rule* (Albuquerque: University of New Mexico Press, 1987) examine the military. For information about authoritarianism and Latin American politics, see Edward Feit, *The Armed Bureaucrats: Military Administration Regimes and Political Development* (Boston: Houghton Mifflin, 1973); David Collier, *The New Authoritarianism in Latin America* (Princeton, NJ: Princeton University Press, 1979); Guillermo O'Donnell, Philippe C. Schmitter, and Laurence Whitehead, eds., *Transition from Authoritarian Rule: Latin America* (Baltimore: The Johns Hopkins University Press, 1986); Francía Elena Díaz Cardona, *Fuerzas armadas, militarismo y constitución nacional en América latina* (Mexico: UNAM, 1988); and Alfred Stepan, *Rethinking Military Politics: Brazil and the Southern Cone* (Princeton, NJ: Princeton University Press, 1988).

5

THE RHETORIC OF NATIONAL SECURITY:

THE GEORGE H. W. BUSH ADMINISTRATION
AND THE NEW WORLD ORDER

James DePalma

F OR NEARLY FIFTY YEARS, the Cold War dominated American foreign policy. In 1991, the end of the Cold War necessitated a reevaluation of America's role in world affairs. No longer would the spread of communism pose the greatest threat to America's security and interests. In the post-Cold War world, the spread of weapons of mass destruction, local or regional conflicts, and even instability itself were the primary threats to peace and order throughout the globe. The purpose of the George Herbert Walker Bush administration's quest for a New World Order was to address these potential threats. Another purpose might have been to find ways for the United States to maintain indefinitely its newfound status as the world's lone superpower. Whether the purpose was more idealistic than selfish in nature is open for debate.

What is clear is that the Bush administration helped undermine its quest for achieving a New World Order. Its idealistic rhetoric often conflicted with and overshadowed pragmatic actions, resulting in the appearance of contradictory and even hypocritical policies that damaged the credibility of the administration's vision. Unfortunately, the perception of contradiction concealed the degree of consistency that actually existed in how the administration determined whether to intervene in an international crisis or not. While the Bush administration and its successors continued to promote principles associated with the New World Order, the term, for all intents and purposes, disappeared from public discourse.

In January 1989, George H. W. Bush became the forty-first president. He entered office with extensive foreign policy experience, including past service as a special representative to China, ambassador to the United Nations, and director of the Central Intelligence Agency. Throughout his term in office, Bush appeared more at ease focusing on foreign rather than domestic policy. His management style was hands-on and stressed expertise and teamwork among a small group of key advisors. Terms often used to describe Bush were "pragmatic" and "competent." The president, however, had an aversion to what he called "the vision thing" and was generally reactive rather than proactive. Analyst Terry L. Deibel argues that the administration's foreign policy reflected "tactical mastery set in a larger pattern of strategic indirection."[1] Deibel dismissed the notion that the New World Order represented a vision.

Not all observers agree that the Bush administration lacked a vision or broad strategy for post–Cold War foreign policy. Political scientist Steven Hurst argues that the New World Order did represent a more coherent and practical strategy than many critics allowed for, particularly given the constraints of the budget deficit and a more assertive Congress that demanded a larger role in crafting foreign policy.[2] He states that a foreign policy strategy consists of a set of objectives and the means to achieve those objectives. The objectives must reflect national interests and the means must be both sustainable and proportionate to the ends. The New World Order, according to Hurst, represented "a relatively coherent and plausible strategy for U.S. foreign policy in the post–Cold War era" because it bal-

1 Stephen F. Burgess, "Operation Restore Hope: Somalia and the Frontiers of the New World Order," in *From Cold War to New World Order: The Foreign Policy of George H. W. Bush*, ed. Meena Bose and Rosanna Perotti (Westport, CT: Greenwood Press, 2002), 260–261; Gullian Peele, "The Constrained Presidency of George Bush," *Current History* 91, no. 564 (April 1992): 151–155; "A Second Chance for Vision," *New York Times* December 17, 1989; Terry L. Deibel, "Bush's Foreign Policy: Mastery and Inaction," *Foreign Policy* 84 (Fall 1991): 3–9.

2 Steven Hurst, *The Foreign Policy of the Bush Administration: In Search of a New World Order* (New York: Pinter, 1999), 3–7.

anced the Bush administration's broad objectives "against the resources available to achieve them."[3]

The ideological heritage of the New World Order dates back to the First World War and the presidency of Woodrow Wilson. Wilson believed that European diplomatic practices tended to result in war and that these practices were dangerous, and due to advances in military technology, outdated. Modern warfare produced unimaginable carnage; therefore, it was vital to create a new order designed to resolve international crises peacefully. Peace would not only produce order in the international system, but it would also help safeguard American interests. As such, Wilson advocated principles that included the promotion of free trade, open diplomacy, disarmament, national self-determination, and a mechanism for collective security. While Wilson's vision was only partially and temporarily realized, his vision had a tremendous effect on the course of American foreign policy throughout the twentieth century. Subsequently, most American presidents advocated Wilsonian principles. The most significant differences between administrations lay not in the ends desired but in the means chosen to implement the principles.

In *America's Mission: The United States and the Worldwide Struggle for Democracy in the Twentieth Century,* Tony Smith characterizes the Bush administration's foreign policy as Wilsonian in nature. Smith provides a useful term, "selective liberal democratic internationalism" or selective Wilsonianism, to describe the policy. He argues that the virtue of such an approach is that "it clearly recognizes the concrete national security interests served by the expansion of democracy abroad, while . . . it has a realistic sense of the limits of American power and the need to work with the world as it is."[4] Unfortunately, the concept of selective Wilsonianism is not without its drawbacks, and these negative aspects will receive attention throughout the remainder of the present study.

For an administration geared toward foreign policy, the Bush administration faced numerous international challenges during its first year in office. It achieved mixed results. Following the Chinese government's brutal crackdown on dissidents at Tiananmen Square, the Bush administration received criticism for resisting sanctions against China and for conduct-

---

3   Hurst, *Foreign Policy of the Bush Administration,* 129.

4   Tony Smith, *America's Mission: The United States and the Worldwide Struggle for Democracy in the Twentieth Century* (Princeton, NJ: Princeton University Press, 1994), 326.

ing secret talks to reassure the Chinese leadership of America's desire for close relations.[5] The administration, in this instance, deemed geopolitical and economic considerations as more important than the promotion of democracy or the advancement of human rights.

In December 1989, the United States intervened militarily in Panama to remove General Manuel Noriega from power. America's one-time client increasingly became an irritant, and the Panamanian dictator faced drug-trafficking charges in the United States. When bureaucratic infighting and mixed diplomatic signals thwarted American efforts to negotiate Noriega's surrender, the United States intervened militarily. The Bush administration also justified intervention on the grounds of defending democracy and safeguarding American lives in Panama. The invasion, referred to as Operation Just Cause, succeeded as Noriega's regime collapsed.

In his memoir, *My American Journey*, Colin Powell states that Operation Just Cause confirmed convictions he had held since the Vietnam War concerning guidelines for military intervention. According to Powell, the invasion underscored the need for the nation (or administration) to have a clear political objective and to maintain the will to sustain that objective and use the proper amount of force to achieve a quick and decisive result. Powell commented that these guidelines, reinforced and validated through Operation Just Cause, were "the bedrock of my military counsel." [6] Many of Bush's advisors shared Powell's convictions and this would become apparent as future international crises confronted the administration.

The significance of the invasion of Panama went beyond the removal of a dictator. Bush risked his credibility because "[i]f the United States could not handle a low-level dictator in a country where it maintained bases and large forces, how would it be able to deal with far more serious international challenges?"[7] More serious challenges lay ahead.

The Bush administration received much criticism for its lack of response to the Tiananmen Square episode and for its confused diplomacy and invasion of Panama. Nonetheless, events unfolding in Eastern Europe during 1989 offered unparalleled opportunities for the administration to demonstrate its aptitude for conducting foreign policy. The end of the

5   Deibel, "Bush's Foreign Policy," 9.

6   Colin L. Powell, *My American Journey* (New York: Random House, 1995), 314.

7   Eytan Gilboa, "The Panama Invasion Revisited: Lessons for the Use of Force in the Post Cold War Era," *Political Science Quarterly* 110, no. 4 (Winter 1995–1996): 558–560.

Cold War and the accompanying challenges it presented preoccupied the Bush administration. The reunification of Germany, the future role of the North Atlantic Treaty Organization, the collapse of the Soviet Union, nuclear proliferation, and, in general, the expansion of democracy and free markets throughout Eastern Europe all required diligent attention.[8] In the wake of such dramatic transformations and challenges, the Bush administration demonstrated competent management. Competent management, however, did not necessarily translate into possessing a vision.

The United States emerged from the Cold War as the world's lone superpower. What international role the Bush administration desired for the United States remained unclear until the Iraqi invasion of Kuwait in August 1990. What follows is an analysis of the administration's response to the Iraqi invasion, to the Yugoslav wars of succession, and to the humanitarian nightmare in Somalia. The reason for selecting these three events is that they occurred during or after the administration's announcement of its quest for a New World Order, its well-publicized foreign policy vision. An analysis of these three episodes also demonstrates how the administration, despite general consistency in decision making, helped undermine its quest for a New World Order.

On August 2, 1990, Iraqi troops invaded Kuwait. There were several reasons for the invasion. Iraq was in debt after its eight-year war with Iran, and Iraqi dictator Saddam Hussein blamed Kuwait and the United Arab Emirates for compounding Iraq's economic woes by producing more oil than OPEC quotas stipulated, decreasing oil prices and, in the process, Iraqi revenue. Iraq and Kuwait also clashed over shared oil fields, and Saddam desired direct access to the Persian Gulf.[9] These grievances precipitated the invasion.

Since the end of the Iran-Iraq war in mid-1988, the United States sought a policy of engagement with Saddam. Once in office, the Bush administration continued the policy. The administration viewed Saddam as a "moderate" in the region and as potentially helpful in influencing the Palestinians and advancing the Middle East peace process. Saddam's weapons program was a concern; however, the administration first desired to use economic and political incentives before taking a tougher stance toward Saddam.[10]

8   For detailed analyses of the Bush administration's reaction to the transformation of Europe, see Bose and Perotti, *From Cold War to New World Order*.

9   Powell, *My American Journey*, 459–460.

10   James A. Baker III with Thomas M. DeFrank, *The Politics of Diplomacy: Revolution,*

Economic and political incentives ultimately failed to moderate his be-havior. In early 1990, Saddam increased his verbal attacks toward Kuwait, Israel, and the United States. In July, he moved troops toward the Iraq-Kuwait border.[11] Secretary of State James A. Baker III later observed that the administration should have realized at an earlier date that it would not be able to temper Saddam's expansionist ideals. Baker stated that the end of the Cold War preoccupied the administration and denied Iraqi policy a more prominent place on the administration's agenda. In addition, less at-tention to its Iraq policy delayed the administration's shift to demand more concessions from Saddam. Baker, however, asserted that no American al-lies in the Middle East, including the Israelis, predicted the Iraqi invasion of Kuwait. Furthermore, Baker argued that the only "realistic chance to de-ter Saddam would have been to introduce U.S. forces into the region—and neither the Kuwaitis, the Saudis, the Soviets, nor the Congress would have supported that cause before August 2."[12]

President Bush declared on August 5, 1990, "This will not stand, this aggression against Kuwait."[13] The stakes were high for the United States in the Persian Gulf. They included preserving the balance of power in the Middle East, defending American commitments and allies in the Gulf, opposing aggression, preventing a hostile power from dominating a large percentage of the world's oil supply, and the opportunity to shape post–Cold War international relations. National Security Advisor Brent Scowcroft states, "In the first days of the crisis we had started self-con-sciously to view our actions as setting a precedent for the approaching post–Cold War world." Administration officials began to talk about a New World Order, a term supposedly coined during a late-August 1990 fishing trip in a conversion between Scowcroft and Bush.[14]

War, and Peace, 1989–1992 (New York: G. P. Putnam's Sons, 1995), 263–264; Hurst, 87–88.

11 Hurst, Foreign Policy of the Bush Administration, 88.

12 Baker, Politics of Diplomacy, 273–274.

13 George Bush and Brent Scowcroft, A World Transformed (New York: Alfred A. Knopf, 1998), 333.

14 George H. W. Bush, "The President's News Conference on the Persian Gulf Crisis," Public Papers, August 30, 1990; Brent Scowcroft in A World Transformed, 400; David Gergen, "Bye-bye to the New World Order," US News & World Report (July 8, 1991): 21; Eric A. Miller and Steve A. Yetiv, "The New World Order in Theory and

The United States and the international community, through the United Nations (UN), quickly condemned Saddam's invasion and demanded the immediate, unconditional withdraw of Iraqi troops from Kuwait. UN sanctions against Iraq followed, diplomatically and economically isolating the country, but it was uncertain whether sanctions alone would compel Saddam to reverse his course. The Bush administration spent the remainder of the summer and fall trying to build support within the American Congress and UN for the possible use of force to expel the Iraqis from Kuwait.

Early in the crisis, the Bush administration ruled out unilateral American intervention against Iraqi forces. Baker stated that the United States had no alternative other than to build an international coalition. Building a coalition aligned the international community against Saddam, especially attracting the support of most Middle Eastern states. Domestic considerations also necessitated building a coalition because the American public and Congress rejected unilateral intervention.[15]

Sanctions ultimately failed to compel Saddam to withdraw his troops from Kuwait. In November 1990, the UN Security Council voted twelve-to-two in favor of sanctioning the use of force, and coalition troops assembling in Saudi Arabia prepared for a confrontation. In a final diplomatic mission, Baker met Iraqi Foreign Minister Tariq Aziz in Geneva on January 9, 1991. He informed Aziz that a war between the international community and Iraqi forces "would be fought to a swift, decisive conclusion." Baker stressed, "This will not be another Vietnam."[16] His mission failed, and in the aftermath, the American Congress authorized the use of force. When the Iraqis did not withdraw from Kuwait by the January 15 deadline, the war began.[17]

The Gulf War featured prominently in President Bush's January 29, 1991, State of the Union address. Bush declared, "What is at stake is more than one small country; it is a big idea: a new world order, where diverse nations are drawn together in common cause to achieve the universal aspirations of mankind—peace and security, freedom, and the rule of law." The president stated that the world answered Saddam's aggres-

---

Practice: The Bush Administration's Worldview in Transition," *Presidential Studies Quarterly* 31, no. 1 (March 2001): 58.

15 Baker, *Politics of Diplomacy*, 279.

16 Powell, *My American Journey*, 489; Baker, *Politics of Diplomacy*, 359.

17 Hurst, *Foreign Policy of the Bush Administration*, 119.

sion through the passage of twelve UN resolutions backed by the forces of twenty-eight countries. Because diplomatic avenues had failed to compel the Iraqis to withdraw from Kuwait, war was necessary. Bush announced, "We will succeed in the Gulf. And when we do, the world community will have sent an enduring warning to any dictator or despot, present or future, who contemplates outlaw aggression."[18] The president's declaration would come back to haunt the administration.

Bush correctly predicted a triumphant outcome in the Gulf War. The coalition's air campaign against Iraqi forces raged from January 16 to February 24, 1991. The land war lasted from February 24 to 27, lasting merely one hundred hours. Coalition forces liberated Kuwait, and Bush declared, "The first test of the new world order has been passed."[19] Though the actual war turned out even better than expected, the aftermath proved quite challenging.

The war ended without coalition troops occupying the Iraqi capital of Baghdad, and Saddam remained in power. One may ask why that was the case. The coalition achieved the primary objectives of the UN resolutions as Kuwait was free and much of Saddam's offensive military capabilities were destroyed. Secretary of State Baker stated that further operations into Iraq would have looked like an American war of conquest, undermining the unity of the coalition, especially among Arab countries, and rallying Iraqi support around Saddam. The continuation of the war would also have increased American casualties, a measure unacceptable to the American public.[20] Furthermore, regime change was never an official objective of the war. Bush's rhetoric comparing the Iraqi dictator to Adolf Hitler, however, elevated public expectations of Saddam's removal. Consequently Saddam's survival diminished the luster of victory because of the false impression Bush gave the public.[21]

The Bush administration also sent mixed signals to the Iraqi people. Following the war, the Kurdish minority in northern Iraq and the Shiite Muslims concentrated in southern Iraq both rebelled against Saddam's

18 George H. W. Bush, "Address before a Joint Session of Congress on the State of the Union," *Public Papers*, January 29, 1991, http://bushlibrary.tamu.edu.

19 George H. W. Bush, "Radio Address to United States Armed Forces Stationed in the Persian Gulf Region," *Public Papers*, March 2, 1991, http://bushlibrary.tamu.edu.

20 Baker, *Politics of Diplomacy*, 436–437.

21 Powell, *My American Journey*, 491; Hurst, *Foreign Policy of the Bush Administration*, 121.

regime. While the administration expressed hope that Saddam's regime would be overthrown and tacitly encouraged the rebellions, the United States did not actively intend to assist the rebels. The administration did not desire to see Iraq fragmented or a new wave of instability ravage the region. It also did not want American troops bogged down in an Iraqi civil war.[22] Ultimately, Saddam's forces violently crushed both uprisings and his regime remained in power.

The Gulf War also demonstrated that the Vietnam syndrome continued to affect American foreign policy. In the days following the war, Bush declared, "The specter of Vietnam has been buried forever in the desert sands of the Arabian Peninsula."[23] The president was gravely mistaken. The legacy of Vietnam may have played a significant role in influencing the decision not to assist the Kurdish and Shiite rebels against Saddam's regime. The administration feared entanglement in a civil war and potential quagmire in Iraq.

Secretary of State Baker focused on a different consequence of the victory in the Gulf. The war against Iraq was a resounding victory completed in a relatively short time with few American casualties. This phenomenon potentially created "its own troubling syndrome." Baker questioned whether the American Congress and public would support future military operations "where massive force is not appropriate."[24] His observation highlighted the complicated nature of post–Cold War conflicts. Saddam's invasion of Kuwait represented a clear case of aggression with one state invading another. Vital American interests, such as securing oil supplies and eliminating Saddam's weapons program, were at stake. Post–Cold War conflicts, however, were increasingly local, regional, and ethnic in nature, and America's vital national interests were not necessarily at risk.[25] The question remained whether Americans would support future intervention in conflicts that did not threaten vital national interests.

----

22   Baker, *Politics of Diplomacy*, 439, 441; Powell, 530–531; Hurst, 121–122.

23   Bush, "Radio Address to United States Armed Forces Stationed in the Persian Gulf Region," *Public Papers*, March 2, 1991. http://bushlibrary.tamu.edu.

24   Baker, *Politics of Diplomacy*, 331.

25   Barry M. Blechman and Tamara Cofman Wittes, "Defining Moment: The Threat and Use of Force in American Foreign Policy," *Political Science Quarterly*, 114, no. 1 (Spring 1999): 27; Thomas L. Friedman, "'Realists' vs. 'Idealists': It's Harder Now to Figure out Compelling National Interests," *New York Times*, May 31, 1992, E5.

The Yugoslav wars of succession during the early 1990s represented a regional conflict with ethnic considerations that did not threaten vital American interests. The Federal Republic of Yugoslavia consisted of the republics of Serbia, Croatia, Macedonia, Montenegro, Slovenia, and Bosnia, and the two autonomous provinces of Kosovo and Vojvodina located within Serbia. A complex mixture of the long-term trend toward political decentralization and an unequal pace of economic development in the various republics contributed to the dissolution of Yugoslavia. In the context of political and economic difficulties, demagogues exploited ethnic, religious, and cultural differences among the Yugoslav people. By the late 1980s and early 1990s, virulent and competing nationalisms undermined the concept of a unified Yugoslav identity. The survival of the Yugoslav federation was in doubt, and few believed that the federation's dissolution would be peaceful.[26]

The Slovenian and Croatian declarations of independence in June 1991 sparked violence in the region. The Serbs traditionally dominated the Belgrade government and most adamantly favored maintaining state unity. The Yugoslav People's Army conducted only a minimal military campaign to prevent Slovene independence; Croatian independence was a more complicated issue. One major differentiating characteristic existed between Croatia and Slovenia: a sizeable ethnic Serb minority lived in Croatia while almost no Serbs lived in Slovenia. The Serbs rejected the notion of the Croatian Serb population falling under the authority of an independent Croatia. The result was a lengthy, bloody conflict that engulfed Croatia and threatened to spread to other republics, most notably Bosnia.[27]

Prior to the secession of Slovenia and Croatia, Secretary of State Baker led a final diplomatic mission to prevent bloodshed and the dissolution of Yugoslavia. Baker called his June 21, 1991, trip to Belgrade "one of the most frustrating I'd had as Secretary of State." He met individually with representatives from all of the republics. Baker later stated, "These people

26   John E. Ullmann, "Appointment in Sarajevo: George Bush, Yugoslavia, and the Prospects of Federalism," in Bose and Perotti, *From Cold War to New World Order*, 281. For a detailed analysis of the dissolution of Yugoslavia, see Sabrina P. Ramet, *Nationalism and Federalism in Yugoslavia, 1962–1991* (Bloomington, Indiana: Indiana University Press, 1992).

27   David Rieff, *Slaughterhouse: Bosnia and the Failures of the West* (New York: Touchstone, 1996), 15–16.

were heading right into a civil war, and yet nothing seemed capable of changing their minds." Baker held the Slovenes, Croats, and Serbs most responsible for the current crisis; the Slovenes and Croats for threatening secession; and the Serbs for violating constitutional procedures. Furthermore, according to Baker, Serb and Croat leaders were among the most virulent nationalists, violating the rights of minorities within their respective republics.[28] In the end, Baker's mission failed and Slovenia and Croatia declared independence, precipitating the wars.

The European Community (EC) and the UN led the international mission to end the Yugoslav wars. The Bush administration did not want a more prominent role for several reasons. The member states of the EC welcomed the chance to lead the mission. At an EC meeting in late June 1991, Luxembourg's Foreign Minister Jacques Poos declared, "This is the hour of Europe." The conflict was located in Europe and more directly threatened European interests. The end of the Cold War also provided European institutions an opportunity to assume greater responsibility for their own security and develop an identity independent of that of the United States. Also, when the Yugoslav wars began, events elsewhere preoccupied the United States. The Bush administration focused on the collapse of the Soviet Union, the issue of nuclear proliferation, and a reinvigorated Middle East peace process. Finally, the Yugoslav wars did not threaten vital American interests.[29]

Baker stated that the Bush administration "felt comfortable with the EC's taking responsibility for handling the crisis in the Balkans" and asserts that the crisis appeared to be one that the EC could manage, but he did not provide evidence as to why the administration placed such faith in the EC's capabilities. He also acknowledged an undercurrent existed in Washington that believed "it was time to make the Europeans step up to the plate and show that they could act as a unified power. Yugoslavia was as good a first test as any."[30]

In April 1992, fighting began in Bosnia. Bosnia was a multiethnic republic inhabited by three national constituent communities, the Bosnian Serbs, the Bosnian Croats, and the Bosnian Muslims. Within the larger context of dissolution and war, the demographics of Bosnia assumed

28   Baker, *Politics of Diplomacy*, 478–483.

29   Alan Riding, "Conflict in Yugoslavia," *New York Times*, June 29, 1991; Baker, *Politics of Diplomacy*, 636.

30   Baker, *Politics of Diplomacy*, 636–637.

greater significance because no ethnic community wanted minority status in either the remaining Yugoslav federation or any subsequent state.
When the vote on Bosnian independence occurred, the Bosnian Croats
and Muslims voted in favor of secession from Yugoslavia. Conversely, the
Bosnian Serbs rejected the notion of independence and separation from
other ethnic Serbs remaining within Yugoslavia. The Bosnian Croat and
Muslim position prevailed, resulting in a bloody and chaotic war.

The question remained as to how the Bush administration would respond to the war in Bosnia. The administration viewed the Bosnian Serbs
and their supporters in what remained of the Yugoslav federation as the
primary aggressors. Baker called the situation in Bosnia a "humanitarian
nightmare" preventable or reversible only through the application of substantial military force with considerable American casualties. The public,
however, would never have supported American military intervention in
Bosnia or in the earlier Yugoslav wars.[31] This was at the center of the
administration's decision to allow the EC and UN to lead the diplomatic
mission.

Prior American experience in both Lebanon and Vietnam influenced
policymakers' perceptions of the current war in Bosnia. In the early 1980s,
Lebanon represented a "poorly-defined mission" for the American military
in an intractable civil war that resulted in the death of over two hundred
American servicemen in a terrorist attack. The Bush administration and,
in particular, General Powell, did not want history to repeat itself in the
present conflict. Administration officials maintained a "deeply-ingrained"
reluctance to interfere in civil wars, and they interpreted the conflict in
Bosnia as a civil war. They also saw no clear American military objective
in Bosnia. The administration feared entanglement in a quagmire, demonstrating that "the specter of Vietnam" remained even after the victory in
the Gulf War.[32]

In his memoir, *Origins of a Catastrophe,* Ambassador Warren
Zimmermann, the last American ambassador to Yugoslavia, criticizes the
Bush administration's decision against the use of force in Bosnia. He ar-
gues that the conflict in Bosnia represented a clear case of aggression and

31   Baker, *Politics of Diplomacy,* 635–636, 640–651.

32   Christian J. Alfonsi, "Improvised Crusades: Explaining the 'Inconsistent' Use of
Military Intervention by the Bush Administration" (Ph.D. diss.: Harvard University,
1999), 350–354, 366–368. Also, see Colin L. Powell, "Why Generals Get Nervous,"
New York Times, October 8, 1992, p. A35.

that the United States "had a moral, perhaps even legal, obligation to deal with it." Although the administration's assessment "was based on an honest perception of the U.S. national interest," Zimmermann declares that the refusal to intervene militarily "was our greatest mistake of the entire Yugoslav crisis." The ambassador argues that American inaction wasted the opportunity to save hundreds of thousands of lives and guaranteed an unjust outcome. He cites three "major" but not "vital" interests that justified American intervention. The first interest was to prevent the conflict from spreading throughout the Balkans, and the second was to demonstrate American leadership and resolve. The third interest was more idealistic. Prior to the war, Bosnia possessed a multiethnic tradition. According to Zimmermann, the United States was the world's most successful multiethnic society and should have recognized the merit of preserving another multiethnic society.[33]

Only months after victory in the Persian Gulf, the Yugoslav wars of succession confronted the administration. For a variety of reasons, especially the anticipated political cost resulting from American casualties, the administration permitted the EC and UN to lead the diplomatic mission to end the fighting. Although Bush's rhetoric raised expectations about forcefully confronting aggressors, the administration practiced selective Wilsonianism. In the wake of American inaction, the president's rhetoric about a New World Order seemed hollow and hypocritical.[34] It did not appear to matter that the administration maintained identifiable guidelines for intervention in crises; what did matter was that the administration abdicated leadership and undermined the credibility of the New World Order through inaction in Yugoslavia.

The Bush administration's handling of the war in Bosnia was an issue during the 1992 presidential election. Democratic presidential nominee Bill Clinton challenged the administration's Bosnia policy and called for a more forceful American response. Nonetheless, domestic issues generally dominated the campaign. For several years Bush received criticism for supposedly neglecting domestic policy. In 1990, *Time* magazine named "the two George Bushes" as its Men of the Year. One profile praised the president's "resoluteness and mastery" in foreign affairs, but another pro-

33 Warren Zimmermann, *Origins of a Catastrophe: Yugoslavia and Its Destroyers: America's Last Ambassador Tells What Happened and Why* (New York: Times Books, 1996), 216–218.

34 Anthony Lewis, "The New World Order," *New York Times*, May 17, 1992, p. E17.

file argued that his domestic agenda demonstrated "wavering and confusion." The negative perception of Bush's handling of domestic issues never abated. The budget deficit, economic recession, and low consumer confidence were key issues among voters.[35]

Although Bush subsequently lost his reelection bid, 1992 proved a crucial year in the development of post–Cold War foreign policy. Two events, the leaking of excerpts from a classified Defense Department memorandum and intervention in Somalia, focused attention on the concept of the New World Order and raised questions about the extent of the Bush administration's commitment to achieve its vision.

The end of the Cold War created a so-called peace dividend. The diminished threat of confrontation between the United States and Soviet Union permitted the reduction of the defense budget. It also, however, necessitated the restructuring of the American military to meet new security challenges. While testimony and debates occurred on Capitol Hill concerning the size and structure of the American military, the task of the requirements were of the early post–Cold War military concerned planners. As such, the classified memorandum titled "Defense Planning Guidance for the Fiscal Years 1994–1999" represented an early Defense Department assessment.

Every few years, the Defense Department creates an internal review called the "Defense Planning Guidance." The purpose of the classified memorandum is to assist with long-term military planning, balancing budgetary concerns with proposed troop levels and weapon systems deemed necessary to protect American interests.[36] The "Defense Planning Guidance for the Fiscal Years 1994–1999" deserves special attention for several reasons. First, the memorandum represented an early post–Cold War military assessment of global threats to American interests. Second, excerpts from a draft of the classified memorandum appeared in the *New York Times* and *Washington Post* during the early months of 1992. The

35   George J. Church, *Time*, January 7, 1991, 20; Andrew Rosenthal with Joel Brinkley, "Bush in a World Remade: Will the Old Compass Do?" *New York Times*, June 25, 1992, p. A1; R. W. Apple Jr., "Few Choices, Fewer Hopes," *New York Times*, August 7, 1992, p. A1; Ann Devroy, "Bush Stresses His Concern over Balkans," *Washington Post*, August 9, 1992, p. A27.

36   For a detailed analysis of the "Defense Planning Guidance," see James Mann, *Rise of the Vulcans: The History of Bush's War Cabinet* (New York: Viking Penguin, 2004), 209–215.

publication of these excerpts proved embarrassing for the Bush administration.

The office of the undersecretary of defense, Paul Wolfowitz, played a
significant role in drafting the memorandum. The memorandum outlined
possible scenarios that might require future American military intervention. The scenarios included an Iraqi invasion of Kuwait and Saudi Arabia;
a North Korean invasion of South Korea; the possibility of the Iraqi and
North Korean crises developing concurrently; a Russian invasion of former Soviet republics or satellites; a coup in the Philippines; and a coup
in Panama that threatened access to the canal. Perhaps the most controversial aspect of the document focused on the suggestion that the United
States prevented the emergence of regional or global competitors, such
as Japan, Germany, and India, that might threaten its position as the sole
remaining superpower.[37]

On February 17, 1992, Patrick E. Tyler of the *New York Times* first wrote
about the "Defense Planning Guidance for the Fiscal Years 1994–1999."
Tyler stated that a Pentagon official leaked the draft in order "to call attention to what he considered vigorous attempts within the military establishment to invent a menu of alarming war scenarios that can be used
by the Pentagon to prevent further reductions in forces or cancellations
of new weapon systems from defense contractors."[38] The ensuing controversy went beyond debates concerning budgets or the possible squan-
dering of the peace dividend. Barton Gellman, who reported about the
"Defense Planning Guidance" for the *Washington Post,* later commented
that the leak occurred because some "within the U.S. defense planning
establishment . . . thought that this thing was nuts, and they wanted a
public debate about it."[39] The heart of the controversy focused on the
question of America's role in the post–Cold War world. Was the United
States rejecting collective security? Was the Bush administration, or at
least certain segments or persons within the administration, renouncing
the New World Order?

....

37   Patrick Tyler, *New York Times,* February 17, 1992, p. A8; Patrick Tyler, *New York
Times,* February 18, 1992, p. A1.

38   Patrick Tyler, *New York Times,* February 17, 1992.

39   Barton Gellman, interviewed by *Frontline:* "The War behind Closed Doors,"
January 29, 2003, http://www.pbs.org/wgbh/pages/frontline/shows/iraq/interviews/
gellman.html.

Examples of the domestic and international reaction reflected the un-settling nature of the information contained within the memorandum. Senator Joseph Biden (D-DE) agreed with some of the objectives listed in the memorandum, but not with the notion of the United States act-ing as the world's policeman or with the necessary accompanying defense budget increases. Political pundit and Republican presidential candidate Patrick Buchanan called on the president to reject the memorandum be-cause it would entangle the United States in countless interventions not vital to American interests.[40] Indian Foreign Secretary J. N. Dixit, in a meeting with State and Defense Department officials, "took issue" with the perception of his country as a potential regional threat to American interests.[41] Historian John Lewis Gaddis summarized the shocking na-ture of the memorandum well when he declared, "I was a little surprised somebody would put this kind of thing down on paper."[42]

During a March 12, 1992, press conference, reporters asked President Bush about the memorandum. The president stated that he had not yet read it, and he cautioned against overemphasis on a leaked report. Nonetheless, President Bush acknowledged that he "was broadly support-ive of the thrust" of the document. When asked if the United States was moving toward or away from a collective security strategy, the president answered that the country "must continue to lead" but "we have worked effectively through multilateral organizations."[43] His answer was charac-teristically pragmatic.

The Defense Department subsequently revised the "Defense Planning Guidance." By the end of May 1992, a new memorandum, one promoting collective security and the maintenance of alliances, was ready. The most significant change was the removal of discussions about efforts to deter or prevent allies from becoming "regional hegemons." Barton Gellman of the *Washington Post* cited an unnamed national security official outside of the Defense Department who could only speculate as to why the revisions occurred. The official offered four possibilities: the revisions produced a document more palatable for domestic and international consumption; there was an unexamined thesis underlying the previous memorandum;

---

40   Patrick Tyler, *New York Times*, March 10, 1992.

41   Barton Gellman, *Washington Post*, March 12, 1992, p. A18.

42   Peter Grier, "Hot Debate over US Strategic Role," *Christian Science Monitor*, March 16, 1992.

43   Barton Gellman, *Washington Post*, March 12, 1992, p. A18.

the thesis was sound, but advocates backed down in the face of criticism; or, in an election year, "the high rollers didn't want to invest the political capital" necessary to defend it. In the end, the official proposed that all four scenarios probably influenced the changes.[44]

The revised memorandum ended the immediate controversy surrounding the "Defense Planning Guidance," and the episode faded from public memory for a number of years.[45] Its effect on the quest for the New World Order is difficult to determine. While the leaked excerpts downplayed collective security, a concept at the center of the New World Order, it never officially became administration policy. Furthermore, regardless of the rationale for the revisions to the memorandum, the Bush administration continued to promote collective security.

As opposed to the "Defense Planning Guidance," the Bush administration's intervention in the East African country of Somalia clearly advanced its quest for a New World Order. Between 1991 and 1992, a humanitarian nightmare unfolded in Somalia. A coup, the collapse of governmental institutions, widespread clan warfare, a drought, and famine created misery and death of unimaginable proportions. By the summer of 1992, an estimated three thousand Somalis were dead and more perished with each passing day. Starvation was the most pressing concern. UN peacekeepers in Somalia tried to provide humanitarian relief, but warring local militias and complicated UN rules of engagement made it difficult for peacekeepers to fulfill their mission. Throughout the summer and fall of 1992, the United States increased the amount of aid and logistical support it provided to the relief mission, but all was in vain. Finally, in late November 1992, the United States, with the backing of the UN, agreed to lead a military mission for the purposes of delivering humanitarian relief.[46]

On December 4, 1992, Bush addressed the nation about the situation in Somalia. He described the harrowing circumstances, including armed

44 Barton Gellman, *Washington Post*, May 24, 1992, p. A1.

45 The ideas expressed in the original memorandum, however, never completely disappear from discourse about the direction of American foreign policy during the 1990s. The terrorist attacks of September 11, 2001, brought renewed attention to the 1992 episode.

46 Jon Western, "Sources of Humanitarian Intervention: Beliefs, Information, and Advocacy in the US Decisions on Somalia and Bosnia," *International Security* 26, no. 4 (2002): 113, 120–123; Don Oberdorfer, "The Path to Intervention; A Massive Tragedy 'We Could Do Something About,'" *Washington Post*, December 6, 1992, p. A1.

gangs harassing UN peacekeepers, looting food shipments, and assaulting aid workers. The president announced that the United States welcomed the offer to lead a coalition into Somalia because only it "has the global reach to place a large security force on the ground in such a distant place quickly and efficiently and thus save thousands of innocents from death." Bush proceeded to reassure the public that the American mission had a limited objective. American troops were to help open supply routes, get food moving, and secure the way for UN peacekeepers to continue the process. Bush announced, "This operation is not open-ended. We will not stay one day longer than is absolutely necessary."[47]

Why did the United States intervene in Somalia, a crisis where vital American interests were not at stake? There are several possible explanations. First, President Bush believed that the United States was the only country possessing the capabilities to deter the warring Somali militias from interfering with the delivery of humanitarian aid, and policymakers and military officials came to view the objective as attainable. Second, before the UN General Assembly on September 21, 1992, Bush stressed the need for the world community, including the United States, to increase support for peacekeeping missions. Enhanced peacekeeping was a component of international cooperation and hence the New World Order. Third, military action in Somalia might lessen criticism for not intervening in Bosnia. In this context, it was an act of redemption. Fourth, growing pressure from international organizations, American politicians, and the media for American intervention to halt the ever-expanding humanitarian nightmare contributed to the administration's decision to act. Fifth, a self-serving factor cannot be disregarded. The decision to intervene occurred weeks after Bush's electoral defeat in November 1992. Involvement on humanitarian grounds might further enhance Bush's legacy.[48] A combination of all of these factors most likely accounts for military action in a conflict that did not threaten vital American interests.

47   George H. W. Bush, "Address to the Nation on the Situation in Somalia," *Public Papers*, January 29, 1991, http://bushlibrary.tamu.edu.

48   George H. W. Bush, "Address to the United Nations General Assembly in New York City," Public Papers, September 21, 1992, http://bushlibrary.tamu.edu; Robert Hunter, "Why Somalia? An Experiment in Redemption; In the Post–Cold War World, A New Role for US Power," *Washington Post*, December 6, 1992, p. C1; Oberdorfer, "The Path to Intervention," *Washington Post*, December 6, 1992, p. A1; Hurst, *Foreign Policy of the Bush Administration*, 220–226.

In "Sources of Humanitarian Intervention: Beliefs, Information, and Advocacy in the U.S. Decisions on Somalia and Bosnia," Jon Western offers another intriguing explanation for American intervention in Somalia. He declares that throughout 1992 the Bush administration lost control over information coming out of Somalia and the ability to frame the argument against intervention. A power shift occurred as liberal humanitarianists, those who advocated widespread intervention in humanitarian crises, increased advocacy and political pressure on the Bush administration to intervene in both Somalia and Bosnia. In the midst of escalated criticism and pressure, Clinton won the presidential election. Many military and Bush administration officials assumed Clinton's election meant the ascendancy of liberal humanitarianism. In particular, they feared that, once in office, Clinton would entangle U.S. forces in Bosnia. Western states, "Given the power shift in Washington and the intensity of mobilized political pressure to respond to humanitarian emergencies, Bush and Powell decided that if the United States was going to commit forces somewhere, it would be in Somalia—not Bosnia. Somalia was the easier of the two missions." By "easier," Western means that military and administration officials believed that the objective of delivering aid in Somalia was achievable and would require fewer American troops as compared with Bosnia.[49]

Western's argument goes beyond the notion that the Bush administration intervened in Somalia to lessen criticism for not acting more forcefully in Bosnia. America's involvement with Somalia was not so much an act of redemption as it was one to forestall continued momentum for entanglement in Bosnia. It reveals just how determined top military and Bush administration officials were to avoid involvement in Bosnia.

Operation Restore Hope, the American-led mission in Somalia, achieved its stated objective, but without complete success. UN forces succeeded in opening up supply routes to deliver aid and saved thousands of lives. The mission, at least temporarily, also furthered the spirit of multilateralism and the cause of the New World Order.[50] Nonetheless, the limited objective of the mission failed to address the larger political problems underlying the crisis. John G. Fox, a Foreign Service Officer extensively involved in the mission, stressed that the initial failure to develop "realistic and meaningful political goals" for the operation resulted in errors that "aggravated tensions between the United States and the UN, between the

49 Western, "Sources of Humanitarian Intervention," 114, 116–118.
50 Hurst, *Foreign Policy of the Bush Administration*, 224–225.

[Somali] warlords, and between regions of Somalia." Unfortunate long-term consequences followed from the initial failure to address the political context of the Somali conflict. The ultimate failure of the international mission, highlighted by the death of eighteen American servicemen in October 1993, "not only forced the end of the operation, it caused the Clinton administration to be more cautious about similar future interventions and less likely to risk U.S. casualties."[51]

In early January 1993, Bush addressed an audience of distinguished civilian and military guests, academy officials, and cadets at the United States Military Academy to recount the outgoing administration's foreign policy record. The president used the occasion to discuss once again the opportunity for achieving a New World Order. He stated, "Our objective must be ... to work toward transforming this new world into a New World Order, one of governments that are democratic, tolerant, and economically free at home and committed abroad to settling inevitable differences peacefully, without the threat of force." Although his remarks were generally positive and optimistic in tone, his message contained a sober reminder about the limitations of American power. American leadership was indispensable in helping to achieve a New World Order, but "[l]eadership should not be confused with either unilateralism or universalism." Bush warned that the United States "should not seek to be the world's policeman." A balance between idealism and pragmatism, between ends and means, was necessary.[52]

In the address, Bush discussed guidelines concerning American military intervention. The guidelines included "a clear and achievable mission, a realistic plan for accomplishing the mission, and criteria no less realistic for withdrawing U.S. forces once the mission is complete." In accordance with the guidelines, America intervened in the Gulf War and, as understood at the time of his speech, in the ongoing Somali operation. The president, however, acknowledged, "Sometimes the decision not to use force, to stay our hand, I can tell you, it's as difficult as the decision to

51   John G. Fox, "Approaching Humanitarian Intervention Strategically: The Case of Somalia," *SAIS Review* 21, no. 1 (2001): 151, 154–156.

52   George H. W. Bush, "Remarks at the United States Military Academy in West Point, New York," *Public Papers of the Presidents of the United States, George Herbert Walker Bush: 1989–1993*, January 5, 1993, http://bushlibrary.tamu.edu.

send our soldiers into battle."[53] He specifically referred to the fighting in the former Yugoslav republics.

Bush went on to say that "there can be no single or simple set of fixed rules for using force" because "every case is unique." He declared that maintaining "rigid criteria" provided "would-be troublemakers a blueprint for determining their own actions."[54] Bush's assertion was only partially correct. The administration did judge each crisis on its own merit. It would have been difficult to predict American intervention in Somalia. Nonetheless, there were principles and experiences that had a tremendous influence on policymakers, particularly the lessons learned from intervention in Vietnam and Lebanon. The crucial point was that these lessons were visible for all to see. Governments, groups, and individuals throughout the world understood that killing Americans often deterred or undermined American interventions. The American public had a low tolerance for American casualties. Such abhorrence affected the decision making of both American administrations and foreign actors.[55] The Bush administration's reluctance to intervene in Bosnia reflects such concerns.

Several weeks after his address at West Point, Bush left office. The end of his administration, for all intents and purposes, marked the end of the New World Order as a symbolic device to characterize the possibilities of the post–Cold War world. What then is the legacy of the Bush administration's quest for a New World Order?

Steven Hurst argues that the New World Order represented a relatively coherent and viable vision from an American perspective, especially given the constraints of the budget deficit and a more assertive Congress. According to Hurst, the concept underlying the objectives associated with the New World Order, such as the promotion of peace, democracy, and free trade, was multilateralism. This is the point where theory and practice diverge. Hurst states that "multilateralism as a pure concept has never been implemented by any U.S. administration that has embraced it." The reason that multilateralism had not been implemented as a pure concept was because of the need for American administrations, including the Bush administration, to achieve concrete goals with finite means. Hurst argues

---

53 Bush, "Remarks at the United States Military Academy in West Point, New York," *Public Papers*, January 5, 1993, http://bushlibrary.tamu.edu.

54 Bush, "Remarks at the United States Military Academy in West Point, New York," *Public Papers*, January 5, 1993, http://bushlibrary.tamu.edu.

55 Blechman and Wittes, "Defining Moment," 5, 27–28.

this qualification did not invalidate multilateralism as "an underpinning element of policy."[56] The Bush administration genuinely desired an international order premised upon Wilsonian principles; however, such a desire represented just that, *a desire*. It was not a universal commitment for action or intervention.[57]

In the article titled "The New World Order in Theory and Practice," Eric A. Miller and Steve A. Yetiv stress that the New World Order was a largely misunderstood concept. They state that the New World Order was idealistic but "accompanied by a good dose of realism." Apparently, Bush and Scowcroft believed that the media misunderstood and distorted the concept, attributing to it more expansive and idealistic qualities than intended. Miller and Yetiv acknowledge that Bush's rhetoric did contribute to confusion about the concept. Nonetheless, the authors contend that Bush never intended for the United States to intervene in all crises or abstain from unilateral action. The administration preferred collective action and the achievement of American interests through such a mechanism, but that "did not mean that it would forfeit national interests or be constrained in pursuing them."[58]

Michael Barone provided an early assessment in a March 25, 1991, article titled "A Realistic New World Order." Barone praises Americans for becoming "more modest about what the nation can achieve and more realistic about inevitable imperfections and inconsistencies in policies." He argues, "Most Americans seem to understand, even if some pundits and politicians don't, that Bush's new order doesn't require the United States to intervene everywhere . . . Vietnam lurks in the background to remind that there are practical limits to what the nation can do."[59] Ironically, only weeks before this article appeared in *US News & World Report,* President Bush declared that the Gulf War buried forever "[t]he specter of Vietnam."[60]

---

56 Hurst, *Foreign Policy of the Bush Administration,* 2–8, 130–134.

57 John Gerard Ruggie, "Third Try at World Order? America and Multilateralism after the Cold War," *Political Science Quarterly* 109, no. 4 (Autumn 1994): 557.

58 Miller and Yetiv, "The New World Order in Theory and Practice," 59–60.

59 Michael Barone, "A Realistic New World Order," US News & World Report (March 25, 1991): 32.

60 Bush, "Radio Address to United States Armed Forces Stationed in the Persian Gulf Region," *Public Papers,* March 2, 1991, http://bushlibrary.tamu.edu.

Barone either disregarded or failed to take account of the Bush administration's rhetoric concerning the quest for a New World Order.

In *America's Mission*, Tony Smith analyzes both the virtue and drawback of utilizing a selective Wilsonian foreign policy approach. A selective approach "clearly recognizes the concrete national security interests served by the expansion of democracy abroad, while . . . it has a realistic sense of the limits of American power and the need to work with the world as it is." Nonetheless, a selective approach was by definition reactive and necessitated judging each case on its own merits. According to Smith, continued hesitation and the lack of boldness threatened to undermine America's credibility and prestige.[61]

The Bush administration's practice of selective Wilsonianism was a pragmatic and realistic approach that unfortunately conflicted with the idealistic rhetoric it utilized in the wake of the Gulf War. The rhetoric heightened expectations about confronting future challenges to peace that the administration had no intention of fulfilling. It resulted in the appearance of inconsistent and hypocritical policies and undermined the credibility of the concept of the New World Order. Subsequent administrations continued to advocate Wilsonian principles, but talk of a New World Order generally disappeared from public discourse.

61   Smith, *America's Mission*, 326.

SECTION TWO:

INTERNATIONAL TERRORISM

W HILE SECTION ONE OFFERS HISTORICAL PERSPECTIVES on American domestic and foreign policy, Section Two begins with a multifaceted portrayal of terrorism and radical violence throughout world history, tracing the evolution of terrorism from a broad spectrum of groups and societies. Terrorism is not a static form of violence. Therefore, any attempt to define terrorism by applying a single universal strategy provides more questions than answers. Throughout history, terrorism has manifested itself in numerous identities, ranging from religious ideologies to revolutionary women and legitimate political parties. In some cases, the difference between legitimate police action and terrorist violence has been difficult to discern.

The first two essays prove that terrorism traverses gender as well as geographical boundaries. Jamie Trnka notes that, in West Germany, some women engaged in forms of non-traditional violence during the second half of the twentieth century. Through her analysis of the media and self-representations of West German terrorists, Trnka provides a more thorough conceptualization of gender and terrorism. Jean Berger continues the discussion of gender and terrorism in her account of the journeys of three Russian women from humanitarian activism to political violence. As late-nineteenth-century Russian laws increasingly restricted the rights of females, some well-educated women turned to violence in order to achieve political and revolutionary ends.

Josh Arinze argues that in Nigeria, terrorism has assumed a different face: that of radical Islamic law. In a nation where the population of Christians and Muslims is roughly equal, the replacement of secular laws with sharia, a form of extreme Islamic fundamentalism, has pitted Christians against Muslims and resulted in state-sponsored terrorism. In the final essay, Benjamin Grob-Fitzgibbon assumes the difficult task of defining terrorism itself as a unique form of violence. This essay also examines the difficulties that arise when a nation's antiterrorist tactics closely resemble that of the terrorist groups it attempts to eliminate. Fitzgibbon traces the changing definition of terrorism over time and discusses growing similarities between the violent actions of terrorist groups and nation states.

6

BEYOND VICTIMS AND PERPETRATORS:
....

WOMEN TERRORISTS TELL THEIR OWN STORIES

Jamie H. Trnka

ENDER AND SEXUALITY were among the most powerful signifiers of terrorist violence in the West German periodical press throughout the 1970s. Media outlets spoke of an "excess of women's liberation" as responsible for the rise of terrorism, a sentiment echoed by some government officials.[1] Terrorists, on the other hand, sought to represent the state itself as marked by violent excess. Insisting on the political quality of social violence understood in its broadest possible terms, they too deployed the language of gender and sexuality to these ends. First-person accounts by women once active in terrorist organizations introduce significant formal and epistemological variation in their choice of expressive genre and articulation of personal and collective political subjects, but they also continue to rely heavily on contemporary discourses of sexuality and violence. Ranging from traditionally structured confessional narratives, to

....

[1] Günter Nollau, Chief of Constitutional Protection, cited in "Gespräch mit Inge Viett," *Die Zeit*, April 4, 1997: 15. In the same document, state officials also refer to a "new girl-militancy" and even "lesbian sponti-militants who scorned the state as an instrument of oppression." See also the state's official *Der Baader-Meinhof-Report. Aus den Akten des Bundeskriminalamts, der "Sonderkommission Bonn" und des Bundesamts für Verfassungsschutz* (Mainz, 1972). All translations are my own.

collaborative narratives and interviews, to participation in documentary film, these accounts have received even less critical attention than media (re)presentations of terrorism, themselves more often invoked than investigated.

I explore how gendered and sexualized images of violence in popular media and personal accounts rely on different but reconcilable assumptions about the relationship of women to the state and to political power. These (re)presentations played and continue to play a constitutive role in popular understandings of West German terrorists, including the Red Army Faction—popularly referred to as the Baader-Meinhof Gang—and the Movement Second June.[2] It is therefore important to explore the terms of their construction and circulation in public debate, including terms of representation that link women's political participation, sexuality, and violence in highly charged discussions of terrorism. It is equally important to draw attention to how disparate memories alternately identify terrorists and the state as perpetrators and victims of violence, obscuring in the process the violent deaths both of individuals targeted by terrorists and casualties of state agents in their hunt for terrorist suspects and suppression of

....

2   Most notably, popular film and artistic retrospective have shaped public discussion and consumption of images of the RAF, but so too has pop cultural marketing of terrorist logos under the rubric of "Prada Meinhof." On the most recent wave of filmic (re)presentations, see especially my article "'The struggle is over, the wounds are open': Cinematic Tropes, History, and the RAF in Recent German Film," forthcoming in *New German Critique 101*; Nora Alter, "Framing Terrorism: Beyond the Borders," *Projecting History: German Nonfiction Cinema, 1967–2000*, (Ann Arbor: University of Michigan, 2002), 43–76; Thomas Elsaesser, "Antigone Agonistes: Urban Guerilla or Guerilla Urbanism? The Red Army Faction," *Germany in Autumn* and *Death Game*; Joan Copjec and Michael Sorkin, eds., *Giving Ground: The Politics of Propinquity* (London and New York: Verso, 1999), 267–302; and Petra Kraus, Natalie Lettenewitsch, Ursula Saekel, Brigitte Bruns, and Matthias Mersch, eds., *Deutschland im Herbst. Terrorismus im Film*, Schriftreihe Münchener Filmzentrum (Munich: Münchner Filmzentrum, 1997). The Institute for Social History has documented responses to the Berliner Kunsthalle's recent, highly controversial exhibit of art inspired by the RAF. See http://www.zeitge-schichte-online.de/md=RAF. On "Prada Meinhof," see the March 2002 *Tussi Deluxe*; Wiebke Brauer, "Tanz den Baader-Meinhof!" *Spiegel Online*, March 5, 2001, http://www.spiegel.de/kultur/gesellschaft/0,1518,120905,00 .html; and Coco Drilo, "Das RAF-Mode-Phantom," [April 2001] March 6, 2002, http://www.salonrouge.de/raf-hype2.html.

so-called sympathizers. By breaking the opposition State-Terrorist, I hope to expand the conceptual space available to casualties, those who survive them, and the role of the West German public itself in both the 1970s and the continuing production of memories about the decade.

The analytic pairing of media- and self-(re)presentations of terrorism serves to draw attention to the processes and implications of how we portray, and thus on what terms we engage with, political violence. By exploring a range of (re)presentations produced by subjects occupying radically different political positions, it is possible to ask what cultural labor different kinds of (re)presentations perform at the hands of different political subjects. As Rita Felski has noted in her work on women's autobiography, the medium and process of writing can come to undermine the authority of the real as much as the real intrudes on written representation. In a field of symbolic and necessarily mediated acts as complex as terrorism, I have no pretense of accessing such a reality, but rather have a more limited interest in what claims to do so suggest about both media and self-(re)presentations of women's political violence.[3]

As a critical counterpoint to popular, masculinist (re)presentations of women's participation in political violence, I bring the recent autobiographical account of former terrorist Margrit Schiller to bear on discourses of terrorism, sexuality, and women's political action more generally.[4]

3 With this point I wish to underscore that in referencing self-(re)presentations, I understand first-person accounts of these women's experiences not as historical fact, but, in keeping with Joan W. Scott's classic essay on experience, both interpretive acts and themselves in need of interpretation. What is more, the truth-content of these and other West German state, media, and terrorist accounts will remain largely unverifiable so long as much government documentation remains unavailable to the public, and existing documentation (for example, regarding conditions of imprisonment) remains extremely contradictory and therefore controversial. That being said, the reported experience of sexual intimidation, innuendo, and slander must be taken seriously as such. I do not consider careful analysis of the language and strategies of sex, violence, and politics to detract from the lived experiences of women terrorists; on the contrary, I hope through such analysis to better understand it.

4 Margrit Schiller: (b.1948) 1970–71: Social work with heroine addicts and loose affiliation with the Socialist Patients Collective. 1971–79: RAF member. During that time, Schiller served two years, eleven months (in two separate terms) for forgery and weapons possession. 1985–91: Cuban exile. 1992: Brief return to Germany. 1993–present: Uruguay.

Neither she nor other women terrorists who wrote autobiographical texts in the 1990s (such as Irmgard Möller and Inge Viett⁵) ascribe a specifically feminist, gendered, or sexually libratory character to any of their violent acts; the experience of violence, and the experience of being a woman, is markedly different in each of their accounts.⁶ There is no consensus at the most basic level in their understandings of the politics of autobiography nor in their retrospective conceptualizations of the subject of their histories. Schiller's "I" is movingly personal and self-reflexive without any diminution of political solidarity among the individuals she describes; Möller rejects a singular subject altogether; Viett alone tells her story from childhood to narrative present, providing the most traditionally structured subject.⁷

5   Inge Viett: (b.1944) 1969: Became integrated into West Berlin subculture. 1972–80: Membership in Movement Second June, which dissolved and integrated into the RAF in 1980. Arrested in 1972 and again in 1975, Viett broke out of prison both times. In 1982, she left the RAF and went into hiding in the GDR. Arrested in 1990 and sentenced to thirteen years prison, she was released in 1997.

6   Irmgard Möller: (b.1947): Möller became active politically in 1967 and joined the RAF in 1971. She served twenty-two years in prison for terrorist activities, and was released in 1994. Möller is the only survivor of the so-called 'Death Night' of October 18, 1977 in Stuttgart's Stammheim prison, when Andreas Baader, Gudrun Ensslin, and Jan-Carl Raspe were found dead under mysterious circumstances. She sustained extensive stab wounds.

7   Margrit Schiller, »*Es war ein harter Kampf um meine Erinnerung*« *Ein Lebensbericht aus der RAF,* Jens Mecklenburg, ed. (Hamburg: Konkret Literatur Verlag: 1999); Irmgard Möller and Oliver Tollmein, »*RAF—Das war für uns Befreiung*« *Ein Gespräch mit Irmgard Möller über den bewaffneten Kampf, Knast und die Linke* (Hamburg: Konkret Literatur Verlag, 1997); Inge Viett, *Einsprüche. Briefe aus dem Gefängnis* (Hamburg: Edition Nautilus, 1996) and *Nie war ich furchtloser* (Hamburg: Edition Nautilus, 1996). The list of women terrorists' accounts could be expanded to include Birgit Hogefeld, *Ein ganz normales Verfahren . . . Prozeßerklärungen, Briefe und Texte zur Geschichte der RAF,* Mit einem Vorwort von Christian Ströbele (Berlin and Amsterdam: Edition ID-Archiv, 1996); Astrid Proll, *Hans und Grete. Die RAF 1967–1977* (Göttingen: Steidel, 1998); and Gabrielle Rollnick's book-length interview with Daniel Dubbe, *Keine Angst vor niemand. Über die Siebziger, die Bewegung 2. Juni und die RAF* (Hamburg: Edition Nautilus, 2003). Accounts by men feature differently constituted subjects that fall outside the scope of this paper; despite the fact that the majority of West German terrorists in the 1970s were women, male terrorist accounts began to emerge significantly

Despite terrorist women's different assumptions about and conditions of autobiographical production, the importance of reading their life narratives together with popular texts that were widely distributed at the time of their active participation in terrorism should not be underestimated. As I have already asserted, the images of terrorism contemporary to terrorist violence in the 1970s continue to inform popular memory and understandings of women and terrorism in Germany. In this sense, my argument is not *about* the 1970s, even as it draws extensively on material from that period.

Let me move to the images themselves. For the purposes of this study, I focus specifically on photographic (re)presentations of women terrorists in my media analysis. The strategic linking of women's political involvement to lesbianism and aggressive heterosexuality and terrorism at play in these images creates a complex system of socially devalued behaviors, in which each element contributed to the delegitimization and criminaliza-

----

earlier, most notably with Michael "Bommi" Bauman's first banned, now classic *Wie alles anfing* [1975]. Mit einem Vorwort von Heinrich Böll und einem Nachwort von Michael Sontheimer (Berlin: Rotbuch Verlag, 1991). The relations among sex, violence, and politics is largely absent from men's accounts, which are structured along the lines of more traditional political and historical chronologies. Instructively, the question of propriety has been central to Viett's story. Like many crafters of life narrative, Viett clearly understood the process of autobiographical telling to be one of taking charge, of presenting a true account rooted in the authority of personal experience (*Nie war ich fürchtloser*, 8). Director Volker Schlöndorff's feature film *Die Stille nach dem Schuss* [*Legends of Rita*] (2001) makes liberal use of material from Viett's own biography. According to him, "I made sure that Inge Viett saw the film before the Berlinale. And then she said she wanted to take legal measures against it, because it's her story. It never came to that, because there are no legal grounds for a suit. When one gets so mixed up in German history as she did, one can't be prissy about it when history strikes back . . . She would have preferred the film not be made. She doesn't accuse the film of being her life, but of not being enough like her life. But we didn't want to tell a 'true story.' A feature film is always fiction, even if I say ten times it was really like that" (Schlöndorff in Daniela Sannwald, "'Die Stille nach dem Schuss.' Frauen sind die besseren Terroristen [Interview]. Politik als Liebesgeschichte: Ein Gespräch mit dem Filmemacher Volker Schlöndorff," *Der Tagesspiegel Online Dienste*, September 13, 2000, http://195.170.124.152/archiv/2000/09/12/ak-ku-fi-14250.html). Because of Schlöndorff's film, Viett's story has received significantly more media attention than the others.

tion of the others. All of the images I discuss appeared repeatedly and in a wide range of papers, in association with a wide range of different events and stories.[8]

Women's participation in radical politics was frequently represented in sexualized terms well before the formation of terrorist groups; its roots run deep in the public imagination. By far the most familiar image of Andreas Baader[9] and Gudrun Ensslin[10] shows them some two years before the formation of the RAF, seated together with their arms over one another's shoulders at their 1968 Frankfurt arson trial, laughing and looking into one another's eyes. Baader is holding a book with its title just visible enough: the Marquis de Sade's *Josephine*.[11] A series of articles published in the boulevard paper *Bild* immediately after Baader's arrest focused primarily on his relationship to Ensslin and included photographs of the two in the courtroom and in bed, making clear the media's obsessive association between political and sexual behavior. In Baader and Ensslin, the media took full advantage of the opportunity to market sex images; sex

---

8 Earlier versions of this work were presented at the 2003 Modern Language Association as part of broader analyses of terrorist images in the print media presented in 2000 at the annual conference "Rethinking Marxism," as well as at the Cornell University Visual Culture Colloquium. "Women's Sexuality and Radical Politics in Popular Accounts of Terrorist Violence," Women in German, MLA Convention, San Diego, December 27, 2003; "Envisioning Terror: Terrorism, Public Spectacle, and Print Media in West Germany of the 1970s," Rethinking Marxism, University of Massachussetts, Amherst, September 24, 2000.

9 Andreas Baader: (1947–1977) 1970: Founding member of the RAF. The group's popular name—'Baader-Meinhof'—derives from the group's formation around his 'liberation' from prison, in which Meinhof was complicit. At the time, he was serving a sentence for arsons committed to protest the Vietnam War, together with Gudrun Ensslin, Thorwald Proll, and Horst Söhnlein, in Frankfurt 1968. Arrested June 1972. Baader was found dead in his prison cell on October 18, 1977.

10 Gudrun Ensslin: (1940–1977): Founding member of the RAF. As a student, Ensslin was active in pacifist and anti-nuclear movements before turning to violent political action around 1967/68. Arrested June 1972. Ensslin was found hanged in her prison cell on October 18, 1977.

11 Matthew Todd Grant elaborates on the significance of "Sadean excess" in visions of the RAF; see "Critical Intellectuals in the New Media: Bernward Vesper, Ulrike Meinhof, the Frankfurt School and the Red Army Faction," Ph.D. diss.: Cornell University, 1994, 202–04.

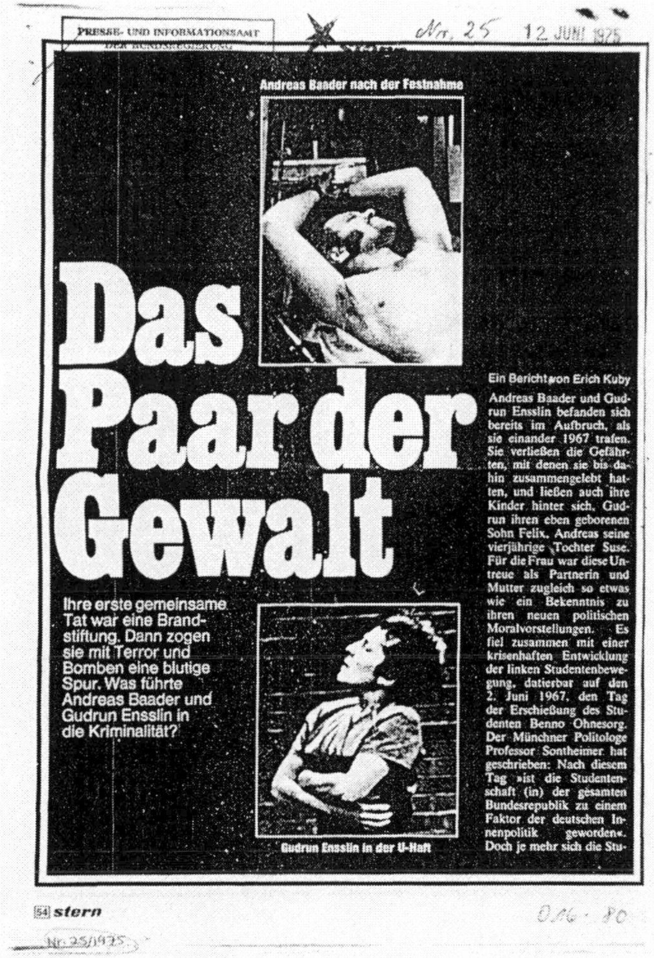
PRESSE- UND INFORMATIONSAMT

Nr. 25 12 JUNI 1975

Andreas Baader nach der Festnahme

Das Paar der Gewalt

Ihre erste gemeinsame Tat war eine Brandstiftung. Dann zogen sie mit Terror und Bomben eine blutige Spur. Was führte Andreas Baader und Gudrun Ensslin in die Kriminalität?

Ein Bericht von Erich Kuby

Andreas Baader und Gudrun Ensslin befanden sich bereits im Aufbruch, als sie einander 1967 trafen. Sie verließen die Gefährten, mit denen sie bis dahin zusammengelebt hatten, und ließen auch ihre Kinder hinter sich. Gudrun ihren eben geborenen Sohn Felix, Andreas seine vierjährige Tochter Suse. Für die Frau war diese Untreue als Partnerin und Mutter zugleich so etwas wie ein Bekenntnis zu ihren neuen politischen Moralvorstellungen. Es fiel zusammen mit einer krisenhaften Entwicklung der linken Studentenbewegung, datierbar auf den 2. Juni 1967, den Tag der Erschießung des Studenten Benno Ohnesorg. Der Münchner Politologe Professor Sontheimer hat geschrieben: Nach diesem Tag »ist die Studentenschaft (in) der gesamten Bundesrepublik zu einem Faktor der deutschen Innenpolitik geworden«. Doch je mehr sich die Stu-

Gudrun Ensslin in der U-Haft

54 stern

Nr. 25/1975

Figure 1 "The Violent Couple," *Stern*, June 12, 1975.

sells better than politics, which is to say that politics sells better disguised as sex.[12] (See fig. 1)

The pairing of Baader and Meinhof[13] as sexually involved draws more on the RAF's popular name than on any substantive physical relation-

12 See Grant, "Critical Intellectuals," 201–02, for similar arguments.

13 Ulrike Meinhof: (1934–1976): Well-known political journalist and co-editor for the leftist magazine *konkret*. Meinhof was active in pacifist and anti-nuclear movements and advocated for social welfare reforms in the FRG prior to her terrorist activity.

Nach der Verhaftung Baaders übernehmen Frauen das Regiment

Wer wird jetzt die neue Führerin der Terroristen?

Wenn Gudrun Ensslin die Kommandeuse wird, ist mit weiteren Anschlägen zu rechnen

Von Horst Zimmermann

SCHON IMMER FÜR UNEINGESCHRÄNKTE GEWALT PLÄDIERT hat Gudrun Ensslin, die 1968 wegen der Kaufhausbrandstiftung in Frankfurt vor Gericht stand.   dpa-Bilder

Figure 2 Headline reads: "Who will be the new lady leader of the terrorists now? After Baader's arrest, the women take over the regiment. If Gudrun Ensslin becomes the commander, further attacks are expected." Photo caption reads: "Gudrun Ensslin has always advocated wanton violence" (*Münchener Merkür*, June 7, 1972).

ship between the two. Nonetheless, their hypothetical involvement was described as the source of tensions between Ensslin and Meinhof. These tensions were supposedly augmented by intellectual egoism, with the media often observing that, were it not for Meinhof, the RAF would be

Founding member of the RAF. Arrested June 1972. Found hanged in her prison cell, May 9, 1976.

Figure 3 Headline reads: "Power struggle between the women in the Baader-Meinhof Gang. Ulrike Meinhof or Baader's lover Gudrun Ensslin—who gives the orders now?" The (very misleading) photo captioning is strikingly parallel, establishing a struggle for political leadership as a struggle over a man: "Abandoned her daughters and husband when she met Baader: Ulrike Meinhof" and "Abandoned her husband and son when she met Baader: Gudrun Ensslin" (*Bild Zeitung*, June 5, 1972).

the Baader-Ensslin Gang. In an article following Baader's arrest, "Power Struggle between the Women in the Baader-Meinhof Gang,"[14] these alleged tensions were used to portray the women as engaged in a petty and personal rather than political struggle for control. Perhaps more importantly, sexually pairing Baader and Meinhof enabled the media to avoid describing them as political partners.[15] (See fig. 2–3.)

14 "Machtkampf der Frauen in der Baader-Meinhof Bande," *Bild Zeitung*, May 5, 1972.

15 It is an unfortunate fact that academic investigations into Red Army Faction terrorism uncritically reinforce the conflation of sexual and political couplings in the RAF. Jeremy Varon's *Bringing the War Home* provides a textbook visualization of the three, in which photos of Meinhof and Ensslin are positioned to gaze at a brooding Baader, who looks away from them both (*Bringing the War Home: The Weather Underground, the Red Army Faction, and Revolutionary Violence in the Sixties and Seventies* [Berkeley, Los Angeles, and London: University of California Press, 2004]). For this example, I thank Andrew

Jamie H. Trnka

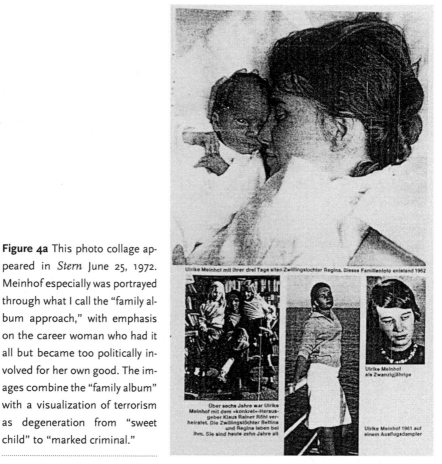

Figure 4a This photo collage appeared in *Stern* June 25, 1972. Meinhof especially was portrayed through what I call the "family album approach," with emphasis on the career woman who had it all but became too politically involved for her own good. The images combine the "family album" with a visualization of terrorism as degeneration from "sweet child" to "marked criminal."

The women of the terrorist group had, however, not always been "sexually deviant" in the media's own terms. Ensslin, whose father was a pastor, was portrayed as a fallen angel of sorts, often referred to as "the pastor's daughter" when she wasn't simply "the Baader-Girlfriend"; Meinhof was portrayed as the woman who had it all—a glamorous career as a journalist, a family, a suburban mansion—and threw it all away because she was too politically engaged for her own good. Hypersexuality is invoked here not as the cause of radical politics, a dubious enough claim, but rather as its symptom. Ironically, the warning voice of the press cautioned against the

Oppenheimer. In an academic climate that, since September 11, 2001, has deemed terrorism a "sexy" topic, sex and violence threaten to become disconcertingly blurred. A detailed analysis of the phenomenon remains the stuff of another article.

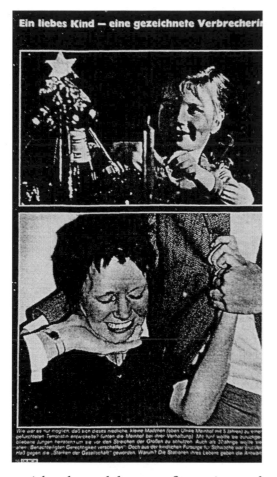

Figure 4b Figures 4b through Figure 7 all appeared as part of the *Quick* magazine series "Ulrike Meinhof and her Cruel Girls," June 28, 1972.

social and moral dangers of terrorism at the same time as it marketed its own highly sexualized images of the terrorists. (See figs. 4-7.)

In stark contrast to these portrayals of terrorists, the media sometimes imaged them as stereotypically androgynous, hinting at queer sexuality. Ensslin, for example, is alternately described as "the torch" (a reference to her involvement in arsons as well as to her supposed sexual insatiability) and as flat-chested, stringy-haired, and possessed of an unparalleled masculine militancy and capacity to dominate. A series of three photos of Ensslin, published in *Der Spiegel*, illustrates these different but related portrayals of Ensslin in the popular press. (See fig. 8.)

The pictures are arranged vertically, one above the other. In the first picture, Ensslin has short-cropped hair and looks androgynous. In the second,

Figure 5 "The unstoppable decline of Ulrike Meinhof"

her hair is long and hangs loose around her shoulders. She is wearing lipstick, and her cheekbones are highlighted dramatically. In the final picture, taken after Ensslin's arrest, she is smoking, her hair has been dyed black and is uncombed, and she is staring blankly into a corner of her dark cell.[16] Similar images combining androgyny or masculinity, heterosexuality and stereotypical feminine beauty, and dark criminality are deployed in various (re)presentations of all of the female terrorists.

While these seemingly different images and the ideologies that inform them are depicted sequentially in this example, my point is that through their frequent repetition, they served to reinforce a cumulative effect on

16 Grant also analyzes these images, describing them as a life chronology (i.e., discrete moments or stages in Ensslin's development taken from the years 1963, 1968, and 1972) rather than a composite image (189).

Figure 6 Captions include: "Two years underground have left their mark on this woman's face" and "Gudrun Ensslin was sexually unsatisfied. In 1969 the pastor's daughter acted in a porn film." Other photos and captions depict Petra Schelm, who was killed by police in July 1971 after she supposedly got involved with the wrong man and, through him, with terrorism. Schelm joined the RAF from the ranks of the broad, West German extra-parliamentary opposition in 1970. She was shot dead by police during the first massive terrorist manhunt in July of the following year. Also pictured: Irene Georgens with her legs spread apart. Georgens first met Meinhof during the journalist's research on foster care facilities. She was active in the RAF from its inception until 1972, when she was arrested and convicted for bank robbery.

the public conscious—an effect that could be described as the trace of an absent referent. What is more, the *composite* image of the RAF suggests the possibility of a subjectivity at once hetero- and homosexual, ugly and beautiful, and politically engaged enough to put one's body at stake in opposition to the democratic German state: a terrifying and destabilizing combination.

The autobiographies that I consider assume a fundamentally different relationship of author, text, and audience: refusing to present either a superficial or a psychologized image of violence, they claim to present authoritative and authentic accounts of women's participation in terrorism and appeal to the reader to locate their political actions within a larger

Figure 7: Headline: "Sowing naked violence" (*Quick*, July 5, 1972). Paperclipped photos and type suggest the authority of police investigative files. Captions include: "They are gangsters with body and soul" and "They know no moral or sexual taboos."

social context that is itself fundamentally characterized by violence, with particular attention to violence against women. Their terrorist acts are, of course, expressions of subjectivity in and of themselves; I choose to address their written self-expression because, like the examples from print media that I have drawn on here, they interpret rather than (re)present the terrorist act. Terrorism communicates through the disruption of public spectacle; at their most productive moments, first-person narratives of terrorism can challenge the spectacle that the (re)presentation of such disruptions itself so often becomes.[17]

17 Arlene A. Teraoka describes terrorism as "an extreme mode of communication" (211) and offers insightful analysis of Ulrike Meinhof's essays and collectively authored RAF communiqués; see "Terrorism and the Essay: The Case of Ulrike Meinhof," *The Politics of the Essay: Feminist Perspectives*, ed. Ruth-Ellen Boetcher Joeres and Elizabeth Mittmann (Bloomington: Indiana University Press, 1993): 208–24. Space dictates that I refrain from a more detailed explication of the rhetoric of terrorism here. My understanding of terrorism as the disruption of public spectacle draws primarily on Guy Debord. His influential *Society of the Spectacle* (1967; trans. Donald Nicholson-Smith [New York: Zone Books, 1995]) emphasizes that spectacle consists not of images

Of the first-person narratives in question, Margrit Schiller's appropriation of the traditionally bourgeois literary form of autobiography lends itself especially well to an analysis of how gender and sexuality are deployed as narrative and rhetorical—that is, not exclusively experiential—categories. With patient, steady self-reflexivity, the political and social significance that she ascribes to elements of her story as a woman and as a terrorist are more explicitly available to the reader in her autobiography than in Möller's or Viett's. (This is largely because it is not shaped by the kind of collaborative (auto)biographical practice that informs their narratives.)

Multiple examples show how Schiller both deploys the categories of sexuality and gender *and* resists the sexualization of her body and political activity in order to refocus attention on the sexual nature of state violence. For instance, she provides a detailed account of her forced press appearance after her first arrest, comparing her treatment to that of a hunting trophy, carried by police, her skirt hitched up, her head held toward the cameras.[18] (See Fig. 9.)

Her account describes a sexualized hunt that took allegedly lascivious women for prey. Ironically, she suggests, her transformation into the sexualized object of the media's gaze should be read as a culmination of the sexual accouterments of her most recent underground disguise: Schiller took on her feminine garb in an effort to evade recognition. She describes in detail the process of making herself up as "feminine," concluding: "I felt costumed, but the search descriptions said that I only ever wore long pants."[19] At the time of her arrest, her sexual persona is not described as an authentic expression of her own sexuality or gender identity, but as a defensive/evasive response to the public gaze cast on another kind of sex-

themselves but of social relationships mediated by images. It should be understood as a "worldview transformed into an objective force" through image-relations (13). He points to what he identifies as the methodological necessity of analyzing the spectacle in its own language in order to "hasten its demise." This is largely what I mean when I point to the terrorists disruption of public spectacle as itself spectacular and yet fundamentally opposed to spectacle. Looking at West German terrorism in the '70s with an eye to these concepts is not only theoretically useful but also historically appropriate insofar as a number of terrorists were closely associated with Situationist groups before going underground.

18   Schiller, »*Es war ein harter Kampf um meine Erinnerung*«, 18.

19   Schiller, »*Es war ein harter Kampf um meine Erinnerung*«, 11.

Studentin Gudrun Ensslin 1963
„Wir haben große Angst gehabt . . ."

Angeklagte Gudrun Ensslin 1968
. . . daß gerade die Baader-Freundin . . ."

Verhaftete Gudrun Ensslin 1972
. . . was ganz Verrücktes machen würde"

Figure 8: *Der Spiegel*, June 25, 1972.

ual body. Forced by the manhunt to sexualize herself, that sexualization is used as a weapon against her by the very state and media authorities who, she says, made it necessary.

To a similar effect, Schiller recalls being forced to strip at the time of her second arrest:

The entire stairwell was full of heavily armed police in protective clothing. I was the only woman. I had to stand naked in the middle of the stairs, surrounded by young policemen. When the initial tension began to dissipate, the pigs around me started to comment on my body. It was about half an hour before a ranking officer put a jacket on me. I felt utterly demeaned and humiliated.[20]

Schiller also describes repeated sexual intimidation by police, guards, and intelligence officers. First housed in a cloister that had been converted into a prison—"a fitting change," she recalls bitterly—she was later transferred to the threatening atmosphere of an all-male prison in dramatic opposition to her initial "cloistering."[21] These state actions are repeatedly framed as narratives of rape or the psychologically torturous effect of potential rape.

Sexualized state violence in sites and conditions of imprisonment finds its narrative corollary in the social violence of Adenauer Germany that Schiller ascribes to her family: her mother violently repressed Margrit's sexuality, beating the backs of her legs black and blue

---

20   Schiller, »*Es war ein harter Kampf um meine Erinnerung*«, 136.

21   Schiller, »*Es war ein harter Kampf um meine Erinnerung*«, 81, 83.

Figure 9: Police forcibly present Margrit Schiller to the press.

with knitting needles. What better metaphor for the gender role assigned her and the consequences of acting on heterosexual desire? Her father's authority is described in terms that suggest he created the threatening atmosphere of a men's prison in Schiller's own childhood bedroom.

By positioning herself as a victim of sexualized social and ultimately state violence, Schiller creates an *ex post facto* justification for terrorist violence even as she narrates away her own agency. This denial of agency exists in tension with a stated interest in using autobiography to reclaim repressed experience and memory, at least in part as a means of taking responsibility for her past actions without renouncing her participation in the RAF. As she employs them, categories and terms of gender and sexuality perform a profoundly destabilizing cultural labor in the history of political violence and its articulation in gendered terms in (West) Germany.

If subjectivity is produced as an effect of writing—that is, if it is not something stable that preexists the process of telling a life story—then writing away agency is an ironic reinscription of the woman terrorist as object, not only (and inevitably) of *self*-reflection, but of a haunting state and media gaze. She exists in tension between subject and object positions implied by the roles of life-author, perpetrator, and victim. Without addressing this tension, one cannot adequately address the question of responsibility that comes with subject-agency and is, in a legal, social, and ethical sense, a necessary precondition for understanding how, when, and why terror is enacted.

Whether or not Schiller and her fellow life-narrators see their own terrorist acts and affiliations as located within or significantly informed by a feminist politics, popular press accounts—which systematically linked women's political initiatives and violence—demand that we analyze all (re)presentations of women's political action—especially terrorism—in these terms. The basis for this link resides in a shared archive of gender (re)presentations across the popular and the personal. By reading women terrorists' stories as part of a longer tradition of confessional narrative, a preferred narrative form in mainstream feminist thought prominent in West Germany of the 1970s,[22] their reliance on gendered categories becomes more immediately apparent.

The conscious articulation of the personal and the political as critical epistemological categories in the West German (and, for that matter, large sectors of the U.S. American) feminist movement(s) in the 1970s is exem-

---

22   While the women terrorist texts under discussion at no point play with the boundaries of fictional protagonist, author, and narrator—a hallmark of women's literature so widely read and discussed at that time—they bear other important formal and thematic affinities to the phenomenon taken as a whole. An important exception might be the collaborative narratives of Astrid Proll and Katharina de Fries by Ulrike Edschmid, *Frau mit Waffe. Zwei Geschichten aus terroristischen Zeiten* (Berlin: Rowohlt, 1996).

plified in confessional narrative.[23] If, with Felski, one asserts a strong relationship between confessional form and its social function, the cultural labor potentially performed in women terrorists' texts is diminished by the relative decline of supposed oppositional communities of readership.[24] Nonetheless, the strong thematic and organizational affinities among these texts (e.g., violation by people and institutions coded as masculine; participation of political and social opposition; extrapolation of familial to broader social-historical relationships) provide some useful insights into their construction. Composed by women who would have been familiar with confessional texts such as Verena Stefan's *Shedding* (1975) and Karin Struck's *Class Love* (1973), they approximate what Eva Keitel describes as "horizontal" relationships between confessional narratives.[25] The "vertical" or structural relationships emphasized vary more widely than might be expected: Schiller, affiliated with the Socialist Patients Collective in Heidelberg before joining the RAF, emphasizes the medical and psychological effects of capitalism; Viett implicitly addresses heteronormative and capitalist structures in relating her experiences as a young sex worker to later vandalism of bridal and porn shops. Feminist scholars, theorizing first-person life narratives in relation to Althusserian and Foucauldian theories of repressive and ideological state apparati, have explored the ways in which women subjects come to understand their social formation in, and through, life narration: "An ideological critique of her engagement in the state apparati is required to understand her own social formation, though such a critique will not undo it."[26] Unsuccessfully, some women subjects of the terrorist act attempt to do precisely that: to explode the physical representatives of social formation in a highly mediated, symbolic act that overreaches critique in a properly productive sense toward something like an undoing. At the risk of pushing the point to its conceptual limit, women terrorists' first-person narratives approximate the "horizontal," terrorism

23 Rita Felski, "On Confession" [1989], *Women, Autobiography, Theory: A Reader*, ed. Sidonie Smith and Julia Watson (Madison: University of Wisconson Press, 1998), 83f, 92; Evelyne Keitel, "Verständigungstexte: Form, Funktion, Wirkung," *The German Quarterly* 56:3: 431f, 448.

24 Outlined by Keitel, "Verständigungstexte: Form, Funktion, Wirkung," 431, 448, and pasim.

25 Keitel, "Verständigungstexte: Form, Funktion, Wirkung," 432.

26 Smith and Watson, *Women, Autobiography, Theory*, 21.

the "vertical" axes of social analysis that Keitel (admittedly schematically) draws in her characterization of confessional narrative.[27]

The autobiographical turn in terrorist communication resumes and resists the rearticulation as "individual."[28] Schiller's titular struggle for personal memory *("It was a hard battle for my memory": A Life Report from the RAF)* intones individual perspective without accepting the formally implied individuation of narrator as social subject. Accountability is conceived as personal, even when individual subjects are not named as such (for naming has legal, institutional consequences that can never be taken for granted in the context of these narratives);[29] personal histories, howev-

....

27 E.g., Keitel, "Verständigungstexte: Form, Funktion, Wirkung," 432.

28 See Smith and Watson, *Women, Autobiography, Theory,* on autobiography as an institution of individuation and interpellation: "For the Althusserian critique understood that 'individual' to be a function of ideology. Students of Althusser directed attention to the ways in which historically specific cultural institutions provide ready-made identities to subjects. 'Autobiography' becomes one such literary institution in the West. It has its tradition (or history); it participates in the economics of production and circulation; and it has its effects—that is, it functions as a powerful cultural site through which the 'individual' materializes" (21). Nonetheless, insofar as the RAF and Movement Second June insisted—and women terrorists' continue to insist—on a collective subject, individual voices resonate differently than many of the subjects considered by theorists of autobiography.

29 Schiller explains: "I think that with our struggle we took on a personal accountability. We stand by it by name. For the most part I name the real names of all the people who are known or dead. The unknown or unrecognized shall remain so: Bernd, Christiane, Christina, Ingrid and Stefan are invented names for people who are not invented" (»*Es war ein harter Kampf um meine Erinnerung*«, 4). Because criminal law is predicated on individual guilt, one of the best defenses of the terrorist suspect is to hold fast to a group identity. Schiller's gesture of renaming or even anonymous naming may be understood as an alternative narrative practice along a spectrum of individual juridical and collective political identifications. For example, the introduction of "crown witness" (*Kronzeuge*) legislation, in which suspects were offered substantial privileges and reduced sentencing in exchange for naming names, was integral to the criminal trial of terrorists, and Ulrike Meinhof described what she viewed as state strategies of "personalization" as fundamentally destructive to the collective in more than just evidentiary terms. By contrast, Schiller's first-person account walks a fine line between personal formation and accountability, and collective affinities (including

er, call out for collective reflection.[30] If feminist confessional, according to Felski and Keitel, represents a failure of intimacy,[31] terrorist confessions (in all of the word's dimensions) represent a failure of communication through the medium of terrorism itself.

Critics like Sigrid Weigel have rightly drawn attention to the aesthetic and political naïveté of the confessional genre;[32] nonetheless, I believe that this naïveté has to be read in tandem with politically calculating moments in autobiographical texts by authors like Schiller. Women terrorists explicitly state a desire to reinscribe themselves into history, to redefine *which* selves are visible (for example, writing the woman as object of state and social violence as well as the active perpetrator of violent acts). In the process, they mobilize categories of gender and sexual identity that had been the object of their own radical critique in the 1970s, albeit to different political ends than popular media deployments of those same categories. This should not be surprising. Since the 1970s, theorists of self-narration have repeatedly emphasized the epistemological limits of narrating

political solidarities, friendships, and sexual relationships).

30   The metaphor of the mirror is intoned by both Jens Mecklenburg's foreword and Argentine author Osvaldo Bayer's afterword to Schiller's text. Möller identifies the problem of individual versus collective histories in explicitly generic terms, drawing attention to the narrative constraints of the one-on-one interview format of her own book, given the RAF's self-understanding as a collective (10).

31   According to Felski in "On Confession": "[T]he production of the text itself functions as an attempted compensation for this failure, generating in the relationship between the reader and author the erotic mutuality which cannot otherwise be realized. Writing, seemingly the most isolated of activities, becomes the means to the creation of an ideal intimacy. As [Judith] Offenbach notes of her own text [*Sonja* (1980)] the confession is a cry for love, allowing the author to express powerful emotional feelings to a reader without fear of rejection. The writing self is profoundly dependent upon the reader for validation, specifically the projected community of female readers who will understand, sympathize, and identify with the author's emotions and experiences" (89–90). Whether the feminist readership these critics posit as a condition for a politicized reception of confessional narrative still exists thirty years after the heyday of feminist confessional narrative is a question that, without more detailed research into reception, I am unprepared to answer.

32   Sigrid Weigel, "'Woman Begins Relating to Herself': Contemporary German Women's Literature (Part One)," *New German Critique* 31: 1984.

memory: "They may contest as well as accept the public rendering but must relate to it and negotiate it."[33] Reconceptualizations of confessional narrative in explicitly political terms by scholars like Felski and Keitel can help us to restate questions about the relationship between feminism and terrorism in media and autobiographical texts. Women and men, perpetrators and victims alike, draw on popular forms and myths in order to narrate their own life experiences.[34] If these categories of sexual and political violence and violation shaped the roles available to Schiller—and they were the predominant roles socially scripted at the time—we should ask what kind of alternate social visions one might work to produce in an effort to escape the material oppositions that constrain representation and, more importantly, lead some subjects to choose violence.[35] This is not a simple question, and the answer is bound to entail broad social change rather than a singular legislative or political intervention.

The material referents in and effects of terrorists' life narratives of course exceed the narrative structures populated by figurative women in the literary texts Felski and Keitel analyze. Nonetheless, the structures and communicative goals of confessional texts invite readers to reconsider the complex production and mediation of the terrorist spectacle in more widely circulated media. Both media and self-(re)presentations provide, to my mind, unsatisfactory accounts of women's participation in political violence, reaffirming an uneasy relationship between feminism and terrorism across a range of authors, texts, and textual forms. Read together,

33   Penny Summerfield, "Dis/composing the subject: Intersubjectivities in oral history," ed. Tess Cosslett, Celia Lury, and Penny Summerfield, *Feminism and Autobiography: Texts, Theories, Methods* (New York and London: Routledge, 2001), 91–106. See also Sidonie Smith and Julia Watson, *Reading Autobiography: A Guide for Interpreting Life Narratives* (Minneapolis: University of Minnesota Press, 2001).

34   See for example Summerfield; M.-F. Chanfrault-Duchet, "Narrative Structures, Social Models and Symbolic Representation in the Life-story," *Women's Words: The Feminist Practice of Oral History*, ed. S. B. Gluck and D. Patai (London: Routledge, 1991); and Luisa Passerini, "Women's Personal Narratives: Myths, Experiences and Emotions," *Interpreting Women's Lives: Feminist Theory and Personal Narratives*, Personal Narratives Group (Bloomington: Indiana University Press, 1989), 189–97.

35   The perception of a choice between socially scripted roles is perhaps clearest not in Schiller but in Rollnick: "[Danial Dubbe]: You could have lived as a housewife with two children in Dortmund, too. [Rollnick]: No, never a housewife. The way it was, with all the mistakes, really was better" (*Keine Angst vor niemand*, 119).

media and self-(re)presentations at least begin to suggest a more complete view of a historical, discursive economy of images and narratives that collectively constitute a gendered epistemology of violence within which terrorism has been and continues to be understood.

WHEN DO WOMEN KILL?

LIFE AND DEATH IN TSARIST RUSSIA

Jean K. Berger

INCE THE SEPTEMBER 11, 2001, TERRORIST ATTACKS on the United States, the subject of political terrorism and the motivations for it have received considerable attention in America. While the subject is relatively new to most Americans, political terrorism is not a new phenomenon. It haunted the dreams of the Russian tsars beginning with the first attempt on the life of Tsar Alexander II in 1866. During the late 1870s and early 1880s political terrorism reached a crescendo in Russia and culminated in the assassination of Alexander II on March 1, 1881. Since that time, volumes of literature have been produced which examine the activities and ideologies of the regicides and the role of women in the Russian revolutionary movement.[1] In spite of the attention, no one has clearly an-

1 Among the many works related to this subject are the following: Dorothy Atkinson, Alexander Dallin, and Gail Warshofsky Lapidus, eds., *Women in Russia* (Stanford, CA: Stanford University Press, 1977); Jay Bergman, *Vera Zasulich: A Biography* (Stanford, CA: Stanford University Press, 1983); Vera Broido, *Apostles into Terrorists* (New York: Viking Press, 1977); Barbara Alpern Engel, *Mothers and Daughters: Women of the Intelligentsia in Nineteenth-Century Russia* (Cambridge, MA: Cambridge University Press, 1983); Barbara Alpern Engel and Clifford N. Rosenthal, eds. and trans., *Five Sisters: Women against the Tsar: The Memoirs of Five Young Anarchist Women of the*

swered the question, what led young Russian women in the 1870s and 1880s to conclude that acts of terrorism were the only possible means of achieving their political and social objectives? This paper attempts to answer that question by examining the progression of three nineteenth-century Russian women from peaceful reformers to terrorists.

By the second decade of the nineteenth century Russia had achieved a position of apparent military invincibility. Napoleon's 1812 invasion of Russia ended in a disastrous retreat for the French. The Russian Army was the largest in Europe, and Russia was a major power broker at the Congress of Vienna. However, this image of power did not take into account the decay at the center of Russian government and society. Russia was an absolute autocracy with no mechanism for progressive elements in society to provide input. The power of the tsar was equated with the power of God. The conservatism of the autocracy was bolstered by the conservatism of the Russian Orthodox Church, which opposed the introduction of Western ideas, books, and technical specialists out of concern for contamination by heretical ideas. The government enforced strict limits on foreign travel and on the number of students admitted to Russian universities. Russian society aimed to produce obedient nobles and passive peasants, not educated citizens or innovative businessmen. Even if the tsar and the church had not opposed progress and modernization, change would have been difficult because the Russian economy was based on serfdom. In 1850 peasants comprised about 84 percent of the Russian population while more than 43 percent of those peas-

1870's (New York: Routledge, 1975); Vera Figner, Memoirs of a Revolutionist (DeKalb: Northern Illinois University Press, 1991); Vera Figner, Zapechatlennyi trud, 2 vols. (Moscow: Zadruga, 1921–1922), Harvard Russian and Soviet Humanities Preservation Microfilms Project; Marcelline J. Hutton, Russian and West European Women, 1860–1939: Dreams, Struggles, and Nightmares (Landham, MD: Rowman and Littlefield Publishers, Inc., 2001); Norman M. Naimark, Terrorists and Social Democrats: The Russian Revolutionary Movement Under Alexander III (Cambridge, MA: Harvard University Press, 1983); Philip Pomper, Peter Lavrov and the Russian Revolutionary Movement (Chicago: The University of Chicago Press, 1972); Philip Pomper, Sergei Nechaev (New Brunswick, NJ: Rutgers University Press, 1979); Richard Stites, The Women's Liberation Movement in Russia: Feminism, Nihilism and Bolshevism, 1860–1930 (Princeton, NJ: Princeton University Press, 1978); S. Tsederbaum, Zhenshchina v russkom revoliutsionnom dvizhenii 1870–1905 (Leningrad: Rabochee izd-vo Priboi, 1927), microfilm; S. S. Volk, Narodnaia Volia, 1879–1882 (Moscow and Leningrad: Nauka: 1966).

ants were unfree serfs who were tied to the land they worked.[2] They owed both labor and dues to their landlords and taxes to the state. These circumstances made a spontaneous industrial revolution similar to that occurring in Western Europe impossible in Russia. Industrialization required free peasants who could migrate to towns in search of opportunities and entrepreneurs with foresight and capital.

Basking in its victory over Napoleon, Russia remained blissfully unaware of its eroding military might. However, when Russia faced off against Britain, France, and Turkey during the Crimean War of 1853–56, the incompetence and backwardness of the Russian military rapidly became apparent. In the decades between the Napoleonic Wars and the Crimean War, Western Europe had experienced the industrial revolution. Steam engines, railroads, and more accurate, longer-range weapons now enhanced the military power of Britain and France. Russia, with its mentally rigid, poorly educated commanders and its illiterate, poorly equipped peasant soldiers, was ignominiously defeated and forced to cede territory to Turkey. This military loss exposed Russia's military weakness for all to see. Russia either had to reform its military or face absorption by its neighbors. However, military reform could not be made without massive economic, social, and political changes to the Russian state.

Facing an impending crisis, Tsar Alexander II issued an emancipation proclamation in 1861 that freed the serfs, who expected immediate release from their obligations to the landlords and ownership of the land they had farmed for generations. Instead, because Alexander II needed to placate the conservative landlords who were losing their valuable human capital, the serfs received only a portion of the land they had farmed and were required to make exorbitant redemption payments to the government for forty-nine years to pay for the land. The peasants rapidly fell in arrears on their payments and were soon in worse condition than they had experienced as serfs.

As the Russian peasantry became disillusioned in the aftermath of emancipation, the progressive, educated element of the Russian nobility also grew embittered. Meanwhile the ideas of utopian socialism, liberalism, Socialism, and Marxism circulated in Western Europe. In order to stem the tide of these ideas flowing into Russia, the government reorganized the educational system by adding extra years of classical studies, rea-

2   David Moon, *The Russian Peasantry, 1600–1930: The World the Peasants Made* (London and New York: Addison Wesley Longman, 1999), 21, 99.

soning that if students were busy learning Greek and Latin they would not have time to think about subversive ideas such as constitutional monarchy. At the same time that education was reorganized, press censorship and police surveillance increased, certain types of legal cases were removed from the authority of ordinary courts, and the government made it clear that the tsar did not intend to ever take steps toward sharing power.

Although conditions in Russia were discouraging to many Russians in the second half of the nineteenth century, they were especially discouraging for women. In marriage a woman could look forward to endless childbearing and a patriarchal legal system that denied women the most basic of rights. An adult woman could not obtain a passport without the consent of her father, if she were single, or the consent of her husband, if she were married. Nor could a woman hope to bypass marriage and become independent by supporting herself financially. Professions required education, but educational opportunities for women were severely limited. Russian universities remained closed to women until the 1870s. Even basic literacy was beyond the reach of most Russian women. In the final years of the nineteenth century, only 13.1 percent of all Russian women could read and write.[3]

Out of this politically repressive, patriarchal milieu emerged women who were not only politically active but who became practitioners of terrorism and assassination as a means to achieve political and social change. A careful examination of the lives of a number of terrorist women yields a pattern. None of these women originally intended to use terror as a tool for social and political change, but each ultimately arrived at the same conclusion. Although social and economic circumstances varied greatly, each woman seems to have passed along the same path from political reformer to terrorist. By examining the steps along that path, the motivations of the women emerge.

Vera Figner is one of the best documented of the reformers-turned-terrorist because she lived long enough to write extensive memoirs. Born in 1852, Figner was brought up in the comfortable surroundings of the Russian minor nobility. While her family was not from the high aristocracy, they were wealthy enough to own substantial property. In her memoirs, Figner claimed that as a child growing up on a rural estate, she was largely

---

3   Rose L. Glickman, "The Russian Factory Woman, 1880–1914," in *Women in Russia*, Dorothy Atkinson, Alexander Dallin, and Gail Warshofsky Lapidus, eds. (Stanford, CA: Stanford University Press, 1977), 73.

unaware of tensions between the serfs that her family owned and her family, the serf-owners. She wrote, "Я ничего не слыхала о барщине, не была свидетьницей каких нибудь притеснений и не слыхала жалоб."[4] [I never heard of barshchina, never witnessed any oppression, and never heard any complaints.][5]

Figner's family had sufficient wealth to send her to a boarding school for girls for six years. After graduation from the school in 1869 at age seventeen, Figner decided she wanted to attend a university and become a medical doctor. According to her memoirs, this decision was influenced by family discussions of the importance of serving society as well as self, by reading literary journals, and by the example of Nadezhda Suslova, the first Russian woman to earn a medical degree in Switzerland. Figner wrote, "Я стала добиваться поступления в университет…лишь бы учиться стать врачем и принести мои знания в деревию, как оружие против болезни нищеты и невежества."[6] [I began to work to obtain admission to a university . . . so that I could study to become a doctor and bring my knowledge to the village as a defense against sickness, poverty and ignorance.] At this point in her life, Figner was not yet influenced by radical ideology and had no proclivity toward violence.

While Figner's desire to study medicine seems benign, both social expectations and the government immediately blocked it. Russian women had petitioned the Minister of Education in 1868 to allow female admission to the universities but had been resoundingly excluded.[7] Since Russian universities were closed to her, Figner decided to study abroad. However, her father refused to allow her to travel abroad to study. To circumvent this obstacle and gain a passport, Figner married Aleksey Filipov, a liberal-minded man who supported her desire to study medicine. In 1872 Figner, her husband, and her sister Lydia arrived at the University of Zurich to study medicine. In her memoirs, Figner related that upon her arrival in Zurich, she wholeheartedly devoted herself to the study of medicine.[8] She also

---

4   Vera Figner, *Zapechatlennyi trud* (Moscow: Zadruga, 1921–22), 23.

5   All English translations in brackets by Jean Berger.

6   Figner, *Zapechatlennyi trud*, 52.

7   Elizaveta Kovalskaia, "Elizaveta Kovalskaia," *Five Sisters: Women against the Tsar*, ed. and trans. Barbara Alpern Engel and Clifford N. Rosenthal (New York and London: Routledge, 1992), 212.

8   Figner, *Zapechatlennyi trud*, 63.

developed an interest in the political debates swirling through the Russian colony there, taking part in the *Fritschi*'s discussions of John Stuart Mill, Fourier, and other thinkers. She became familiar with the ideas of Lavrov and Bakunin, which were hotly debated by the Russian students.[9] By this point in her life, Figner was interested in political reform theories but was not yet taking any action to support change.

Late in May 1873, the Russian government created a new obstacle to Figner's education. An official decree ordered the termination of all studies by Russian women in Zurich:

> The government warns . . . all Russian women visiting the university and the polytechnical school of Zurich that those of them who after January 1 of the coming year 1874 continue to attend lectures in these institutions, will not be admitted to any occupations the permission for which is dependent on the government, or to any examination or Russian institution of learning.[10]

Some Russian students scattered to other European universities while others began returning to Russia to put theory into action. Figner went to the University of Berne where she continued studying medicine until December 1875.[11]

Figner's return to Russia was motivated by a sense of duty to improve the lot of the peasants and to refill the ranks of reformers who had been arrested for attempting to spread political ideas among factory workers. Among those arrested were Figner's sister Lydia and many of her friends from the Fritschi circle. Figner wrote, "Когда я вспомнила, что эти люди томятся в тюрьме и уже испытывают тяжелую долю... подумала о том что в настоящий момент уже обладаю знаниями необходимыми для врача."[12] [When I remembered that these people languished in prison and already experienced an oppressive lot . . . I realized that in that moment I already possessed the knowledge necessary for a doctor.]

9   Amy Knight, "The Fritschi: A Study of Female Radicals in the Russian Populist Movement," *Canadian-American Slavic Studies* 9, no. 1 (1975): 6.

10 Jan M. Meijer, *Knowledge and Revolution: The Russian Colony in Zuerich (1870–1873): A Contribution to the Study of Russian Populism* (Assen, Netherlands: Van Gorcum and Co., 1955), 142.

11   Figner, *Zapechatlennyi trud*, 79.

12   Figner, Zapechatlennyi trud, 80.

On her return to Russia, Figner became part of the Land and Freedom political group which resulted in her decision to go "to the people." The "to the people" movement advocated living among the masses of uneducated Russian peasants and doing peaceful propaganda work as a means to bring about political change. Since Figner initially believed that informing the masses would bring about this change, her first revolutionary activity consisted of an attempt to live among rural peasants and provide them with medical care. She believed that working as an assistant physician would bring her in contact with the masses of ordinary Russian peasants, allowing her to do political propaganda work with them while treating their physical ailments. Consequently, in August of 1877, Figner took a position as an assistant physician in rural Russia.[13]

Figner's first attempt at peaceful propaganda through medical practice rapidly taught her the weaknesses of this approach. Figner was appointed to work in the province of Samara. In her memoirs, she discussed the burden of her working conditions. She was assigned to provide medical care to twelve villages which entailed being away from home for eighteen days out of each month. The extremely heavy workload was the least part of the problem. The illnesses, poverty, and squalor of the Russian peasants proved overwhelming. She wrote:

Я останавливалась обыкновенно в избе, называемой вьезжей, куда тотчас же стекались больные, оповещенные подворно десятским или старостой. 30-40 пациентов моментально наполняли избу; тут были старые и молодые, большое число женщин, еще больше детей всякого возраста, которые оглашали воздух всевозможными криками и писком. Грязные и истощенные,—на больных нельзя было смотреть равнодушно; болезни все застарелые: у взрослых на каждом шагу—ревматизмы, головные боли, тянущиеся 10-15 лет; почти все страдали накожными болезнями; в редкой деревне были бани; в громадном большинстве случаев они заменялись мытьем в русской печке; неисправимые катарры желудка и кишек, грудные хрипы, слышные на много шагов, сифилис, не щадящий никакого возраста, струпья, язвы без конца, и все это при такой невообразимой грязи жилища и одежды, при пище, столь нездоровой и скудной, что останавливаешься в

13 Figner, *Zapechatlennyi trud*, 98.

отупении над вопросом: есть ли это жизнь животного или человека?

[I usually stopped at a hut, designated as the visiting hut where immediately thronged thirty or forty patients apprised of my arrival by the village elder or his assistants. There were old and young, a large number of women and even more of children of all ages, who filled the air with all possible types of screams and squeaks. It was impossible to look indifferently on the dirty and emaciated patients. Their illnesses were all chronic. Adults on every side had rheumatism and headaches which dragged on for ten to fifteen years. Almost all of them suffered from skin diseases. Bath houses were rare in villages. In the vast majority of cases they washed themselves in the Russian oven. There were incurable catarrhs of the stomach and intestines; wheezing chests, audible from many steps away; syphilis which spared no age; scabs and sores without end; and all this with such unimaginably filthy dwellings and clothes, and with such unhealthy and insufficient food that one stopped oneself in stupefaction with the question: is this the life of animals or of humans?][14]

Figner had encountered the first of the problems with this approach to political reform. The peasants were so ground down by poverty, filth, ignorance, and exhaustion that ideas of political reform were incomprehensible to them. After three months, Figner fled from Samara to avoid arrest. A compromising letter to her had been found in the possession of another revolutionary. That fact alone would have been sufficient grounds for her arrest.

Not deterred by the lack of revolutionary results in her first attempt at medical practice and propaganda, in 1878 Figner made a second attempt to live among the peasants, taking a position as a rural assistant surgeon in the Saratov region. Although Figner held the official position of assistant surgeon, her younger sister Evgeniia, who had also recently passed the assistant surgeon examinations, came to live with her and assist her both with the medical and propaganda work.[15]

Figner's second attempt to provide medical care and revolutionary ideas to the masses introduced her to hostility from the clergy and official ha-

----

14   Figner, *Zapechatlennyi trud*, 100–101.

15   Figner, *Zapechatlennyi trud*, 107.

Jean K. Berger

rassment by local government officials. The peasants, however, initially met her medical practice with an overwhelming response:

> Бедный народ стекался ко мне как к чудотворной иконе целыми десятками и сотнями около фельдшерского земского домика стоял с утра до позднего вечера целый обоз скоро моя слава перешла за пределы трех волостей которыми я заведывала а потом и за пределы уезда[16]

> [The poor people thronged to me by the tens and hundreds like I was a miracle-working icon. A string of carts surrounded the doctor's hut from morning until late at night. My fame quickly spread beyond the boundaries of the three counties which I served and even beyond the boundary of the *uyezd*.]

Figner reported that she provided care to eight hundred patients during the first month of her practice and that during her ten months of service in Saratov she saw five thousand patients.[17] Figner's sister, Evgeniia, assisted her in the care of this large number of patients.

In addition to their successful medical practice, the Figner sisters opened a free school for the peasants of the area. Evgeniia Figner taught without charge and provided the books and supplies so that the students' families would not incur any expense. Since there was not a single school in the three counties that the Figners served, their school rapidly became very popular both with young students and with adults who wanted to learn basic arithmetic.[18] The Figners' third activity while they were in the Saratov region was also well received by the peasants. In the evenings, the sisters would visit a village and read works of Russian literature aloud to the peasants. As Figner described it:

> Покончив занятия в аптеке и школе … мы брали … книгу и шли на деревню к кому-нибудь из крестьян. В том доме в тот вечер был праздник; хозяин бежал к шабрам и родственникам оповестить

---

16   Figner, *Zapechatlennyi trud*, 108.

17   Figner, *Zapechatlennyi trud*, 109.

18   Figner, *Zapechatlennyi trud*, 109.

их, чтобы и они пришли послушать. Начиналось чтение; в 10-11 ча-
сов хозяева все еще просили почитать еще.[19]

[Finishing our work in the dispensary and school . . . we took . . . a book
and went to the village to the house of one of the peasants. In that house
that evening was a holiday. The host ran to his neighbors and relatives to
tell them so that they could come and listen. The reading began. At ten or
eleven o'clock the hosts still begged us to continue reading.]

The Figners hoped the readings would spark conversation, during
which revolutionary propaganda might find an opening. Although the sisters were providing much-needed medical care to the peasants of the district, Evgeniia was offering them the rudiments of basic literacy without
charge, and the readings provided free entertainment, as well. After ten
months, Vera and Evgeniia had to flee to avoid arrest.

The first source of opposition to the Figners' humanitarian activities
came from the village priest who apparently feared that the success of the
medical clinic would undercut his authority as a faith healer. He began
telling the villagers that the Figner sisters were illegal fugitives without
passports or proper papers and also began a rumor that they had no legitimate medical training. Furthermore, he refused to allow them to be god-
mothers to the villagers' babies, claiming he didn't know enough about
the sisters.[20]

Opposition from the local priest was only the beginning of the Figners'
problems. Local government officials began to harass children who attended the school and peasants who came for medical care. Officials asked
the school children if Evgeniia was teaching prayers to them. At the time,
teaching prayers in school was common in Russia. Although Evgeniia
taught the children prayers, official complaints were lodged that she was
teaching the children, "Бога нет, а царя не надо."[21] [There is no God and
the Tsar is unnecessary.]

Official hostility intensified when the county administration rumored
that the Figners were harboring fugitives. Subsequently, whenever peasants
came to their house for medical care or education, a policeman would soon
show up and keep watch, frightening away patients and pupils. Peasants

---

19   Figner, *Zapechatlennyi trud*, 109.
20   Figner, *Zapechatlennyi trud*, 112.
21   Figner, *Zapechatlennyi trud*, 112.

tried to sneak to their house by back routes to avoid being seen. Hostility increased still more when a provincial official, Prince Chegodayev, began a rumor, "Что мы ходим из избы в избу и читаем прокламации, что мы не пропускаем ни одного болного, чтоб не растолковать ему, что во всем царит неправда и что все чиновники-взяточники."[22] [That we were going from peasant hut to peasant hut, reading proclamations, that we didn't allow even one patient to pass without explaining to him that falsehood reigned everywhere and that all government officials were bribe-takers.] This official harassment grew to the point that the women could no longer carry out their work. According to Figner's memoirs, "Оставаться долее в деревне было бесполезно и невыносимо." [23] [To remain in the village longer was useless and unbearable.] The lives of the Figner sisters were further complicated by the fact that their friend, Alexander Solovyev, made an unsuccessful assassination attempt on the life of the tsar in April 1879. When the police began tracking down all of Solovyev's acquaintants, the Figners fled from the village, narrowly escaping arrest.

From her experiences in Saratov province and her earlier experiences in Samara, Vera Figner concluded in 1879 that it was impossible to carry on peaceful propaganda work among the people. It was not feasible to bring about political change in Russia by peaceful means:

> Так кончилось наше пребывание в Саратове, с надеждами в нача-ле, с минусом в конце. Но, если на вопрос возможна ли желаемая нами деятельность в народе? Мы, в силу внешних условии, опу-тывавших деревню, пришли к ответу отрицательному и к выводу, что, прежде всего, необходимо сломить эти самые условия ...[24]

> [Thus ended our stay in Saratov, from hope in the beginning to despair in the end. To the question, "Are our desired activities among the people possible?" we gave a negative reply because of the external conditions entangling the village. We concluded that, first of all, it is essential to smash the very conditions . . .]

The third factor in Figner's conversion to terrorism was her witness of the many lives destroyed or devastated by the tsarist government's fear

---

22 Figner, *Zapechatlennyi trud*, 112.

23 Figner, *Zapechatlennyi trud*, 118.

24 Figner, *Zapechatlennyi trud*, 119.

of ideas. She lost many friends to imprisonment, exile, or execution for their reform/revolutionary activities. Figner's sister Lydia was arrested in 1875 for working in a factory as a way to gain access to the peasants and spread revolutionary ideas. She was sentenced to five years at hard labor because she was found to be in possession of revolutionary literature. In addition, many of Figner's fellow students and acquaintances from her university days in Zurich were arrested and sentenced to imprisonment or exile for their activities. Sofia Bardina, Betia Kaminskaia, Aleksandra Khorzhevskaia, Anna Toporkova, Evgeniia Tumanova, Olga Liubatovich, and Nadezhda Subbotina, among others, were arrested in 1875 for working in factories and attempting to spread propaganda among the workers.[25] Figner later commented:

Наряду с партией, но в более грандиозных размерах, практиковалось насилие правительства: сковывалась мысль, запрещалось слово, отнималась свобода и жизнь: административная ссылка была обычным явлением, тюрьмы были переполнены; казни считались десятками. Вместе с тем, на Каре практиковались побои, в центральных тюрьмах—унизительное обращение; по всем тюрьмам грубое насилие; в доме предварительного заключения высекли Боголюбова и оскорбляли стыдливость женщин.[26]

[Side by side with the violence practiced by the party, but in more grandiose dimensions, was the violence practiced by the government. It fettered thought, prohibited speech, and took away freedom and life. Administrative exile was an ordinary occurrence, the prisons were overfilled, and executions were counted by the tens. Together with this, in Kara the prisoners were beaten, and in the central prisons humiliating treatment was used. In all the prisons crude violence was common. In the House of Preliminary Detention, they flogged Bogoliubov and insulted the modesty of women prisoners.]

In the spring of 1879, impelled by the combined weight of her earlier experiences, Figner became an active supporter of terrorism as a means of political change. When the Land and Freedom Party dissolved over the issue of using violence, Figner joined the People's Will, which supported

25   Knight, "The Fritschi," 14–15.
26   Figner, *Zapechatlennyi trud*, 227.

assassinating the tsar as a way to bring about political change. Figner's transformation from reformer to terrorist was complete.

What steps had occurred along the way? First, Figner had been blocked by societal values and by the government from even training to make a positive contribution to society. Russian society believed that a woman did not need a serious education but she did need the supervision of a man. The tsarist government had attempted to block Figner's study of medicine both in Russia and in Zurich, and her father had tried to block her from studying abroad. Secondly, Figner was blocked by the ignorance and poverty of the peasants, the conservatism of the church, and the harassment of the government from carrying out peaceful reform by practicing medicine. Finally, Figner saw the fate of those who attempted to bring about reform peacefully. Thus, frustration over a society and government that tried to prevent women from contributing to society, frustration over a government that blocked even benign reform efforts, and frustration over the devastated and destroyed lives of those who attempted peaceful reforms combined to convince Figner that peaceful means did not yield positive results.

After Figner fully converted to the necessity of terrorism as a means to bring about change, she took part in making the bombs that killed Tsar Alexander II on March 1, 1881, for which she was arrested in February of 1883. After being held in prison for twenty months, she was tried and sentenced to execution by hanging for her revolutionary activities. This sentence was commuted to "каторгой без срока"[27] [penal servitude for life]. Figner was held in solitary confinement from October 12, 1884, until her sentence was commuted and she was released on September 28, 1904.[28]

In 1879, at about the same time that Figner became a proponent of terrorism, Elizaveta Nikolaevna Solntseva-Kovalskaia, the second of the three women to be examined in this paper, also made the transition from peaceful reformer to terrorist. Kovalskaia began her life under quite different conditions than Figner. Because she was the illegitimate daughter of a serf woman and a nobleman, Kovalskaia was treated as a serf during the early years of her childhood. Consequently, she became aware of her legal inequality at a very young age. She later wrote, "Мне не было еще 6 лет, вероятно, когда мне стало известно, что существуют помещики

27   Figner, *Zapechatlennyi trud*, 325.

28   V. N. Figner, "Figner, Vera Nikolaevna," in *Deiateli SSSR i revoliutsionnogo dvizheniia Rossii: entsiklopedicheskii slovar' Granat* (Moscow: Sovetskaia entsiklopediia, 1989), 252.

и крестьяне-крепостные … что мой отец может продать мою мать соседнему помещику, а меня другому, разлучив нас. Но моя мать не может продать моего отца."[29] [I probably was not yet six years old when I became aware that landowners and serfs existed … I became aware that my father could sell my mother to a neighboring landowner and sell me to a different one, separating us. But my mother couldn't sell my father.]

Kovalskaia was also made painfully aware of the distinction between legitimate and illegitimate children. Thus, she found that in the eyes of society there were three reasons to devalue her humanity—she was serf-born, she was illegitimate, and she was a woman. Although she was completely unaware of it at the time, she had already taken the first step toward eventual terrorism when she realized that society limited her options in life because of the labels it placed upon her.

When Kovalskaia was about seven years old, her father used his political connections to have her legal status and the legal status of her mother changed to that of free peasants. He began to educate Elizaveta as a young noblewoman rather than allowing her to remain illiterate, as was the norm for virtually all serf women. She attended a boarding school for girls and, when that closed, attended a gimnazia. Thus, Kovalskaia was well educated for a girl in Russia.

Kovalskaia's formal education was supplemented by two other sources that heightened her awareness of social injustice. As a student, she set up a reading circle with other students to read and discuss the literature available to them. According to her memoirs, "Занимались мы преимущественно общественными вопросами, но рядом с этим бывали рефераты по естественным наукам: по астрономии, по физике и другим отраслям знаний."[30] [We mainly studied social questions, but along with those we read papers in the natural sciences, in astronomy, in physics, and in other branches of knowledge.]

Theoretical issues acquired names and faces when the girls attended the public courtroom in Kharkov after school each day. Kovalskaia later recalled, "Перед нами проходили крестьяне, обделенные землею при освобождении, судившиеся за бунты; женщины-убийцы своих мужей, не

29   E. N. Kovalskaia, "Kovalskaia, Elizaveta Nikolaevna," in *Deiateli SSSR i revoliutsionnogo dvizheniia Rossii: entsiklopedicheskii slovar' Granat* (Moscow: Sovetskaia entsiklopediia, 1989), 109.

30   Kovalskaia, *Deiateli SSSR*, 110.

стерпевшие своего рабства, санкционированного законом."³¹ [In front of us passed peasants who had been cheated out of their share of land during emancipation and who were now being tried for rebellion, and women who murdered their husbands because they could not bear their legally sanctioned slavery.]

Since Kovalskaia already possessed a well-developed awareness of social issues as a schoolgirl, it was not surprising that she became involved in reform activities soon after her graduation from the gimnazia. Her father died shortly after she graduated, thus removing a potential source of opposition to her activities. Furthermore, he had left her a sizeable inheritance which freed her from mundane financial concerns.³²

All of Kovalskaia's initial reform efforts focused on improving literacy and education, especially education for women. Since Russian universities were still closed to women, one of her projects in the late 1860s was the organization of free classes for women seeking higher education. She allowed the women's classes to meet in one of the houses she owned in Kharkov, known as the Pink House, and arranged for an assistant professor and some university students to serve as instructors.³³Courses offered included physics, chemistry, cosmography, natural sciences, political economy, history, and higher mathematics.³⁴ Unfortunately, these courses could only convey knowledge; they could not grant any type of certification.

Kovalskaia also belonged to the Kharkov Society for the Promotion of Literacy, which operated Sunday schools that focused on basic literacy for factory workers. Kovalskaia personally taught literacy classes for women and used the classes to screen students for more politically oriented classes. She taught classes for factory women on Socialism and women's rights at the Pink House. Since these classes were more concerned with conveying political ideas than with basic literacy, Kovalskaia read to her students rather than teaching them to read.³⁵

Kovalskaia's other activities in Kharkov in the late 1860s included organizing both a women's study circle and a men's study circle in her house

31 Kovalskaia, *Deiateli SSSR*, 110.

32 Kovalskaia, *Deiateli SSSR*, 110.

33 Richard Stites, *The Women's Liberation Movement in Russia: Feminism, Nihilism, and Bolshevism, 1860–1930* (Princeton, NJ: Princeton University Press, 1978), 130.

34 Kovalskaia, *Deiateli SSSR*, 110.

35 Kovalskaia, *Deiateli SSSR*, 110.

for the discussion of literature and social issues, organizing pedagogy conferences for village schoolteachers, and participating in a petition drive to persuade the Minister of Education to open Russian universities to women. All of Kovalskaia's reform activities in the 1860s were nonviolent; some of these actions did not involve the exchange of any political ideas at all. Others were politically motivated but did not advocate the use of violence. Richard Stites described her as "[a] typical *intelligentka* of the 1860's, she held 'advanced' ideas and was a staunch apostle of women's rights. She and her husband, Kovalsky, became the center of Kharkov's leftist intellectual life."[36] In spite of the peaceful nature of her activities, she was forced to terminate them because of government harassment.

Kovalskaia described one of these situations—a police raid on one of her pedagogy conferences for village schoolteachers. She wrote:

Во время одного из таких собраний в нашем доме появился жандармский полковник Ковалинский со своею свитою, увидев разложенные на столах географические карты, таблицы для наглядного обучения, удивленно заявил нам: "Все это очень хорошо, вы делаете полезное дело, и ничего противозаконного я не вижу, но, по предписанию свыше, должен все ваши собрания прекратить, а в случае возобновления их, вынужден буду вас арестовать." Пришлось все приостановить.[37]

[During one of these conferences, Colonel Kovalinskii of the police appeared with his retinue in our house. Catching sight of the maps and visual displays spread on the tables, he was astonished and declared to us, "All this is very well, you are doing a useful work and I see nothing illegal in it. However, according to the orders of superiors, you must break off all your conferences, and in the event of a renewal of them, I will have to arrest you." Everything had to come to a halt.]

After the police shut down Kovalskaia's schools and literary circles, she moved to St. Petersburg where she enrolled in the Alarchinskii free classes for women and became involved in the Chaikovsky circle.[38] Before the

---

36   Stites, *The Women's Liberation Movement in Russia*, 130.

37   Kovalskaia, *Deiateli SSSR*, 111.

38   Barbara Alpern Engel, "From Separatism to Socialism: Women in the Russian Revolutionary Movement of the 1870s," *Socialist Women: European Socialist Feminism*

Chaikovsky circle could begin its first project, distributing books at low prices, Kovalskaia became seriously ill, most likely with tuberculosis, and was ordered by her doctors to go to southern Russia to restore her health. From there, doctors sent her to Zurich.[39]

In Zurich, Kovalskaia developed a greater interest in and awareness of political ideas. She was influenced by the ideas of Bakunin and Lavrov. Previously, her interests had focused on education and improving the lives of women. She now saw the importance of political change and became interested in the "to the people" movement.

Kovalskaia realized that her frail health precluded her from laboring in fields or factories; upon her return to Russia, she took a position as a rural schoolteacher in a school located close to a factory. This gave her access to the village youth who worked in the factory. In addition to teaching, she distributed revolutionary pamphlets among the factory workers and engaged in propaganda work. Although her actions had become decidedly political, they were still nonviolent. Just as police harassment had ended her earlier educational activities, imminent arrest ended her career as a rural schoolteacher and propagandist. Kovalskaia fled abruptly when she learned she was about to be arrested.[40]

Kovalskaia began to move further along the path from peaceful reformer to terrorist. Each time she was blocked from pursuing a reform activity, her next activity was more radical. After fleeing arrest, Kovalskaia moved back and forth between St. Petersburg and Kharkov, distributing illegal literature and organizing political discussion groups among factory workers. By this time in her life, Kovalskaia clearly met the second of the conditions that all of these women experienced in their progression from reformer to terrorist: she had been repeatedly blocked by government authorities from carrying out peaceful reform activities.

In March 1878, the Russian government literally forced its repressive nature onto Kovalskaia's head. She was severely beaten by police for being in the wrong place at the wrong time. Following Vera Zasulich's acquittal by a jury for the attempted political assassination of General Trepov, the St. Petersburg police had beaten demonstrators and onlookers on the streets. According to her own account, "Во время демонстрации после суда над

in the Nineteenth and Early Twentieth Centuries, eds. Marilyn J. Boxer and Jean H. Quataert (New York: Elsevier North Holland, Inc., 1978), 57.

39 Kovalskaia, Deiateli SSSR 111.

40 Deiateli SSSR, 111.

Засулич я была сильно избита жандармами, уехала в Харьков, где около года пролежала в постели."[41] [During the demonstration following Zasulich's trial, I was violently beaten by the police. I went to Kharkov where I spent almost a year in bed recovering.]

In spite of this, in 1879 when the Land and Liberty Party split into two new parties, the People's Will and the Black Repartition, Kovalskaia joined the less extreme group. She wrote, "Твердо убежденная в том, что социалистическая революция может быть совершена только самим народам, что центральный террор в лучшем случае приведет только к плохенькой конституции, которая поможет окрепнуть русской буржуазии, я вступила в Черный Передел."[42] [Having a firm conviction that the Socialist revolution could be completed only by the people themselves, that terror aimed at the center of the state—in the best case—brings only a poor constitution which would help to strengthen the Russian bourgeoisie, I joined the Black Repartition.] The Black Repartition focused on the economic plight of the peasants, their need for land, and the necessity of generating mass consciousness among the peasantry so that a social revolution would spontaneously occur.

Kovalskaia continued her revolutionary activities, focusing much of her energy on procuring, operating, and protecting a printing press so that pamphlets could be illegally printed. She also worked very closely with Nikolai Shchedrin to organize the Union of Russian Workers of the South. The initial purpose of the union was to increase the political awareness of factory workers. Since most Russian factory workers were peasants who returned periodically to their villages, Kovalskaia and Shchedrin hoped that arousing the political awareness of the factory workers would, in turn, lead those workers to take their ideas to the peasants in the villages. The desired result would be a popular revolution.

While Kovalskaia was engaged in these activities, some of her colleagues were arrested. Others of her associates, such as Zharkov, turned out to be government informers. In addition, atrocities continued to occur to the peasants, the factory workers, and Russian society as a whole as the government became more repressive in response to assassination attempts. By early 1880, the governor-general of Kiev felt under siege by the revolutionaries to such an extent that he ordered executions for nonviolent crimes such as possession of a single illegal document or

41   *Deiateli SSSR, 111.*

42   *Deiateli SSSR, 111.*

proclamation.[43]Kovalskaia had now clearly reached the third condition that each of these women passed through on her way to supporting terrorism: she witnessed the lives of many reformers and revolutionaries being devastated or destroyed for their nonviolent attempts to reform society.

As a result, Kovalskaia began to advocate what she called economic terror. She wrote, "Political terror directed at the center of the system was too remote for [the peasants] to comprehend. Economic terror . . . defended their immediate interests."[44] By "economic terror," Kovalskaia meant the murder of police officials, government officials who were in daily contact with the people, abusive factory owners, and other local oppressors of the people. Like Figner, she had been transformed from a peaceful reformer to an advocate of terror. Unlike Figner, Kovalskaia never progressed from the stage of advocating terror to actually committing terrorist acts, as she was arrested in October 1880 and sentenced in May of 1881 to hard labor for life in Siberia. In 1903, after twenty-three years, her sentence was commuted and she was released.[45]

The third Russian woman who followed a similar progression from reformer to terrorist and who will be examined in this essay is Vera Zasulich. Zasulich was born to a poor gentry family in 1849. Her father died when she was very young, and her impoverished mother sent her to live with wealthier relatives who could provide for her. Although she was materially provided for, Zasulich felt that she was an outsider and unloved. She wrote, "The older I grew, the more I became convinced that I was indeed an alien: I didn't belong. No one ever held me, kissed me, or sat me on his knee; no one called me pet names. The servants abused me."[46]

Zasulich's alienation grew when she realized that society had already determined the only acceptable position in life for her as an impoverished gentry woman. She wrote, "I was repelled by the fate that my social position held in store for me . . . I was to become a governess."[47] Thus, by age fifteen, Zasulich already had a grievance against the rigidity of Russian society.

---

43 Kovalskaia, *Five Sisters*, 228.

44 Kovalskaia, *Five Sisters*, 226.

45 Kovalskaia, *Deiateli SSSR*, 113.

46 Vera Zasulich, "Vera Zasulich," *Five Sisters: Women against the Tsar*, eds. and trans. Barbara Alpern Engel and Clifford N. Rosenthal (New York and London: Routledge, 1992), 65.

47 Zasulich, *Five Sisters*, 69.

Although Zasulich felt unloved by her relatives, they provided her with a respectable yet shallow education. They sent her to a girl's boarding school in Moscow to learn the necessities for being a governess. While she was attending the boarding school, Zasulich first became interested in political ideas. She was introduced to the ideas of populism and Socialism and, through her older sister Ekaterina, she was introduced to members of the Ishutin revolutionary circle.[48] At this point in her life, Zasulich's interest in political and social reform was purely theoretical.

Just as the appalling living conditions of the peasantry had been a catalyst in Vera Figner's political development, awareness of the condition of the peasantry also influenced Zasulich's political consciousness. Zasulich passed the examinations to become a governess and procured a job working for a justice of the peace. She now saw the legal problems and miseries of the peasants on a daily basis.[49] When her job with the justice of the peace ended, she moved to St. Petersburg and worked at a variety of jobs, including in a seamstresses' artel and a bookbinding artel.[50]As Zasulich became more interested in political ideas, she became involved in the campaign to simultaneously spread literacy and raise political consciousness among factory workers by teaching literacy classes.[51] Zasulich still was not a terrorist, not even a revolutionary. The most revolutionary activity she had undertaken thus far was to teach basic literacy to factory workers. In fact, she was not quite clear what her own political views were.

However, the Russian government was about to speed up Zasulich's political education and assist in her transformation to a terrorist. Zasulich had the misfortune to meet Sergei Nechaev at the house of her friend, Anna Tomilova. Nechaev charmed Zasulich and then casually asked for her address. According to Zasulich's memoirs, she gave Nechaev her address because she wanted to help the revolutionary cause. "I could imagine no greater pleasure than serving the revolution."[52] Nechaev used Zasulich's address for some of his revolutionary correspondence: Zasulich passed along letters to the designated recipients. Eventually, a letter with Zasulich's

48 Jay Bergman, *Vera Zasulich: A Biography* (Stanford, CA: Stanford University Press, 1983), 5–6; and in Zasulich, *Five Sisters*, 71.

49 Bergman, *Vera Zasulich*, 8–9.

50 Bergman, *Vera Zasulich*, 9.

51 Zasulich, *Five Sisters*, 71.

52 Zasulich, *Five Sisters*, 73.

address and with revolutionary content fell into the hands of the police. Zasulich's activity of passing letters was clearly illegal, although not violent. For this nonviolent activity that she hoped might contribute to a better Russia, Zasulich was arrested in April 1869 and imprisoned for two years in the Litovskii fortress.[53] After that, she was sent into administrative exile until September 1875.[54] Six years of enduring the tender mercies of the tsarist prison system prepared Zasulich to become a full-fledged terrorist.

Upon her release from prison, Zasulich joined a revolutionary group in Kiev. Many years later, the revolutionary Sergei Iastremskii remembered meeting Zasulich in the winter of 1875–76. "Предприняв зимою 1875-76 г поездку в Киев ... я в Киеве познакомился с кружком ... где были ... В. Засулич ... и др."[55] [Having undertaken a journey to Kiev in the winter of 1875–76, in Kiev I became acquainted with the group which included V. Zasulich and others.] After spending time in the Kievan revolutionary group, Zasulich moved back to St. Petersburg in 1876 and worked as a typesetter for an illegal printing press.[56] In July 1877, Arkhip Bogoliubov was flogged in the St. Petersburg House of Detention for failure to remove his hat when he encountered General Trepov, the governor of St. Petersburg, in the prison exercise yard. Bogoliubov was in prison because he had been arrested and sentenced to fifteen years at hard labor for the crime of being an onlooker at a street demonstration.[57]

When Zasulich heard of Bogoliubov's flogging, she took the final step along the path to terrorism. Zasulich had both witnessed and personally experienced the devastation and destruction of lives by the repressive nature of the tsarist government while she was in the prison system. Although Zasulich had never met Bogoliubov, she identified with him as another life destroyed by the government. She determined to send a warning to the government that such abuse would meet with retaliation. At her trial she testified, "There was nothing to stop Trepov, or someone just as powerful as he, from repeating the same violence over and over. I resolved at that

53 Zasulich, *Five Sisters*, 78.

54 Bergman, *Vera Zasulich*, 20.

55 S. V. Iastremskii, "Iastremskii, Sergei Vasilevich," *Deiateli SSSR i revoliutsionnogo dvizheniia Rossii: entsiklopedicheskii slovar' Granat* (Moscow: Sovetskaia entsiklopediia, 1989), 337.

56 Zasulich, *Five Sisters*, 78.

57 Bergman, *Vera Zasulich*, 33.

point, even if it cost my life, to prove that no one who abused a human being in that way could be sure of getting away with it."[58] Accordingly, Zasulich went to the governor's office in the guise of a petitioner. She pulled a revolver from under her cloak and shot Trepov at close range. Zasulich was arrested, tried, and acquitted by a sympathetic jury. Before the tsarist authorities were able to rearrest her, she escaped to Switzerland.

While Zasulich's path to terrorism varied slightly from that of Figner and Kovalskaia, the essentials remained the same. Zasulich had been blocked by societal values from pursuing any other course in life but that of a governess. She engaged in the nonviolent reform activity of teaching literacy to factory workers and the nonviolent—although illegal—activity of passing along revolutionary correspondence. Her activities were abruptly ended by her imprisonment. Finally, she witnessed the devastation of the lives of other nonviolent reformers. Like Figner and Kovalskaia, Zasulich concluded that only acts of violence could change Russia.

Although this paper has focused on only these three women, there were in fact a number of other women who trod the same path from reformer to revolutionary in the nineteenth century. For example, Sophia Perovskaia, famous for orchestrating the assassination of Tsar Alexander II, had at first engaged in literacy activities and medical practice. In 1872 she had tried to bring about change in Russia by working in a village school and later by vaccinating peasants against smallpox. From 1874 to 1877 Perovskaia had worked as an aide in a hospital.[59] Similarly, Olga Liubatovich began her reform career in 1875 by doing propaganda work among factory workers and ended it by participating in the attempts by the People's Will to assassinate the tsar.[60]

Figner, Kovalskaia, and Zasulich all belonged to political discussion groups and political parties at various times in their lives. However, it appears that their decisions to participate in terrorist acts were less influenced by ideology than by frustration over their inability to bring about change through peaceful means. Each of the women was already aware of the full range of political theories during her reformer stage, and each ap-

58 Zasulich, *Five Sisters*, 78.

59 Engel, "From Separatism," 70, 72.

60 Olga Liubatovich, "Olga Liubatovich," Vera Zasulich, "Vera Zasulich," *Five Sisters: Women against the Tsar*, eds. and trans. Barbara Alpern Engel and Clifford N. Rosenthal (New York and London: Routledge, 1992), 143-201.

pears to have chosen an ideology which fit her actions rather than tailoring her actions to fit the ideology. Kovalskaia recorded an occasion when her actions did not conform to party ideology:

> When he [Pavel Akselrod] learned that we intended to plot the murder of Khludov, he got indignant and tried to prove to us that it was an impossible, undesirable, and even harmful project. He proceeded to read us the new program he had drawn up for Black Repartition. It was a very diffuse draft for something in between populism and Marxism—an impossible mixture . . . Akselrod saw how stubborn we were about this. Gently but firmly, he declared: "But you don't have the right to act in this way without the consent of the party." . . . "In any case," we told Akselrod, "we're leaving the party and we're going to act independently."[61]

Kovalskaia also records that another Black Repartition member, Mikhail Popov, told her, "People here don't care much about theory; everyone wants to do revolutionary work . . ."[62]

The great question, of course, is, what can we learn from the lives of these nineteenth-century Russian women that is applicable to the post–September 11 world? While ideology and religious fundamentalism, both Christian (as in the case of abortion-clinic bombers) and Muslim (as in the case of suicide bombers) are clearly major components of the motivation for modern terrorism, it may also prove useful to remember the motivations of historical terrorists. If Vera Figner had been allowed to peacefully practice medicine, would she have ever helped to build bombs? If Elizaveta Kovalskaia had been allowed to peacefully develop her efforts toward women's education, would she have ever advocated the use of terror? If Vera Zasulich had not given six years of her life for the appearance of her name on an envelope, would she have shot General Trepov? Certainly, the evidence presented in this essay demonstrates *reactionary* rather than merely ideological and religious motives to violence. Thus, amid the contemporary focus on ideology and religion as catalysts for terrorism, scholars and government leaders would be wise not to overlook the role of sheer human frustration with life conditions of those who choose the path of violence.

---

61   Kovalskaia, *Five Sisters*, 224-225.

62   Kovalskaia, *Five Sisters*, 225.

8

A TROUBLED PAST, AN UNCERTAIN FUTURE:

RADICAL ISLAMISM AND THE PROSPECTS FOR NIGERIA'S STABILITY

Josh Arinze

Among the Igbo people of Nigeria, there is an age-old story about a young man who disliked his new stepmother. Time-honored tradition—to say nothing of his father's feelings—made it necessary for the young man to treat his stepmother with courtesy. Still, he could not stop looking for an opportunity to start a fight with her, vent his resentment, and accuse her of some wrongdoing. The stepmother, however, refused to grant him the excuse he wanted, so the young man created one. One day, after she offered him a snack of palm nuts, he demanded that she also give him some palm oil. When the stepmother asked why anyone would need palm oil to eat palm nuts (which would be like saying that one cannot eat an apple unless there is a glass of apple juice to go with it), the young man began shouting insults at her. He then went about telling the neighbors what a bad stepmother he had. "This is a terrible woman my father has married," he said. "She's so wicked she refuses to give me palm oil to go with my palm nuts."

As we will see shortly, the essence of this story is relevant in understanding a major religious uprising that devastated the northern Nigerian city of Kaduna from November 20 to 23, 2002. It was one of several bloody clashes between Christians and Muslims that have shaken northern Nigeria since many states in the region began enacting Islamic law—known as *sharia*—in place of the country's secular laws. According to the Nigerian Red Cross, at least 220 people were killed in the November 2002 clashes in Kaduna. More than five hundred others suffered injuries serious enough to need treatment in hospitals. Over five thousand people lost their homes to the fighting, and more than thirty thousand were forced to flee their neighborhoods. A local civil rights group reported that sixteen churches and nine mosques were burned during the unrest.

About 45 percent of Nigeria's 130 million people are Muslim, and about 45 percent are Christian, with some 10 percent following various forms of African traditional religion. Like other major world religions, Islam has adherents who, while firm in their beliefs, still manage to treat people of other faiths with tolerance and respect. Like other religions, Islam also has its share of zealots: fundamentalists who have little patience for those who either have not seen the "light" or are not quite devout enough. In the opinion of some Islamists (the reference of choice in this essay for Muslim fundamentalists), the message of Prophet Muhammad as revealed in the Holy Qur'an ought to be the guiding principle, not just of religious observance and practice, but of politics and interpersonal relations as well. Islamism, to borrow the definition offered by one scholar of Islamic culture, is "the effort to order society and create government based on Islamic law."[1]

To understand why this attitude is so pervasive among Islamists, it is worth noting that in Islam, there is no well-established tradition of separating politics from religion. Since the founding of Islam, the powers that control mosque and state have always been essentially the same. As historian Bernard Lewis has observed, Prophet Muhammad was not just a preacher; he was also a soldier and a head of state: "In the experience of the first Muslims, as preserved and recorded for later generations, religious truth and political power were indissolubly associated: the first sanctified the second, the second sustained the first . . . The very notion of something that is separate or even separable from religious authority, expressed in Christian languages by terms such as *lay*, *temporal*, or *secular*, is totally alien to Islamic thought and practice."[2]

---

1 See "The Democracy Dilemma in the Middle East: Are Islamists the Answer?", The Washington Institute for Near East Policy, *Policy Watch #990* (Special Forum Report), May 3, 2005.

2 Bernard Lewis, *The Crisis of Islam: Holy War and Unholy Terror* (New York: The

Of course, it goes without saying that not all Muslims are Islamists. Even among devout adherents of Islam, there are those who believe that it is neither practical nor desirable to regulate all facets of life according to narrow interpretations of the Qur'an. However, the voices of such moderates are not usually as loud and clear as those of the Islamists. One Muslim commentator offered an explanation for this: "Most Muslims today believe that the Qur'an is the final and therefore perfect manifesto of God's will. Consequently, when abuses take place in the name of Islam, even moderates are often unable to debate such justifications, given the fact that they have never been introduced to the possibility of raising questions about their holy book."[3] This observation is no less true of Nigeria's Muslims than it is of Muslims in the Arab world.

"A Parade of Nudity"

The November 2002 violence in northern Nigeria began when Muslim youths, protesting Nigeria's hosting of the Miss World beauty pageant, lit bonfires on the streets of Kaduna, looted shops, and attacked churches, hotels, and the homes of Christians in the city. The uprising did not come as a surprise. For months, Nigeria's Islamists had been expressing opposition to the beauty pageant, which they described as "a parade of nudity" that flouted the teachings of the Qur'an. Media reports stated that what ignited the attacks was a newspaper article suggesting that Prophet Muhammad might have approved of the beauty contest, or even married one of the contestants.

The story in question appeared on Saturday, November 16, 2002, in *ThisDay*, a newspaper based in the southwestern city of Lagos. It was part of a package of articles the paper published that day about the Miss World contest. In discussing the stand many Muslims had taken against Nigeria's hosting of the pageant, *ThisDay* reporter Isioma Daniel wrote, "The Muslims thought it was immoral to bring 92 women to Nigeria and ask them to revel in vanity. What would Mohammed think? In all honesty, he would probably have chosen a wife from one of them."[4]

Modern Library, 2003), 3–28.

3   See "A 'Muslim Refusenik' in Pursuit of Reform in Islam," *The Washington Institute for Near East Policy, Policy Watch #897* (Special Forum Report), September 13, 2004.

4   Isioma Daniel, "The World at their Feet," *ThisDay*, November 16, 2002.

Nigeria being what it is—a country troubled by deep ethnic and religious fault lines, an artificial nation whose testy citizens are locked in a union they didn't choose—it might be fair to criticize this reporter's comments as indiscreet or reckless. However, were those thirty-seven words of Isioma Daniel the real reason more than two hundred lives were lost in Kaduna in November 2002? Few people who followed events leading up to the violence believed that Daniel's comments, however tasteless anyone considered them, were the real cause of the Kaduna upheaval. In blaming *ThisDay* and its reporter for the violence they initiated on November 20, 2002, Nigeria's Islamists were in fact latching on to a convenient excuse for acts of belligerence they had been planning for months.

In other words, blaming Isioma Daniel's comments for the violence in Kaduna is about comparable to declaring that the stepmother in the earlier-mentioned Igbo anecdote was responsible for her stepson's hostile and premeditated behavior. In February 2000, as will be detailed later in this essay, some three thousand people died in the same city of Kaduna when demonstrations for and against the introduction of *sharia* sparked a much bloodier round of clashes between Christians and Muslims. That conflict had nothing to do with a newspaper article.

The same is true of other bloody upheavals that have plagued northern Nigeria since the so-called Miss World riots[5] of November 2002. During the first two weeks of May 2004, as many as one thousand people died in tit-for-tat clashes between Christians and Muslims in two of Nigeria's northern states: Kano and Plateau. Long-standing Christian-Muslim disputes had flared into a Muslim attack on a church during Sunday service in the Yelwa-Shendam area of Christian-majority Plateau state in early May 2004; more than twenty Christians died. Several days later, a Christian militia launched a revenge attack on the Muslim community in the same area; more than fifty Muslims were killed. Shortly thereafter, the violence spread to the Muslim-majority state of Kano, and hundreds of Christians lost their lives. On May 18, 2004, Nigeria's President Olusegun Obasanjo imposed a state of emergency on Plateau State, dis-

---

5 The word "riot(s)" implies an essentially spontaneous outbreak of public disorder. Christian/Muslim clashes in Nigeria—or, for that matter, acts of mass violence motivated by ethnic animosity, such as the anti-Igbo pogroms that have plagued Nigeria (especially the north) for years—are often premeditated actions, not the spontaneous outbreaks that their planners usually try to make them look like.

solving the state's legislature and suspending the elected governor from office for six months.[6]

These instances of inter-religious clashes are typical episodes in a pattern of furious violence that has plagued Nigeria for decades. Using the November 2002 Kaduna uprising as a signature case, this essay will probe the roots of this disturbing pattern of bloody sectarian clashes, which have been particularly prevalent in northern Nigeria. It will focus on how and why the expansion of *sharia* constitutes a significant danger to Nigeria's prospects for sustaining a stable democracy. It will also discuss the major threat that radical Islamism poses to the very survival of Nigeria as we know it.

Usman dan Fodio and the Legacy of Radical Islamism

The southernmost parts of what we now know as Nigeria came under British control in the 1860s, with English-speaking traders and explorers first establishing themselves along a coastline washed by the Atlantic, and extending their sphere of influence inland as the years progressed. In 1903, a British military expedition defeated the army of the sultan of Sokoto, the Muslim paramount overlord of what is now northern Nigeria. Before this overthrow of the sultan's political domain, known as the Sokoto caliphate, Islamic law was supreme in much of the region.[7]

The Sokoto caliphate had been founded in 1804, almost exactly a century before the British subdued it. Its founder was Usman dan Fodio, a Muslim cleric of Fulani ethnic stock, who hailed from the town of Sokoto, in what is now northwestern Nigeria. Usman dan Fodio launched his movement and kingdom by declaring a *jihad* against local Hausa rulers, whom he accused of polluting Islam. Within four years after the fighting began, Usman dan Fodio and his followers had taken over much of what later became the Northern Region of Nigeria. They established a feudal system in which all-powerful rulers (known as "emirs," with the sultan of Sokoto sitting atop the rigid hierarchy) were the final authorities on political and religious matters. It was oligarchy in its purest form, rooted in an Islamic equivalent of the doctrine of "divine right of kings," which medieval European monarchs had used to control their serfs. Under the

6   See *ThisDay*, May 1–20, 2004.

7   Elizabeth Isichei, *A History of Nigeria* (London: Longman Group Limited, 1983), 368–369.

feudal structure put in place by dan Fodio and his descendants, the power of *sharia,* as defined by the ruler and his minions, was total. The peasants (or *talakawa,* as they are known in the local Hausa language) were expected to know their place and to accept their lowly status as the wish of Allah. They quickly learned to do just that.[8]

After the British takeover in 1903, the sultan and his emirs were kept firmly in place as part of the colonial system of Indirect Rule. However, the application of *sharia* was restricted to civil matters. *Sharia* was used to decide such issues as marriage, divorce, and inheritance. Criminal cases were tried under secular laws the British had introduced, not just in northern Nigeria, but in southern Nigeria as well. Although British colonial authorities amalgamated Nigeria's north and south in 1914, they did this mostly for administrative convenience, for they continued to run the two entities under very different rules. For instance, Christian missionaries were allowed to open schools in southern Nigeria but were barred from doing so in the north, in deference to the wishes of the sultan and his emirs.[9]

The use of *sharia* as civil law in the north continued after 1960, when colonial rule ended in Nigeria. The status quo remained after military rule was introduced in 1966, quickly followed by the Nigeria-Biafra war of 1967 to 1970, and the continuation of military rule, which lasted until 1979. In 1978, when a Constituent Assembly was meeting to draft a new constitution in preparation for the return of democracy in 1979, a dispute over *sharia* captured national attention. Some Constituent Assembly delegates from predominantly Muslim northern states pushed for *sharia* to be extended to the federal level, well beyond its application as civil law in northern states with large or predominantly Muslim populations. Other delegates resisted this move, which they saw as a violation of the key principle of keeping the Nigerian state separate from church and mosque while protecting the rights of all citizens to freedom of religion.[10]

At some point during the heated debate, a number of Muslim delegates walked out of the meeting hall in protest. Among those who walked out was Shehu Shagari, who later became Nigeria's president during the Second Republic (1979 to 1983). Ultimately, the delegates decided in fa-

8   Isichei, *A History of Nigeria,* 202–204.

9   See Toyin Falola, *The History of Nigeria* (Westport, CT: Greenwood Press, 1999), 70–74.

10   Falola, *The History of Nigeria,* 164–168; Isichei, *A History of Nigeria,* 471–478.

vor of the status quo: *sharia* as civil law in northern states with large or predominantly Muslim populations, but no application of *sharia* in the realm of criminal law, and no expansion to the federal level. Things stayed this way until 1999, when democracy returned to Nigeria after yet another long period (this time, more than fifteen years) of military rule.[11]

A Troubled Country

Since it gained independence from British rule in 1960, Nigeria has suffered many bouts of bloodshed. Without question, the most serious trauma in the country's history was the Nigeria-Biafra war of 1967 to 1970, which killed no less than 2 million people. That war was preceded by massacres of ethnic Igbo, which reached their peak in 1966,but have happened several times since. While not exclusive to northern Nigeria, the 1966 massacres of ethnic Igbo, in which as many as fifty thousand may have died between May and October of that year, were particularly intense in the north. As for the more recent acts of deadly violence equally rooted in Nigeria's deep ethno-religious divide, these are not just particularly intense in the north; the vast majority of them have happened in that region.[12]

During the 1980s and 1990s, in nearly every major town and city in northern Nigeria, there were bloody confrontations between rival Muslim sects. A prominent example of the clashes between Muslim groups took place in 1980 in Kano (the largest city in northern Nigeria and capital of a state of the same name), when Mohammadu Marwa, a hard-line Islamist preacher also known as Maitatsine, provoked a showdown that quickly overwhelmed the police. It took the firepower of the Nigerian Army to defeat Maitatsine and his well-armed followers, whose possession and skillful use of automatic weapons shocked many Nigerians. Some four thousand people died.[13]

From Kano, the clashes between rival Muslim groups spread to other northern cities and towns in almost-regular two-year cycles—Maiduguri, Gombe, Yola, Bauchi, and, of course, Kaduna. In 1982, there was another

---

11   Falola, *The History of Nigeria*, 221–230.

12   Isichei, *A History of Nigeria*, 471–478.

13   Marwa, who claimed to be the one true prophet of Allah, was killed during the fighting. See Anthony Oyewole and John Lucas, *Historical Dictionary of Nigeria*, 2nd ed. (Lanham, MD, and London: The Scarecrow Press, Inc., 2000), 328.

uprising in Kano, not essentially between Muslim sects, but triggered by a political dispute involving Abubakar Rimi, the then governor of Kano State, and Ado Bayero, the emir of Kano. Among the grisly events in that uprising was the burning alive of Governor Rimi's political advisor (a young college professor) by an angry mob loyal to the emir of Kano.[14] In 1988, there was a flare-up in the northwestern city of Sokoto, touched off by a dispute over the selection of a new sultan. Sokoto's Christian ethnic Igbo residents were in no way involved in the dispute over the selection of a sultan, but scores of Igbo people were killed during that unrest as some members of Sokoto's Muslim community took advantage of the crisis to scapegoat their Igbo neighbors.[15]

To its frustrated citizens, Nigeria can sometimes feel like a bad experiment. As currently constituted, the country is highly susceptible to ethnic, religious, and political turmoil. While such turmoil can be held in check by firm, fair-minded, and honest leadership, very few of Nigeria's leaders, particularly since independence, can convincingly be said to have shown these qualities. In all the instances of violence that Nigeria has experienced over the past half-century, three factors are never far below the surface: ethnic animosity, religious fanaticism, and bitter rivalry for political power among the various groups that make up the fractious federation. Because all three factors are sometimes at play, it can be difficult—especially for foreigners—to get to the root of these conflicts.

In the days following the November 2002 upheaval in Kaduna, several Nigerian commentators argued that foreign media reports oversimplified the causes of the violence. Chuks Iloegbunam, a columnist for Lagos-based *Vanguard*, noted that attributing the deadly upheaval to *ThisDay*'s article "appears plausible but it happens to be wrong." Iloegbunam argued that a feeling of outrage over supposedly disrespectful treatment of religious icons was not an acceptable ground for violence. He wrote:

> When Martin Scorsese, the American film director, released *The Last Temptation of Christ* in 1988, the last thing that crossed the minds of those offended by the blasphemous film was that he should be lynched. No one believed that his temerity should elicit burning and killing and looting . . . Even Chris Ofili, a Nigerian-born artist, drew the Madonna and titled it *The Holy Virgin Mary*. Yet it was a pornographic work partly rendered with ele-

14 Oyewole and Lucas, *Historical Dictionary of Nigeria*, 100, 462.

15 For more information see Falola, *The History of Nigeria*, 187–193.

phant dung. People never thought that . . . Ofili should be beheaded or that private homes and places of worship . . . should be torched as a result.[16]

Pini Jason, another *Vanguard* columnist, dismissed the emphasis on the much-cited commentary published in *ThisDay:* "So much heavy weather has been made of the slip in the *ThisDay* newspaper story . . . How many of the *almajiris* [students from Koranic schools, who were key participants in the uprising] read that story? Who were those who interpreted the story to [them]? If the *ThisDay* story was the problem, the riots would have been spontaneous. But the riot did not start until . . . five days after the article [appeared], and during which *ThisDay* had published repeatedly its apology."[17]

Apologies Made no Difference

After the controversial comments appeared in *ThisDay* on November 16, 2002, Muslim groups demanded an apology. The newspaper published the first apology on November 18. The next day, the Nigerian Supreme Council for Islamic Affairs, one of the most prominent pressure groups representing Nigeria's Muslims, issued a statement rejecting the apology. *ThisDay*'s "purported apology," the Council said, was "indirect, terse and lame."[18] It gave the newspaper until November 23 to publish a more extensive statement of remorse. Other Muslim groups and imams made similar demands.

ThisDay quickly complied. In a much stronger statement of regret that it published for three days (November 20, 21, and 22), the newspaper said, *inter alia:*

> To all our Muslim brothers and sisters, Assalamu Alaikum Wa Rahamatul-Llahi Wa Barakatuhu. May the peace and blessing of Allah be upon you all. With all sense of responsibility, sensitivity and respect for all Muslims, the staff, management, editors and Board of THISDAY Newspapers apologise for the great editorial error in last Saturday's edition on [the] Miss World

16   Chuks Iloegbunam, "The Nigerian Nation as Hostage," *Vanguard*, November 26, 2002.

17   Pini Jason, "A Bloody Pageant," *Vanguard*, November 26, 2002.

18   "Blasphemy: NSCIA Gives ThisDay 7-Day Ultimatum," *Daily Trust*, November 20, 2002.

Beauty Pageant . . . We are sorry that the portrayal of the Holy Prophet Mohammed [Peace Be Unto Him] in a commentary written by one of our staff was not only unjustified, but utterly provocative . . . At THISDAY, we have no reason to denigrate Muslims or the Holy Prophet. Why should we? Key members of our management are devoted Muslims . . . Beyond that the offensive paragraph runs against the grain of our beliefs and what we stand for at THISDAY as we show sensitivity to the complexity of our nation . . . Saturday November 16 was our error, for which we feel very sorry. We recognise the gravity of this error, and we have handled it with all the seriousness it deserves, including very strong disciplinary measures for those who failed in their duties . . . May the Almighty Allah, the God of infinite wisdom, continue to guide us aright. Ma-Assalam, and Ramadan Kareem.[19]

It may have been the most profuse apology ever published in a Nigerian newspaper. Unfortunately, it made no difference. On November 20, 2002, the same day *ThisDay* began printing it, Muslim youths launched the mayhem in Kaduna. The Associated Press described the situation on November 22:

Sporadic gunshots rang out in the northern city of Kaduna where most of the fighting has taken place. Christians retaliated Friday after enraged Muslim mobs in previous days stabbed and set fire to bystanders they believed were Christian, and set fire to at least four churches. Plumes of black smoke rose above Kaduna, a tense, religiously mixed city of several million people. Authorities extended a round-the-clock curfew—although many ignored the order. Young Muslim men shouting "Allahu Akhbar," or "God is great," ignited makeshift barricades of tires and garbage. Others chanted, "Down with beauty" and "Miss World is sin."[20]

The same news dispatch also noted that violence spread on that day to Abuja, Nigeria's capital, where the final event of the Miss World pageant was scheduled to take place on December 7: "Muslim protesters armed with sticks, machetes and daggers burned cars and attacked pedestrians outside the city's plush international hotels after gathering outside the

---

19 *ThisDay*, "An Apology to All Muslims," November 22, 2002, 1.

20 D'Arcy Doran, "Religious riots over Miss World pageant spread to Nigeria's capital," Associated Press, November 22, 2002.

central mosque following afternoon prayers. Rioters pulled a local journalist off a motorcycle and told him he would be killed unless he could recite verses from Islam's holy book, the Quran. The crowd released him unharmed when they realized he was Muslim."[21]

A Shortage of Courage

Prominent Muslim leaders in Nigeria were not in a hurry to help quell the bloody uprising in Kaduna: the Nigerian Supreme Council for Islamic Affairs waited until November 23 before issuing a statement declaring its acceptance of *ThisDay*'s apologies. Meanwhile, Nigerian Muslim Umma, an umbrella group of Islamist clerics, declared a "serious religious emergency" and called on Nigeria's government to stop the pageant. Interestingly, the statement did not call on Muslim youths brandishing deadly weapons in the streets to go home.

The behavior of Nigeria's federal government verged on hypocrisy. On November 21, in its first reaction to the violence, the Obasanjo administration announced that it would punish those associated with the newspaper report, "which without doubt exceeded the bounds of responsible journalism by making [a] provocative publication on the Holy Prophet."[22] President Olusegun Obasanjo himself emphasized this point, saying, "The beauty queens should not feel that they are the cause of the violence. It could happen at any time irresponsible journalism is committed against Islam."[23]

Obviously, in the president's opinion, *ThisDay*'s "irresponsible journalism" was a bigger offense than the acts of deadly violence committed by the Islamist radicals who initiated the rampage. There were no reports quoting Nigeria's president as expressing equally strong condemnation for the irresponsibility of religious fanatics fomenting havoc in the streets of Kaduna and Abuja. Nigeria's president and his administration quickly condemned a journalist who wrote something that upset some people, but

---

21   Doran, "Religious riots over Miss World pageant."

22   Statement by Ufot Ekaette, Secretary to the Government of the Federation; broadcast on Radio Nigeria, November 21, 2002 (supplied by BBC Worldwide Monitoring, November 23, 2002).

23   Alan Cowell, "Religious Violence in Nigeria Drives Out Miss World Event," *New York Times*, November 23, 2002.

they had no harsh words for the militants who, even as the president was speaking, were still stabbing and killing innocent people.[24]

President Obasanjo's pronouncements reflected an attitude he had shown since many states in northern Nigeria began supplanting the country's secular laws with *sharia*. A Baptist who likes to describe himself as a "born-again Christian," Obasanjo consistently demonstrated a lack of courage in dealing with the *sharia* issue. He resisted calls to seek a Supreme Court ruling on the constitutionality of *sharia*, arguing that a definitive ruling could split Nigeria. "I think sharia will fizzle out," Obasanjo said in August 2000. "To confront it is to keep it alive."[25]

President Obasanjo seemed to believe that *sharia* would go away if Nigeria's federal government ignored it long enough. When the northwestern state of Zamfara formally introduced *sharia* in January 2000, the first state to do so, Obasanjo dismissed the move as a gimmick. He also said at the time that the movement would soon "fizzle out." It did not. By December 2002, *sharia* had spread to twelve of Nigeria's thirty-six states. By then, Obasanjo had another incentive to ignore the *sharia* issue—he sought a second term in elections scheduled for April 2003. With an eye on the votes of Muslims in northern Nigeria, Obasanjo did not want to be seen as changing his policy on *sharia* from smug acquiescence to vigorous opposition.[26]

Chronicle of a Carnage Foretold

At least three months before any of the Miss World contestants arrived in Nigeria, Muslim groups had already threatened to disrupt the event. In August 2002, Nigeria's tourism minister, Boma Bromillow-Jack, warned the contestants to avoid visiting parts of the country where *sharia* was being enforced. "We have told the [organizers] not to allow the ladies to go to Zamfara and other Shariah states because of the risks involved," the minister said. This warning became necessary after several Muslim groups de-

24   See *ThisDay*, November 21–30, 2002.

25   Douglas Farah, "Islamic Law Splits Nigeria: Move by Northern States to Reassert Muslim Identity Ignites Sectarian Violence and Threatens Democracy," *The Washington Post*, August 31, 2000.

26   For coverage see *ThisDay*, December 2002.

nounced the pageant as immoral and vowed to foil it. None of the groups specified how they were going to do so.[27]

In deference to the views of Nigeria's Muslim community, the organizers of the pageant moved the final event from November 30 to December 7, ensuring it did not happen during the Islamic holy month of Ramadan. The participants had been scheduled to meet Nigeria's president. To avoid offending Muslims, the president's office canceled that appointment. The final event was to be held in Nigeria's capital, Abuja, which was not under *sharia* law. All the other events in the Miss World pageant took place in southern states with predominantly Christian populations, such as Rivers and Cross River. No events were scheduled for Kaduna or any of the other states that had enacted *sharia* law. In all the venues, security remained tight. Having realized they could not breach security in any of the places where the Miss World events took place, the Islamists chose a customary stomping ground: Kaduna. Their plan proved successful. After more than two hundred people were killed in Kaduna, the organizers of the pageant moved it to London.[28]

One of the most remarkable aspects of the Miss World fiasco was the skillful way Nigeria's Islamists seized upon a mundane show-business event and used it to flex political muscle, kill innocent people in the name of Allah, and, along the way, display flagrant disrespect for the laws of a diverse, multireligious country. Many Nigerians felt it painful to think that hundreds of lives were lost because of something so frivolous.

By forcing the Miss World event to flee, the Islamists were seeking to create the impression that Nigeria is a Muslim country. Nigeria's Christians and other non-Muslims find this impression deeply disturbing. Their concern grows when they have reason to suspect that the rest of the world falls for this fallacy.

In a country whose population, by most estimates, is split nearly evenly between Muslims and Christians, pursuing a reckless quest for Islamization is a surefire formula for serious strife. It is difficult to think of a better strategy for anyone seeking to destroy Nigeria, an artificial coun-

---

27 "Miss World in Nigerian Islam scare," *Irish News*, August 12, 2002.

28 Alan Cowell, "Religious Violence in Nigeria Drives Out Miss World Event," *New York Times*, November 23, 2002, 1. See also "Beauty pageant flees to London," *The Gazette* (Montreal), November 23, 2002, A1.

try cobbled together by the British in 1914, which has struggled for nearly a hundred years to hammer out a shared sense of nationhood among its many peoples. The zealots waving the banner of radical Islamism do not show any sign of concern about the danger of serious conflict or loss of lives. What they do show are signs of a resolve to impose what they consider the will of God, whatever the cost.

The first crisis that faced the plan to hold the Miss World pageant in Nigeria was also *sharia*-related. After an Islamic court ruled that Amina Lawal, a thirty-one-year-old Muslim woman, should be stoned to death for having a baby out of wedlock, some contestants announced plans to boycott the pageant. Amina Lawal was not the first Muslim woman to be so sentenced, but her case was the most recent as of November 2002. Following assurances from the Nigerian government that such a sentence would not be carried out, ninety-two participants in the beauty pageant arrived in Nigeria on November 11. However, contestants from at least five countries stayed away.

Nigeria's Islamists even found a way to use *ThisDay*'s profuse apology to further their agenda. First, they watched the newspaper run it for at least two days and did nothing to pull back the *almajiris* rampaging through Kaduna. Then they celebrated as the Miss World organizers announced late on November 22 that the pageant was moving to London. Finally, on November 23, Lateef Adegbite, secretary-general of the Nigerian Supreme Council for Islamic Affairs, declared that the council had accepted *ThisDay*'s apology. In doing so, Adegbite made a point of feeding more humble pie to a newspaper that had already eaten a lot of it.

"I call on all Nigerian Muslims to forgive *ThisDay* newspapers," Adegbite said. "It was an abomination, and such a thing should never be done again. And it should also be a lesson to all others." Adegbite added, "Islam is a very serious religion . . . You would recall what happened to Salman Rushdie, who wrote that stupid book, *Satanic Verses*. Some of the people in the Western world thought the Muslims went too far by pronouncing a death sentence on him, but you see, they did not appreciate the gravity of what he had done. I only sincerely hope [*ThisDay*'s apology] was genuine, and as I said, we have accepted it in good faith and it would be a lesson [so] that such a thing does not happen again."[29]

---

29 "Supreme Council Accepts THISDAY apology," *ThisDay*, November 24, 2002.

Theocracy by Default

Nigeria's Islamists quickly moved from condescension to recklessness. At a rally of Muslim faithfuls on November 25, 2002, Zamfara state's deputy governor, Mahmoud Dallatun Shinkafi, declared a *fatwa* (an Islamic judicial ruling)[30] pronouncing a death sentence on *ThisDay*'s reporter, Isioma Daniel. "Like Salman Rushdie, the blood of the ThisDay writer can be shed," Shinkafi stated. The following day, another state official clarified the declaration. "What we are saying is that the Holy Quran has clearly stated that whoever insults the Prophet of Islam, Mohammed, should be killed," said Zamfara's commissioner of information, Umar Dangaladima Magaji. "It is a fatwa . . . based on the request of the people. Being a leader, you can pass a fatwa."[31]

On November 28, Jama'atu Nasril Islam, a Muslim organization closely allied with the Nigerian Supreme Council for Islamic Affairs, issued what news reports called an "order," telling Muslims to ignore the Zamfara state government's *fatwa*. The organization said the Zamfara state government had no authority to issue a *fatwa*. Only the Jama'atu Nasril Islam and the Nigerian Supreme Council for Islamic Affairs, both headed by the sultan of Sokoto (usually regarded as the paramount Nigerian Muslim leader), had the power to issue a *fatwa*, the statement said. It went on to say that the sultan had directed the *fatwa* committee of the two bodies to meet and deliberate on Isioma Daniel's article. "The fatwa committee, which comprises members from the 36 states of the federation and Abuja shall soon meet."[32]

The critical point to keep in mind is that Jama'atu Nasril Islam and the Nigerian Supreme Council for Islamic Affairs did not oppose Zamfara's *fatwa* on the ground that they considered it unacceptable or illegal to ask Nigerian Muslims to kill a fellow citizen. They opposed it on the ground that the instruction to kill had come from the *wrong source*. Of course, under Nigerian law, it is a crime to incite the murder of another person. However, this failed to register with the Islamists, who evidently believed that Islamic law supersedes Nigeria's constitution and secular penal code. This statement from Jama'atu Nasril Islam, which the Obasanjo admin-

30 John L. Esposito, *Unholy War: Terror in the Name of Islam* (New York: Oxford University Press, 2002), 169.

31 *New York Times* online/Reuters, November 26, 2002.

32 *Washington Post* online/Reuters, November 28, 2002.

istration allowed to go unchallenged, clearly underlines the serious problem that *sharia* represents for Nigeria's future. Emboldened by "victories" such as this, Nigeria's Islamists are likely to keep demanding more concessions. Nigeria's Christians, meanwhile, grow more and more nervous. This heightens the danger that escalating religious acrimony, mixed in with long-standing ethnic tensions, could tear the country apart.

It is a testimony to Nigeria's unfortunate situation that an elected official and a state government functionary would publicly call for the murder of another person and get away with it, without as much as losing their jobs, let alone being prosecuted. A culture of impunity among holders of public office has always been a big part of Nigeria's problems, and the expanded application of *sharia* makes the situation increasingly worse in this respect. More to the point, *sharia* seems to be on a collision course with Nigeria's secular constitution and legal code. Cosmetic half-measures and timid negligence could delay the collision for a number of years, but they are not likely to be enough to prevent it.

In October 2001, Zamfara state governor Ahmed Sani went as far as announcing that the governors of *sharia* states were contributing money into a fund dedicated to the purchase of arms to defend the Islamic faith. The northern Nigeria chapter of the Christian Association of Nigeria expressed concern about this statement and called on the federal government to investigate. There was no such investigation.[33]

When Nigeria's Christians express fear that prominent leaders in Nigeria's Muslim community are pursuing a vision of turning the country into an African equivalent of Saudi Arabia or Afghanistan, people in the West often view this as an overreaction. However, this fear is grounded in Nigeria's history and the pattern of events since October 1999. Nigeria's Christians are not the only ones worried about the spread of radical Islamism. Although many Nigerian Muslims have embraced *sharia* especially in the north, some Muslims (including some in states that have adopted *sharia*) are concerned about what the rule of rigid Islamic law would mean for them and their families.

It is also important to understand that there are millions of Nigerians who are neither Christian nor Muslim. One prominent example is the playwright Wole Soyinka, who won the Nobel Prize for Literature in 1986. Although raised by Christian parents, Soyinka identifies much more with

33 *Vanguard* newspaper online/BBC Summary of World Broadcasts, October 13, 2001.

the traditional Ifa religion of his Yoruba people. Soyinka's comments about the November 2002 Kaduna uprising and Zamfara's *fatwa* ruling emphasized a concern he has expressed several times in the past. "In this country, religion is being used—and it has been used—for short-sighted, narrow-minded political ends," he said during a book event in Lagos on December 11, 2002. "This is not how to practice religion. This is sheer scramble for domination, authority . . . These murderous tendencies which we have seen have a long history."[34]

Stressing that this was not the first time a *fatwa* death sentence was decreed in Nigeria, Soyinka said the only difference this time was that the November 2002 *fatwa* was pronounced in public. He said previous *fatwa* rulings had been pronounced in secret and, in some instances, subsequently carried out in public. He cited the case of Gideon Akaluka, a Christian businessman from the Igbo ethnic group, who was beheaded by Islamists in the northern city of Kano in December 1994.[35]

Some Muslims had accused Gideon Akaluka's wife of desecrating a copy of the Qur'an by using a page from the holy book to clean her baby. By all accounts, Akaluka's wife had done this in error: she did not know that the page in question was from the Qur'an. Nonetheless, her husband, who had been out of town during the incident, was arrested after he returned and detained for about a month at a police station in Kano. A few days before he was to be released, a Muslim mob invaded the police station where Gideon Akaluka was being detained, beheaded him, and paraded the streets of Kano displaying his severed head on a stick.[36] An Islamist group, Jama'atu Tajdidi Islamiyya, claimed responsibility for the murder of Akaluka. By June 1995, this group was issuing statements threatening to cleanse Kano of all non-Muslims, and pronouncing "impending calamity" if Christians and other non-Muslims failed to move out of the area.[37] No one was ever prosecuted for the murder of Gideon Akaluka.

34 South African Press Association/Agence France Presse, News24.com, December 11, 2002.

35 South African Press Association/Agence France Presse, News24.com, December 11, 2002.

36 "Tensions High After Muslims Accused of Beheading Christian," Associated Press, January 3, 1995. See also "Why Gideon Akaluka's death has set Christians trembling," *Manchester Guardian Weekly*, March 26, 1995; and Karl Maier, "Beheading stirs Nigerian tension," *The Independent*, August 16, 1995.

37 "Pamphlets call on non Moslems to leave Kano," Agence France Presse, June 16,

Soyinka suggested that the November 2002 violence in Kaduna had something to do with the pursuit of a long-term vision to turn Nigeria into an Islamic country. "There is an attempt to cow this nation, an attempt to terrorize this nation into accepting the norm of one religion . . . Whenever terror is unleashed by Islamic hoodlums, I don't see them being called to order. I do not hear a strong language of condemnation being pronounced unto those who brutalize their fellow humanity for no reason whatsoever."[38]

Lawful Dissent vs. Criminal Intolerance

In every country, indiscreet comments in the media that annoy or offend some citizens are not just commonplace; they are inevitable. This is particularly true of countries as multiethnic and multireligious as Nigeria. Words can generate outrage, but it is hard to argue that such feelings of outrage constitute legitimate grounds for killing people or destroying property. In a democracy—which Nigeria is supposed to be—respect for freedom of expression (including tasteless expression) is as critical as respect for the religious beliefs, or non-belief, of others. In fact, in making their case for full-scale *sharia*, Nigeria's Islamists have repeatedly argued that they have the right to demand *sharia* because Nigeria is now a democracy.

Citizens who encounter disagreeable commentary in a newspaper would be expected to make their views known to the writer and the newspaper's editors. They could respond by presenting a different opinion—in very strong words, if they so desire. Some true believers have been known to go as far as organizing a boycott or petition drive against publications that offended their (religious) beliefs or other cherished opinions. Such boycotts or petition drives have happened in Nigeria. (In the late 1980s, for example, a few Christian preachers tried to mobilize their followers to boycott the Concord group of newspapers, whose publisher they accused of using his media organization to promote an Islamist agenda.[39] The

1995.

38   Wale Olaleye and Emeka Monye, "Soyinka Alleges Plan to Foist One Religion on Nigeria," *ThisDay*, December 11, 2002.

39   See "Pastor-Scholar Agbali looks at inculturation and contextual theology as aspects of Christianity in Africa," US/Africa Dialogue, No. 96: African Christianity, University of Texas at Austin [Internet, accessed July 13, 2006, http://www.utexas.edu/conferences/africa/ads/96.html]. See also "Theological Ambivalence and Democratic

boycott campaign was not particularly successful.) In any case, even when individual citizens cross the line and take the law into their hands, respectable governments are not expected to condone such behavior. More to the point, respectable governments usually do not make excuses for the actions of those who organize or join killer mobs. Unfortunately, this is what happened in Nigeria in November 2002.

It is easy to come across arguments that such basic rule-of-law norms that other countries respect and enforce are not necessarily relevant in Nigeria. Because Nigeria is a big developing country with big problems, the argument often goes, it needs (or, better still, deserves) to be allowed the time to get its own affairs in order. For various reasons, interested parties within and outside Nigeria have been peddling this opinion—and the elaborate excuses that go with it—for the better part of a century. British administrators were quick to make such excuses during the years of colonial rule. The same excuses were commonplace in the early 1960s, when elected leaders played petty politics while Nigeria slipped into corruption and disorder. Those same excuses were prevalent in the 1980s and 1990s, when military dictators held Nigeria in a grip of venal brutality.

Nigeria is once again a democracy, and its leaders are recycling the same old excuses to explain away what has now become a culture of ineptitude. The case must be made, however, that to keep excusing Nigeria from aspiring to the same high standards that underpin enlightened law and public policy in much of the rest of the world is to consign Africa's most populous country to ramshackle backwardness.

Devotion to Islam is not a prerequisite for disliking beauty contests. While Christians cannot necessarily prove that Jesus expressed any opinion about beauty shows, many Christians also regard such shows as somewhat ridiculous. So do feminists, who tend to consider beauty pageants an anachronism. Obviously, to refuse to have anything to do with beauty pageants is within the bounds of reason. However, to threaten or carry out violent protests because a beauty pageant is being held somewhere in a country where one lives is unreasonable, especially in a country like Nigeria, defined by its laws as a secular state.

Accountability" (Summary of Presentation by Sam Amadi at the Pentecostal-Civil Society Dialogue, October 18, 2004), Heinrich Boll Foundation, Nigeria [Internet, accessed July 13, 2006, http://www.boellnigeria.org/documents/Sam%20Amadi%20 -%20Theological%20Ambivalence%20and%20Democratic%20Accountability.pdf].

Josh Arinze

Sharia's Impact on Non-Muslims: The Case of Zamfara

Heated debates about how much leverage *sharia* should command in Nigeria's constitution and jurisprudence are not new. As noted earlier in this essay, this was a contentious issue during the constitution-drafting sessions leading up to the restoration of democracy in 1979. The major difference between 1979 and 1999 in this respect was that in the later year, some state governors opted to raise the stakes by championing the enactment of laws that made *sharia* the preeminent legal code in their states.

Among the new governors who took office in May 1999 was Ahmed Sani, who was elected governor of the northwestern state of Zamfara. Sani had used the promise of full-scale *sharia* to rally support during his campaign for governor, and he moved quickly on this front after he took office. On October 9, 1999, he signed two new laws extending *sharia* into the realm of criminal law in Zamfara, effectively supplanting Nigeria's secular statutes and, some have argued, the country's constitution. Among other provisions, Zamfara's new *sharia* laws stipulated such punishments as amputation of limbs for serial thieves, floggings for the consumption of alcoholic drinks, and death by stoning for those found guilty of fornication.[40]

On October 27, 1999, at a rally of Muslim faithfuls in Gusau, the state capital, Governor Sani formally proclaimed the introduction of *sharia* in Zamfara. He announced that the full implementation of *sharia* would begin on January 27, 2000, after the installation of Islamic judges trained in Saudi Arabia. "Without sharia, Islamic faith is valueless," Sani told the crowd. He urged other states in northern Nigeria to follow Zamfara's example.[41]

Although the Zamfara state government cites January 27, 2000, as the day it formally began full implementation of Islamic law, key aspects of *sharia* were already being enforced at the time Sani addressed the rally in Gusau on October 27, 1999. As of that date, the sale of alcohol had been banned all over Zamfara, and hotels, video parlors, and movie theaters were being closed. Also as of that date, students in Zamfara's public schools were already being segregated by gender, women-only taxis and buses had been introduced, and women had been banned from playing soccer or using motorcycle taxis, a common means of transportation.[42]

40   See *The Tide and Vanguard*, October 10, 1999.
41   Mohammed Rufai, Reuters/*The Toronto Star*, October 28, 1999.
42   Rufai, Reuters/*The Toronto Star*, October 28, 1999.

As of October 27, 1999, Christian congregations in Zamfara were already being denied permits to build new churches. Some churches had already been demolished by the Zamfara state government, which said they were built without the required permits. These facts notwithstanding, on January 27, 2000, Governor Sani repeated what he had said before—that *sharia* would apply to Muslims only. "Nothing will change for Christians," the governor said. "They have nothing to fear."[43]

"Shariah is fundamental human rights," Zamfara's deputy governor, Mahmoud Shinkafi, told the *New York Times* in a report published in December 1999. "Now we are in a democracy. Whatever we want, we have the right to." The report also stated: "The prospect of shariah has already infringed on the rights of non-Muslims, said people attending Mass one recent Sunday morning at Our Lady of Fatima Roman Catholic Church in Gusau. Christian women said they were refused entry into the green-and-yellow taxis because their heads were not covered."[44] These were the same taxis already designated for women only.

By February 1, 2000, Radio Nigeria reported that Christian programs or announcements of any type were no longer allowed on Zamfara state radio and television stations. Simon Bana, the Anglican bishop of Zamfara, told a Radio Nigeria interviewer that he himself experienced discrimination in housing when he arrived for his new assignment, just after the launching of full-scale *sharia* in Zamfara state. "After paying the money [for a new house], and immediately they found that it is a bishop that is going to stay there, they would say no, take back your money," Bana said.[45]

In November 1999, the *Dallas Morning News* reported: "In September, local authorities tore down the walls of the small Wesley Methodist Church in Gusau because they said the church had failed to obtain the proper licenses. 'The government here is very hostile to churches,' said the Rev. Chijioke Nnaji, Wesley's minister. He said he had submitted the requested documents, but the state government had not responded." Nnaji disagreed with the governor's claim that Islamic law would not affect non-

43   Barnaby Phillips, "Islamic law has Christians up in arms," *Calgary Herald*, January 28, 2000.

44   Norimitsu Onishi, "A Nigerian State Turns to the Koran for Law," *New York Times*, December 8, 1999.

45   "Bishop complains of religious discrimination in Zamfara state," BBC Summary of World Broadcasts/Radio Nigeria, February 3/February 1, 2000.

Muslims. "When women and men can't travel freely, you can't tell us that *sharia* is not going to affect us," he said.[46]

In December 1999, Zuma Hotel, owned and run by a Christian businessman, was abruptly shut down, as were many others. "I wasn't given any notice that they would close me down," said Zuma's owner Vincent Umeadi, whose earnings from the hotel helped put his ten children through school. "Sharia has affected us badly. If it was a thing for Muslims only, then they would not have forced me to close down."[47] All the same, Zamfara's government officials continued to state that Christians and other non-Muslims had nothing to fear.

"I Woke Up without a Hand"

In June 2000, Buba Bello Jangebe, a forty-three-year-old man whom a *sharia* court had found guilty of stealing cattle, became the first person to lose a limb under Zamfara state's Islamic code. News reports suggested that Jangebe was a well-known miscreant. As one newspaper put it, Jangebe "spent years dodging the law and running cattle rackets." But did he deserve to have his right hand cut off for stealing? Nigeria's secular laws say no. Zamfara's *sharia* judges said yes. *Sharia* prevailed. "They took me from the prison to the hospital, and that's all I remember," Jangebe said in a report published in November 2002. "I woke up without a hand." Labaran Mohammed, an Islamic-law judge in Gusau, Zamfara's state capital, said his conscience was at peace with pronouncing such punishments as amputation of limbs, or stoning. "We are slaves to Allah," the judge said. "We must comply. There is no debate."[48]

By the end of 2002, eleven other states in northern Nigeria had followed Zamfara's example. One Islamist, Ibrahim Datti Ahmad, president of a group calling itself the Supreme Council for Sharia in Nigeria, was predicting that *sharia* would eventually spread to at least nineteen of Nigeria's thirty-six states.[49]

---

46 Andrew Maykuth, "Nigeria strained as state adopts Islamic law," *Dallas Morning News*, November 25, 1999, 57A.

47 Ann M. Simmons, "Nigerian State's Embrace of Islamic Law Triggers Alarm," *Los Angeles Times*, February 23, 2000.

48 Janine di Giovanni, "Terror for Nigerians as Sharia marks its victims," *The Times* (London), November 19, 2002.

49 Farah, "Islamic Law Splits Nigeria."

In November 2004, *Daily Champion*, a Lagos-based newspaper, reported that in Bauchi, another state that had enacted *sharia*, twenty-nine convicts were in prison awaiting amputation, as were two others sentenced to death by stoning. One of the convicts sentenced to amputation was asking that the sentence be carried out. Adamu Shu'aibu, twenty-nine, whom a *sharia* court found guilty of stealing, told an official of Nigeria's Legal Aid Council "that he preferred being amputated to remaining in endless imprisonment." Shu'aibu said, "If there is anything the Legal Aid Council can do for me, it is to accelerate the amputation of my hand so that I can leave the prison and carry on with [my] life."[50]

Sectarian Violence in Kaduna, February 2000

In February 2000, barely a month after the official beginning of full-scale *sharia* in Zamfara state, agitation for a similar move sparked a major explosion of violence in Kaduna, the same city that later suffered the worst of the Miss World riots of November 2002. The one major difference between the two outbreaks in Kaduna was that many more lives were lost in February 2000 than in November 2002.

Trouble began when Kaduna's Muslims, having observed how events unfolded in Zamfara, began calling on the Kaduna state government to introduce full-blown *sharia*. (Both the state and its capital are called Kaduna.) However, unlike Zamfara, whose population is, by many accounts, no more than 20 percent Christian, Kaduna state's Christian population is much bigger: about 50 percent. After Muslims marched in the city of Kaduna, calling for *sharia*, Christians organized their own march to show their opposition to *sharia*. As is often the case in such matters in Nigeria, accounts differ about how the violence began. By the time it was over, some three thousand people were dead, and large parts of the city were in ruins. De-facto segregation of Christian and Muslim neighborhoods has since become a fact of life in Kaduna, a result of continuing tension and distrust between the two communities.

A large number of the Christians who died in Kaduna in 2000 were ethnic Igbo. (Nearly all ethnic Igbo are Christian.) After hundreds of Igbo dead were taken home for burial in Igboland (in southeastern Nigeria), the anger boiled over. Northern Muslims living in Aba, a southeastern city, were attacked. News reports said as many as two hundred people

---

50 "Sharia Convict Pleads for Amputation," *Daily Champion*, November 22, 2004.

may have died in Aba. What happened in Aba was unprecedented. In a long history of ethnic violence in which tens of thousands of ethnic Igbo had been killed in northern Nigeria, it was the first time northerners were targeted in backlash attacks in Igboland. It was a clear sign that the cycle of violence was making it much harder to keep the lid on grievances that had been simmering for decades.

The Politics of Intimidation

During the period between the Kaduna clashes of February 2000 and November 2002, another major flare-up occurred elsewhere in northern Nigeria. This one began on September 7, 2001, in Jos, a city that has been known since the 1970s as one of the most tolerant in northern Nigeria. The capital of Plateau state, Jos is a majority-Christian city with a substantial Muslim minority, and it had not seen such furious ethno-religious bloodshed since the anti-Igbo pogroms of May to October 1966.

In 1991, when a Christian-versus-Muslim uprising devastated the nearby town of Bauchi, thousands of Bauchi residents of both faiths took refuge in Jos. Many Bauchi-based business people moved their operations to Jos because it was considered a much safer, more welcoming city. (Jos also boasts a beautiful, hilly terrain, and much cooler weather that feels like autumn for a good part of the year.) In addition, in July 2001, when the introduction of *sharia* in Bauchi state triggered sectarian clashes reported to have killed up to one thousand people, many Bauchi state residents fled to Jos for safety. Now, just two months later, simmering tensions exploded into sectarian violence in Jos, following the federal government's appointment of a Muslim to head Plateau state's poverty alleviation program. For some reason, the appointment added fuel to long-simmering tensions between the city's Christian and Muslim communities.

Of course, there were conflicting accounts of how the killings began. The (London) *Guardian* reported: "Some say [the violence] was set off by an old Christian woman who offended Muslim men at prayer. Others say a group of Muslim youths set fire to a church and provoked a backlash. But within days, hundreds were dead. The killings flared again Wednesday [September 12, 2001], apparently revived by Muslims publicly celebrating the terrorist attacks in the U.S. A fleeing resident of Nasarawa district told the Lagos Guardian that some people were killed by men wielding machetes and shouting Islamic slogans . . . The Inter-Religious Council condemned the 'unbelievable carnage in one of Nigeria's most peaceful cities.'"[51]

Between May 1999 and December 2004, some ten thousand Nigerians died in the country's religious and ethnic conflicts. Most of these deaths happened in northern Nigeria during sectarian uprisings ignited by disputes over *sharia*. Although there were deadly fights in Lagos and elsewhere in the southwest between ethnic Hausa northerners and Yoruba southwesterners, nearly all the deaths occurred in often-volatile northern Nigeria. Of course, ethnic killings and religious intolerance in Nigeria predate the introduction of full-blown *sharia* in twelve northern states. But *sharia* has substantially increased tensions and made the clashes more frequent and, in some respects, more deadly than before.

There is no reason to believe the violence that stems from Nigeria's ethnic and religious fault lines are over. Granted, not all governors and legislators in northern Nigerian states with big Muslim populations are enthusiastic about *sharia*. However, under intense pressure from Islamist clerics and their followers demanding *sharia*, state governors and legislators do not want to be seen as not being Muslim enough. They realize that refusing to jump on the *sharia* bandwagon could lead to political defeat, or worse.

For obvious reasons, Nigeria's Muslim politicians would go to great lengths to avoid being denounced as enemies of Islam. President Obasanjo is not a Muslim, but he appears to have succumbed to intimidation all the same, demonstrating a lack of courage in dealing with the fanatical propagators of radical Islamism. With a large number of elected officials in appeasement mode, Nigeria's Islamists feel empowered to continue playing high-stakes hardball. As good students of history know, appeasement often fails to deter aggression.

------

51   Chris McGreal, "Militants wrestle for the soul of Nigeria: Hundreds of deaths in new religious clashes have revived the fear of civil war," *The Guardian* (London), September 15, 2001.

IS TERRORISM UNIQUE?

A TACTICAL AND IDEOLOGICAL APPRAISAL

Benjamin Grob-Fitzgibbon

The terrorist attacks of September 11, 2001, in Washington D.C., New York City, and Pennsylvania were acts of war against the United States of America and its allies, and against the very idea of civilized society. No cause justifies terrorism . . . The enemy is not one person. It is not a single political regime. Certainly it is not a religion. The enemy is terrorism.

National Strategy for Combating Terrorism[1]

Terrorism is an abstract phenomenon of which there can be no real essence which can be discovered and described . . . In the field of terrorism, there is no agreement about any single definition.

Alex P. Schmid, Political Terror[2]

hen the administration of George W. Bush came to power in January, 2001, it was not particularly interested in the threat that terrorism posed to the United States, nor did it place countering terrorism high on its list of priorities. Indeed, one of the first acts of

---

1 *National Strategy for Combating Terrorism*, The White House (February 2003), 1.

2 Alex Schmid, *Political Terror: A Research Guide to Concepts, Theories, Data Bases and Literature* (New Brunswick, NJ: Transaction Books, 1983), 110.

National Security Advisor Condoleezza Rice was to downgrade the National Coordinator for Counterterrorism from the Principals Committee to the Deputy Secretaries Committee.[3] Yet when the Al-Qa'ida terrorist organization attacked the United States nine months later, on September 11, 2001, the administration's domestic and foreign policy was radically reappraised. Suddenly, terrorism became a matter of extreme national significance and the administration proclaimed that the U.S. government had "no more important mission than protecting the homeland from future terrorist attacks."[4] Francis W. Taylor, the new Coordinator for Counterterrorism, commented that "those murdered on 9/11 [would not be] lost in vain," and announced that the United States had "launched a worldwide campaign against terrorism."[5]

Taylor spoke these words with candor. An unparalleled campaign against terrorism did indeed begin, and within two years of the September 11 attacks, the government was able to report that two-thirds of the senior Al-Qa'ida "leaders, operational managers, and key facilitators" had been killed or taken into custody.[6] In Operation Enduring Freedom, the United States military uprooted the Taliban regime in Afghanistan and disrupted Al-Qa'ida's safe haven there, and in Operation Iraqi Freedom the U.S. military invaded Iraq and deposed of the regime of Saddam Hussein, claiming that Iraq was "the central front for the war on terror."[7] In addition to these military endeavors, the U.S. Department of Justice charged over 260 individuals "uncovered in the course of terrorist investigations," 140 of whom were convicted or pled guilty.[8] The government also established a cabinet-level secretary of homeland security whose primary mission was to "prevent terrorist attacks within the United States; reduce America's vulnerability to terrorism; and minimize the damage and recover from attacks that do occur."[9] Finally, in the years 2001 to 2004, the State

....

3 Richard A. Clarke, *Against All Enemies: Inside America's War on Terror* (New York: Free Press, 2004), 230.

4 *Progress Report on the Global War on Terrorism*, The White House (September 2003), 2.

5 *Patterns of Global Terrorism 2001*, United States Department of State (May 2002), v.

6 *Progress Report on the Global War on Terrorism*, 3.

7 *Progress Report on the Global War on Terrorism*, 5.

8 *Progress Report on the Global War on Terrorism*, 4.

9 *Securing our Homeland: U.S. Department of Homeland Security Strategic Plan*, United

Department published an unprecedented forty-three fact sheets relating to terrorism and distributed no fewer than seventy-four press releases on counterterrorism initiatives.[10]

Despite this improved attention, however, there has been a disconnect between the way the government has officially defined *terrorism* and the way it has interpreted terrorism in practice. For example, both the Central Intelligence Agency (CIA) and the State Department draw their definition from Title 22 of the U.S. Code, Section 2656f(d): "The term 'terrorism' means premeditated, politically motivated violence perpetrated against noncombatant targets by subnational groups or clandestine agents, usually intended to influence an audience."[11] The Federal Bureau of Investigation (FBI) uses the definition found in the Code of Federal Regulations (28 C.F.R. Section 0.85), which states that terrorism is "the unlawful use of force and violence against persons or property to intimidate or coerce a government, the civilian population, or any segment thereof, in furtherance of political or social objectives."[12] If the State Department and CIA's definitions were to be strictly adhered to, however, many of the acts of violence committed by the insurgency in Iraq could not be classified as terrorism, as this violence is directed at U.S. and coalition forces who are not "noncombatants." Likewise, the CIA, State Department, and FBI stipulate that terrorism has to be perpetrated for political or social reasons, and thus inadvertently rule out the actions of Al-Qa'ida, which are committed primarily for religious reasons. Because of this lack of clear classification, a sense of confusion surrounds the war on terrorism, with the enemy neither plainly defined nor easily identifiable.

Elsewhere, I have explored this discrepancy and have argued that for the war on terrorism to have any constructive utility, *terrorism* must not be defined within a single category but rather as four distinct categories: na-

States Department of Homeland Security (2004), 3.

10   Releases, Counterterrorism Office, United States Department of State, http://www .state.gov/s/ct/rls/.

11   *Patterns of Global Terrorism 2003*, United States Department of State (April 2004), vii, http://www.cia.gov/terrorism/faqs.html.

12   *Terrorism 2000/2001*, FBI Publication #0308, http://www.fbi.gov/publications/terror/terror2000_2001.htm. The FBI further notes that "a terrorist incident is a violent act or an act dangerous to human life, in violation of the criminal laws of the United States, or of any state, to intimidate or coerce a government, the civilian population, or any segment thereof, in furtherance of political or social objectives."

tional terrorism (offensive and defensive), revolutionary terrorism, reactionary terrorism, and religious terrorism.[13] My purpose in making such distinctions was to show that the motivations and end goals of those who are collectively called terrorists have been (and still are) dramatically different.[14] This paper intends to take that analysis a step further, asking not only if terrorists differ from each other (the answer is clearly yes) but if and how terrorists differ from other people who use violence and are not called terrorists. What, for example, makes Osama bin Laden a terrorist and the pilot of the *Enola Gay* not? What makes the actions of the Irish Republican Army terrorism yet those of the CIA sabotage? Put another way, is there any truth in the old adage "One man's terrorist is another's freedom fighter"? There are three parts to this problem: first, does terrorism differ tactically from other forms of violence; second, are terrorists

13   Benjamin Grob-Fitzgibbon, "What is Terrorism? Redefining a Phenomenon in Time of War," *Peace and Change* 30, no. 2 (April 2005). National terrorism is used by those whose aims concern national boundaries. It can be further divided into two categories: offensive national terrorism and defensive national terrorism. The former seeks to change existing national boundaries through violent means directed at the state currently upholding those boundaries. The latter seeks to use violence to maintain the national status quo, to prevent the state or an offensive national terrorist group from changing the existing national boundaries. Revolutionary terrorism aims to change the philosophical or political nature of a government and/or society and is not limited to a single state. It is concerned with regional, continental, or even worldwide change. Reactionary terrorism works in direct contrast to revolutionary terrorism. It seeks to prevent change in government or society or both. It is concerned with either preserving the present structures or returning to a "golden age" that it views as tainted by revolutionary or evolutionary change. Finally, religious terrorism uses violence for religious reasons, to religiously convert or cleanse a people or nation, or to bring about revolutionary or reactionary religious change within a single state, region, or continent.

14   I write: "There is a great deal of difference between the young Irish Republican Army volunteer who shoots a British soldier for the purpose of ending British rule in Northern Ireland and the Weather Underground recruit who sets fire to a police car in Chicago to bring about worldwide Marxist revolution. To classify all those 'people-from-below' who use violent means to secure their desired ends with the single designation of 'terrorist' belies the complexity of political and religious violence and hints at a simplicity of purpose that should not be accepted by a serious scholar" (Grob-Fitzgibbon, "What is Terrorism?", 236).

ideologically exclusive from non-terrorists; and third, is terrorism therefore a unique form of violence?

Terrorism, like all violence, is limited in its capabilities by the technology available to its practitioners. Indeed, terrorists have seldom had the funds available for large-scale research and development. Consequently, terrorists have usually followed in the footsteps of the military, only utilizing technology once it has already been developed and perfected by the State. As such, at first glance at least, terrorist tactics have seldom shown much innovation or distinction. For example, guns, although used by the military as early as the fourteenth century (their use becoming widespread by the seventeenth), were only first used by terrorists in the late eighteenth century, during the American Revolution and the French Reign of Terror.[15] While rapid-fire weapons dated from the late nineteenth century, terrorist groups only adopted them after the First World War. Fully automatic weapons, pioneered during the Second World War, did not become common among terrorists until the 1960s.[16]

The same replication can be found with the use of bombs. Gunpowder bombs, although as old as the gun itself, were only first used by terrorists in the late eighteenth century, after they had already been adopted by the military.[17] The first use of a gunpowder bomb with any effect did not come until 1858 when Felice Orsini attempted to take the life of Napoleon III. Although Napoleon himself was not killed, Orsini's bomb did kill eight others.[18] Nine years later, in 1867, the Fenians, an Irish republican terrorist group, killed 12 and injured 120 during a bomb attack on Clerkenwell Prison, where some of their comrades were being held.[19]

---

15 For more on the early history of firearms, see Kenneth Chase, *Firearms: A Global History to 1700* (Cambridge, MA: Cambridge University Press, 2003).

16 Herbert K. Tillema, "A Brief History of Terrorism and Technology," in Tushar K. Ghosh, Mark A. Prelas, Dabir S. Viswanath, Sudarshan K. Loyalka, eds., *Science and Technology of Terrorism and Counterterrorism* (New York: Marcel Dekker, Inc., 2002), 23.

17 Tillema, "A Brief History of Terrorism and Technology," 23.

18 Walter Laqueur, *The New Terrorism: Fanaticism and the Arms of Mass Destruction* (New York: Oxford University Press, 1999), 41. For more detail on Orsini's assassination attempt, see Michael St. John Packe, *Orsini: The Story of a Conspirator* (Boston: Little, Brown and Company, 1957).

19 See T. W. Moody, ed., *The Fenian Movement* (Dublin: Mercier Press, 1978); and R. V. Comerford, *The Fenians in Context: Irish Politics and Society, 1848–82* (Dublin:

Nitroglycerin, pirric acid, and combustible derivatives of petroleum were developed as weapons in the early nineteenth century, but they were only first used by terrorists (the Russian anarchists) in the late nineteenth century.[20] Dynamite was first developed by Alfred Nobel in 1866,[21] but it was only first used by terrorists (the Russia organization *Narodnaya Volya*, or People's Will) in the 1880s.[22] After the use of explosives was perfected by the State during the First and Second World Wars, terrorists adopted them in typical copycat fashion. TNT was first used by terrorists in the years after 1918, and plastic explosives, chiefly Semtex, became a terrorist weapon of choice only after 1945.[23] Now that governments have used weapons of mass destruction during war, most notably when the United States Air Force dropped the atomic bomb on two Japanese cities during the Second World War, there is real concern that terrorists are also trying to acquire chemical, biological, and nuclear devices.[24]

Yet this replication by terrorists of what has first been done by the State tells only part of the story, the part concerned with the use of technology. Terrorist target-selection, in contrast to weaponry, has tended historically to vary greatly from the target-selection of legitimate governments. While in the nineteenth century the State largely conducted its violence on battlefields, with soldiers killing soldiers, terrorists actively sought out for assassination those traditionally considered off-limits, such as police officers, civil servants, and government officials. In the first half of the twentieth century, when guerilla warfare became a more common form of force utilized by the State, terrorists escalated their violence still further, targeting those on the home front who were not actively engaged in combat operations. Finally, in the second half of the twentieth century, terrorists actively and indiscriminately targeted civilians during peacetime in their home environments, such as at shopping

---

Wolfhound Press, 1985).

20 Tillema, "A Brief History of Terrorism and Technology," 23.

21 Tillema, "A Brief History of Terrorism and Technology," 23.

22 Laqueur, *The New Terrorism*, 41.

23 Laqueur, *The New Terrorism*, 42.

24 See Laqueur, *The New Terrorism*; and Nadine Gurr and Benjamin Cole, *The New Face of Terrorism: Threats from Weapons of Mass Destruction* (New York: St. Martin's Press, 2000).

centers and railway stations. Typically, governments have sought to avoid such areas when targeting violence.[25]

The weapons used by terrorists, then, have shown little distinctiveness when compared with the weapons used by the State. Terrorists have tended merely to utilize the weapons popular at the time. Terrorist target-selection, in contrast, has traditionally been exceptional, with terrorists consistently elevating their violence to a level that shocks the societal sensibilities of the day. In certain situations, however, the State has itself mimicked the targets chosen by terrorists. Most are familiar with the civilian deaths that occurred during the targeted bombing raids of the Second World War, where the Allied Forces determined that the intentional killing of civilians was a price worth paying for victory in the larger war.[26] It is not necessary, however, to look only at Dresden and Hiroshima to find occurrences of Western governments killing civilians, accidentally or otherwise. A cursory glance at the newspaper headlines from the 1980s and 1990s shows that there is much that has been done by Western governments that resembles terrorism. This can be separated into two categories, intentional and non-intentional killing. We will turn first to non-intentional killing, more commonly referred to as *collateral damage*.

Collateral damage, or the unintended civilian deaths that occur as a consequence of attacks on more legitimate targets, is a relatively recent phenomenon in war. Of course, in most modern wars, some civilians have lost their lives as a consequence of military action, but in the staged battles of the seventeenth, eighteenth, and nineteenth centuries, such deaths were usually the result of wayward soldiers who were duly punished when caught. Very few civilians were killed by an armament gone awry.[27] Collateral dam-

25   For more on the development of armed conflict, see John Keegan, *The Face of Battle: A Study of Agincourt, Waterloo, and the Somme* (New York: Viking Press, 1976); Richard A. Preston, Sidney Wise, and Alex Roland, *Men in Arms: A History of Warfare and Its Interrelationships with Western Society*, 5th ed. (New York: Holt, Rinehart, and Winston, 1991); Theodore Ropp, *War in the Modern World*, rev. ed. (Baltimore: Johns Hopkins University Press, 2000); and Russell Frank Weigley, *The American Way of War: A History of the United States Military Strategy and Policy* (New York: Macmillan, 1973).

26   For more on this, see Tami Davis Biddle, *Rhetoric and Reality in Air Warfare: The Evolution of British and American Ideas about Strategic Bombing, 1914–1945* (Princeton, NJ: Princeton University Press, 2002).

27   See Geoffrey Best, *Humanity in War* (New York: Columbia University Press, 1980);

age, in the sense of accidental civilian deaths, has grown only with the development of long-range artillery weapons and the use of air power. Only as soldiers have been able to kill without seeing their enemy has it been possible for civilians to be accidentally killed instead of the intended target.[28] An example of such collateral damage occurred in April 1986, when at least five bombs went astray during a U.S. raid on Libya. These missiles hit the French Embassy and several civilian homes, resulting in numerous unintended civilian deaths.[29] Other well-reported instances of collateral damage occurred during the 1999 NATO campaign in the former Yugoslavia. Within a two-week period, twenty-six civilians were killed during bombing raids in the town of Aleksinac, twenty-seven passengers lost their lives when a civilian train was accidentally bombed, and sixty Albanian refugees were mistakenly killed while fleeing the war zone.[30]

The September 11 terrorist attacks and the subsequent war on terrorism have brought renewed attention to the problem of collateral damage. With the commencement of American and British bombing raids on Afghanistan in October 2001, the problem of civilian deaths became a reccurring theme in the media. The first such deaths were reported in the *New York Times* on October 14, exactly a week after the campaign began. A navy jet had

Michael Howard, *Restraints on War: Studies in the Limitation of Armed Conflict* (Oxford: Oxford University Press, 1979); and Quincy Wright, *A Study of War*, Second Edition (Chicago: University of Chicago Press, 1965). Of course, there have been exceptions to this notion of limited civilian deaths before the twentieth century, most notably during the American Civil War. In most of these cases, however, civilian deaths occurred as an intentional part of larger military strategy. They were not, therefore, collateral damage. For an example of this, see Mark Grimsley, *The Hard Hand of War: Union Military Policy toward Southern Civilians, 1861–1865* (Cambridge, MA: Cambridge University Press, 1995).

28   See Biddle, *Rhetoric and Reality in Air Warfare*; R.J. Overy, *The Air War, 1939–1945* (Chelsea, MI: Scarborough House, 1991); Michael S. Sherry, *The Rise of American Air Power: The Creation of Armageddon* (New Haven, CT: Yale University Press, 1987).

29   George C. Wilson, "Stray Bombs Called Unavoidable: U.S. Raid on Libya Was Bound to Miss Some Targets, Experts Say," *Washington Post*, May 11, 1986, A31.

30   Robert Fisk, "War in the Balkans: NATO Stained with Blood of Civilians," *The Independent* (London), April 15, 1999, 2 (News section); Col E. D. Doyle, "Unthinkable Quickly Becomes the Norm: As the War over Kosovo Escalates, the Western Public's Sense of Shock at 'Collateral Damage' has been Replaced by a Dull Acceptance of Inevitable Civilian Casualties," *Irish Times*, April 15, 1999, 16 (News Features).

accidentally dropped a two-thousand-pound bomb on a residential neighborhood in Kabul, killing at least four people and injuring eight others. Earlier in the week, the article reported, a bomb had also killed four civilian employees of a United Nations mine-clearing agency, and it was rumored that a further two hundred civilians had been killed in attacks on Jalalabad.[31] The following day, the *New York Times* reported that a five-year-old boy had been killed in Kandahar when an American missile hit a munitions dump half a mile from his home, sending shell fragments and rocks throughout the surrounding neighborhood.[32] A week later, a thousand-pound bomb missed its intended target (a vehicle storage depot) and instead hit a senior citizen's home three hundred feet away, resulting in at least one hundred civilian deaths, most of whom were residents of the home.[33]

Reports of mistaken bombings continued to haunt the Pentagon at press conferences throughout the remainder of 2001, so much so that in the early days of 2002, U.S. Secretary of Defense Donald Rumsfeld was forced to publicly defend the U.S. campaign, claiming, "I can't imagine there's been a conflict in history in which there has been less collateral damage, less unintended consequences."[34] Considering the relatively recent development of collateral damage, his comments were somewhat disingenuous. Regardless, after only three months of bombing, the civilian toll of Operation Enduring Freedom continued to grow, with estimates of civilian deaths ranging from 1,300 (by the Project on Defense Alternatives, a Cambridge, Massachusetts, think-tank) to over 4,000 (by a University of New Hampshire study). The latter estimate, notably, was higher than the number of people killed during the terrorist attacks of September 11.[35]

31 Eric Schmitt and Michael R. Gordon, "A Nation Challenged: The Fighting; Pentagon Says an Error Led to Bombing of Houses That Killed Four in Kabul," *New York Times*, October 14, 2001, sec. 1B, col. 1, p. 5 (Foreign Desk).

32 Douglas Frantz, "A Nation Challenged: The Child; Father Mourns an Unintended Victim, Age 5," *New York Times*, October 15, 2001, sec. B, col. 4, p. 4 (Foreign Desk).

33 Rupert Cornwell, "Pentagon Admits US Jets Bombed Old People's Home in Afghan City," *The Independent* (London), October 24, 2001, 1.

34 Sudarsan Raghavan and Tom Infield, "U.N. Critical of U.S. Bombing it Claims Killed Dozens of Civilians," *San Diego Union-Tribune*, January 4, 2002, A2.

35 John Donnelly, "Fighting Terror Global Impact/Casualties: US is Probing Cause, Degree of Civilian Toll," *Boston Globe*, January 19, 2002, A12. See also Ian Traynor, "The Unfinished War: Afghans are Still Dying as Air Strikes Go On. But No One is

Although these civilian deaths were all accidental, to the people on the receiving end of the errant missiles and to the families of those killed, the actions of the West could have been seen as no different from the terrorist acts that the bombs were intended to combat.

These unintentional deaths are, nevertheless, quite different from the intentional killing of civilians, which is what traditionally has distinguished terrorism from state violence.[36] Such intentional killing by governments, however, has been on the rise in recent years. In October 1984, for example, the media released a CIA document titled "Psychological Operations in Guerrilla Warfare." This document explicitly instructed Nicaraguan rebels in the use of political assassination, in tactics for killing fleeing civilians and government officials, and in kidnapping techniques that they could use to their advantage.[37]

That same year, White House aide Lt. Col. Oliver North suggested that President Ronald Reagan authorize "neutralizing" suspected terrorists, essentially advocating assassination.[38] In May of 1985 the New York Times linked the CIA to a Lebanese group that exploded a car bomb in a Beirut suburb, killing more than eighty civilians. The bomb was an unsuccessful attempt on the life of Mohammed Hussein Fadlallah, a Shiite leader thought responsible for terrorist attacks against U.S. installations in the Middle East. The CIA had been working with Lebanese counterterrorism

Counting: Bombing Blunders and Misleading Information on the Ground Keep the Civilian Toll Rising in Afghanistan," *The Guardian* (London), February 12, 2002, 4; Indira A.R. Lakshmanan, "Fighting Terror/The Military Campaign Kabul: Afghans Call For Compensation For US Strikes, Seek Audience with Senators But to No Avail," *Boston Globe*, April 2, 2002, A10; and David Wood, "Civilian Casualties Set Back America's War on Terrorism," *San Diego Union-Tribune*, July 5, 2002, B7.

36   For more on this, see Igor Primoratz, "State Terrorism and Counter-terrorism," in Igor Primoratz, ed., *Terrorism: The Philosophical Issues* (New York: Palgrave Macmillan, 2004).

37   John M. Goshko and Margaret Shapiro, "CIA Manual for Guerrillas Denounced by Rep. Boland; Contras Instructed in Assassination," *Washington Post*, A1; Joel Brinkley, "President Orders 2 Investigations on C.I.A. Manual," *New York Times*, October 24, 1984, sec. A, col. 4, p. 1.

38   Dan Morgan and Charles R. Babcock, "North Reprimanded on Idea to 'Neutralize' Terrorists; CIA Official Angered by Choice of Words," *Washington Post*, February 22, 1987, A1.

in combating Fadlallah, and the *New York Times* showed that the techniques taught by the CIA to Lebanese counterterrorism officials had been used by the group directly responsible for the bombing.[39]

The recent war on terrorism has seen a rise in instances of such behavior. For example, the commander of the USS *Enterprise* battle fleet in the Arabian Sea stated during a press conference that the U.S. objective was "to terrorize the terrorists."[40] Although he later claimed that his words had been ill-chosen, the use of the word "terrorize" seemed greatly at odds with the expressed American goal of eliminating terrorism. Just days after September 11, Rumsfeld told the Pentagon press corps that actions would be taken in the war on terrorism to which the press and public would never be privy. This, taken together with the Senate's support for repealing the 1976 ban on foreign assassinations (a ban that was ultimately never repealed), cast an ominous shadow over the war for those concerned about human rights and the correct use of international law.[41] Only weeks later, an unnamed senior Washington official told the *Washington Post* that "the gloves are off" in dealing with Al-Qa'ida and that "lethal operations that were unthinkable pre–September 11 are now underway."[42]

CIA covert teams were also deployed shortly after the September 11 terrorist attacks, and some of their tactics were uncomfortably close to what the Western world would consider terrorism. In late October 2001, the CIA claimed the administration had ruled that the 1976 ban on assassinations did not prevent an American president from ordering the deaths of specific terrorists by covert action.[43] The first public example of this tac-

---

39   Stuart Taylor Jr., "Lebanese Group Linked to C.I.A. is Tied to Car Bombing Fatal to 80," *New York Times*, May 13, 1985, col. 3, p. A1. See also Mark Tran, "Reagan 'issued license to kill,'" *The Guardian* (London), October 6 1988 (Washington section).

40   Geoff Cumming, "Air Strikes Aim to 'Terrorize the Terrorists," *The New Zealand Herald*, October 10, 2001 (World News section).

41   Peter Beaumont, "Military Options: The Dirty War: CIA Gets Go-ahead for a Return to Murderous Cold War Tactics," *The Observer* (London), September 23, 2001, 8 (special supplement).

42   Rupert Cornwell, "Dark Deeds Herald a New Kind of Ground War," *The Independent* (London), October 22, 2001, 3.

43   Barton Gellman, "CIA Weighs 'Targeted Killing' Missions; Administration Believes Restraints Do Not Bar Singling Out Individual Terrorists," *Washington Post*, October 28, 2001, A01.

tic was evident a year later, in November 2002, when an unmanned CIA Predator drone targeted the car of a suspected Al-Qa'ida terrorist with a missile while he was traveling in Yemen, killing its target and five others. The U.S. government acknowledged that they were responsible for this assassination.[44]

In the war on terrorism alone, then, Western governments have employed targeted bombing, the use of assassination, and, unintentionally, the killing of civilians through collateral damage. When looking only at the tactic of terrorism—at the specific acts of violence perpetrated, regardless of the motivations or ideology behind those acts—it seems that such violence (or, at least, violence that is very similar) has been used not only by terrorists but also by governments. With the exception of collateral damage, of course, those killed by the West differ from those killed by the terrorist in that they have been shown to be, however inadequately, guilty in some way of a crime or wrongdoing. They are generally not the unaware civilian on the train or in the marketplace. The killing is thus not indiscriminate. Nevertheless, the appearance of terrorism is created by such attacks and can be manipulated for greater effect than if no attack had taken place. In the case of collateral damage, although the intent behind the violence is quite different from the terrorist (civilians are not deliberately targeted in collateral damage), to the families of those who perish, there seems little to separate collateral damage from terrorism. The end result is the same. Consequently, as the twenty-first century progresses, violence that is terrorist and violence that is not terrorist, from a tactical point of view, looks increasingly similar. While historically there has been a gulf between these two forms of violence, in recent years this gulf has been narrowing.[45]

This reduced distinction is troubling and raises some difficult questions. If the tactics used by all parties can be described as terrorist, how can any particular moral abhorrence be attached to those whose violence is

---

44   Adrian Hamilton, "Campaign Against Terror: It is Wrong to be Judge, Jury, and Executioner," *The Independent* (London), November 6, 2002, 2; Caroline Daniel, "Murky Tactics Surface in War on Terror: Attack on al-Qaeda Suspects Raises Question of Whether US Has Revived the Banned Use of Assassination," *The Financial Times* (London), November 22, 2002, 9.

45   For more on the narrowing gap between conventional war and terrorism, see the recent *Human Security Report 2005: War and Peace in the 21st Century*, University of British Columbia, 2005.

specifically called terrorist (as opposed to governmental violence which resembles terrorism)? Could not some terrorist actions rightly be described as useful, and even moral, while others not, just as some acts of war are good and others bad? If terrorist tactics resemble tactics used as much by Western governments as by those designated terrorist, how can a war on terrorism be seen as anything but hypocritical? After all, if followed through to its logical conclusion, a true war against the tactic of terrorism (putting aside terrorist ideology, for the time being) would need to bring action against elements within the Western power structure itself. When looking at the tactic of terrorism alone, then, there can be only two conclusions: either legitimate governments are becoming more terrorist in their tactics, or terrorism cannot be defined solely in tactical terms. We must ask, therefore, what, if anything, makes terrorism more than a mere tactic? What is ideologically unique about that group of individuals who are collectively called terrorists? And what fundamentally sets these terrorists apart from those who are called soldiers?

A little-known German journalist, Karl Heinzen, was the first to articulate a specifically terrorist ideology. In his essay "Murder" (published in 1849), and its later version "Murder and Liberty" (published in 1853), Heinzen works from a single, central premise: that murder has been "the principal agent of historical progress."[46] He sees all intentional killing as murder, no matter the method used, and considers governments the chief executers of this murder.[47] For him, all violence that ends in death

46   Karl Heinzen, *Murder*, in Walter Laqueur, ed., *Voices of Terror* (New York: Reed Press, 2004), 57. For a more detailed analysis of Karl Heinzen, and for excerpts from his *Murder and Liberty*, see Benjamin Grob-Fitzgibbon, "From the Dagger to the Bomb: Karl Heinzen and the Evolution of Political Terror," *Terrorism and Political Violence* 16, no. 1 (Spring 2004).

47   Heinzen writes: "A wide variety of names have been coined for the art of obliterating one's enemy. In one country they have him put to death 'legally' by an executioner and call it the death penalty. In another, they lie in wait with stiletto blades behind hedges and call it assassination. In another they organize obliteration on a grand scale and call it war. Examined in the clear light of day, these various appellations appear for what they are, entirely superfluous, being all expressions of what is fundamentally one and the same thing, and whether I am executed or assassinated or torn to pieces, the end effect is the same. I am dispatched to the other world and this dispatching to the other world was the purpose of my enemy" (Heinzen, *Murder*, 57).

is morally equivalent—all murder.[48] This being the case, he argues that revolutionaries (he does not call them terrorists) should also adopt the tactics of murder, just as governments have done. The revolutionaries, however, should not murder as governments have (primarily through war). Rather, they should be more creative with their killing and should devote themselves "to the study of murder and refine the art of killing to the highest possible degree."[49] As all methods of murder are equally valid, and all are morally equivalent, the desired ends are the sole consideration when killing, and these ends will always justify the means. All limitations should, therefore, be removed from violence: "The revolutionaries must try to bring about a situation where the barbarians [government] are afraid for their lives every hour of the day or night . . . For them, as for us, may fear be the herald and murder the executor."[50] If this unlimited violence achieves its desired ends, it will be moral, no matter the means used.[51]

Heinzen was writing in the immediate aftermath of the failed 1848 European Revolutions, and he was thus well aware of the consequences of waging traditional warfare. He dismissed any notion of restricted violence

48   Interestingly, Heinzen does not see murder, in its original form, as morally justi-fied. He writes that "any voluntary killing of another human being is a crime against humanity," "no one under any pretext whatsoever has the right to destroy another's life," and "anyone who does kill another or has him killed is quite simply a murderer." However, Heinzen also believes that the revolutionary is "able to achieve previous little with our humanity and our ideas of justice." Therefore, he argues, "Let us, then, be practical. Let us call ourselves murderers as our enemies do, let us take the moral horror out of this great historical tool . . . If to kill is always a crime, then it is forbid-den equally to all; if it is not a crime, then it is permitted equally to all." See Heinzen, *Murder*, 58.

49   Heinzen, *Murder*, 67.

50   Heinzen, *Murder*, 67. Heinzen specifically recommends, for this terrorism, the derailing of trains "by a thimbleful of fulminating silver placed under the rails," bombs "placed beneath paving stones," "containers filled with poison, which burst in the air," and "underground rooms full of fulminating silver [that] can blow whole towns into the air, complete with their one hundred thousand murderous slaves."

51   Heinzen writes: "To have a conscience with regard to the murdering of reactionar-ies is to be totally unprincipled . . . Even if we have to blow up half a continent or spill a sea of blood, in order to finish off the barbarian party, we should have no scruples about doing it" (Heinzen, *Murder*, 62).

because he had seen it to be ineffective against the powerful nation-states of Europe. He was not himself, however, a terrorist, nor did he ever plan or carry out any of the violent atrocities he so enthusiastically advocated. His successor in terrorist ideology, Sergey Nechaev, was quite different, himself a member of a terrorist circle and a proved killer.[52] In 1869, twenty years after Heinzen's "Murder," Nechaev published his *Catechism of the Revolutionist* (like Heinzen, he did not use the term *terrorist*). In this piece, Nechaev intimately explores the psychology of the terrorist, writing that, "Everything in him is absorbed by a single exclusive interest, a single thought, a single passion—the revolution."[53]

Like Heinzen, Nechaev considers that the achieved end, rather than the means to achieve those ends, should be the sole consideration when using violence. Thus, he argues that "everything is moral which assists the triumph of revolution. Immoral and criminal is everything which stands in its way."[54] In picking the targets of terrorism, Nechaev states that "the guiding principal must be the measure of service the person's death will necessarily render to the revolutionary cause . . . [A]ll those must be annihilated who are especially harmful to the revolutionary organization, and whose sudden and violent deaths will also inspire the greatest fear in the government."[55] For Nechaev, a terrorist act is justified, and the deaths it causes moral, if that terrorism services the final goal towards which the terrorist is moving. Both Heinzen and Nechaev see fear as the chief means of achieving their ends, and the greatest fear, in their opinion, is induced by violent death.

Following Nechaev, the next significant terrorist philosophers were both members of the Russian terrorist organization People's Will, whose main purpose was to assassinate the tsar, a task it eventually accomplished in 1881.[56] A year prior to this assassination, Nikolai Morozov and G. Tarnovski

----

52   For more on Nechaev's life, see Phillip Pomper, *Sergei Nechaev* (New Brunswick, NJ: Rutgers University Press, 1979).

53   "Catechism of the Revolutionist" in Laqueur, *Voices of Terror*, 71.

54   "Catechism of the Revolutionist," 71.

55   "Catechism of the Revolutionist," 74.

56   For a complete background on Russian terrorism, see Deborah Hardy, *Land and Freedom: The Origins of Russian Terrorism, 1876–1879* (New York: Greenwood Press, 1987). For more on the assassination of the tsar, see David Footman, *The Alexander Conspiracy: A Life of A. I. Zhelyabov* (LaSalle, IL: Library Press, 1944, 1968).

each published a pamphlet assessing Russian terrorism. Significantly, in contrast to Heinzen and Nechaev, both Morozov and Tarnovski used the term "terrorist" in their articles, a title they accepted for themselves with no guilt or shame and, indeed, preferred to the softer "revolutionary."

Morozov explains in his piece that the chief advantage the terrorist organization has over a larger revolutionary army is that it is a smaller and more secretive group, and thus cannot be easily combated.[57] This is for the terrorist organization a distinct advantage: "it can act unexpectedly and find means and ways which no one anticipates. All that the terroristic struggle really needs is a small number of people and large material means."[58] The key weapon of the terrorist, according to Morozov, is political assassinations, which "always hit their target" and are thus a more moral tactic than the massive revolutionary armies.[59] Finally, Morozov argues that terrorism must become more than a mere tactic, but an actual creed: "Success of the terroristic movement will be inevitable if the future terroristic struggle becomes a deed of not only one separate group, but of an idea, which cannot be destroyed by people. Then in place of those fighters who will perish, new ones and new revolutionaries will appear until the goal of the movement is achieved."[60] For Morozov, what chiefly distinguishes terrorism from other forms of violence is a belief system, based on clandestine action and assassination, which transcends any in-

57 Morozov writes that the terrorist group is "not afraid of bayonets and the government's army because it does not have to clash, in its struggle, with this blind and insensible force, which strikes down those whom it is ordered to strike. This force is only dreadful to the obvious enemy. Against the secret one it is completely useless" (Morozov, "The Terrorist Struggle," in Laqueur, *Voices of Terror*, 76–77).

58 Morozov, "The Terrorist Struggle," 77.

59 He argues, "The [terrorist] movement punishes only those who are really responsible for the evil deed. Because of this the terroristic revolution is the only just form of a revolution" (Morozov, "The Terrorist Struggle," 77).

60 Morozov, "The Terrorist Struggle," 79. Morozov also writes: "When a small handful of people appears to represent the struggle of a whole nation and is triumphant over millions of enemies, then the idea of terroristic struggle will not die once it is clarified for the people and proven that it can be practical . . . [T]he ideas of the revolutionaries will live in the memories of the masses, and every manifestation of violence (on the part of the government) will bring forth new terroristic groups. (Morozov, "The Terrorist Struggle," 81.

dividual person or group. Terrorism can thus be recycled time and time again as the need arises. Furthermore, consistent with both Heinzen and Nechaev, Morozov sees the ends as justifying the means. Political assassination by a small group is more effective than large revolutionary wars, and thus its use becomes inherently moral as a system of bringing about a desired end.

Tarnovski takes this theme one step further, explicitly examining terrorist morality. He argues that terrorists "have the right to ignore public conscience."[61] The reason for this, he claims, is that anyone engaged in revolution "must be able to renounce conventional morality and raise himself to the natural laws of justice and morality. And from this point of view of the highest justice, all revolution as a means of liberating the people is moral—already moral—because it gives the people the possibility of living a moral way of life." Since, according to Tarnovski, a free society is the only one in which personal morality can be properly practiced, any means used to attain that free society are not only legitimate but inherently moral also: "[I]n the social sense only that is moral which furthers society's freedom, development, and material benefit. Everything hostile to this is immoral and destined to destruction."[62] For Tarnovski, anything not directly aiding the terrorists in accomplishing their goals can be seen as thwarting those goals, and is therefore a legitimate target for annihilation.

Despite this extremism, however, with the exception of Heinzen and Nechaev, these early terrorist theorists did not directly advocate the murder of civilians (although they would certainly have seen this as a legitimate tactic if it furthered the implementation of their end goals). They were primarily concerned with halting the operation of governments, and thus above all else advocated the killing of those people associated with governments. This terrorist inattention to civilian destruction did not last long, though. Johann Most, an exiled German anarchist who lived in the United States, began advocating the killing of civilians in his radical newspaper *Freiheit* (Freedom) in the 1870s. In 1884 (just four years after Morozov and Tarnovski published their treatises), he serialized his book *The Science of Revolutionary Warfare* (also called *Military Science for Revolutionaries*), in which he provides for his followers precise details of how to carry out terrorist attacks, including his own invention, the letter

---

61 Tarnovski, "Terrorism and Routine," in Laqueur, *Voices of Terror*, 84.

62 Tarnovski, "Terrorism and Routine," 85.

bomb.[63] In particular, Most describes scenarios in which not only government officials would be killed but also any civilian in larger society who was deemed to be against the revolution.[64] In an interesting addendum to this saga, on September 7, 1901, the day American President McKinley was assassinated, Most re-printed Heinzen's "Murder," demonstrating a direct link in terrorist ideology from 1848 to 1901.[65]

In the twentieth century, the pace of terrorist actions increased substantially, yet ideological statements of this terrorism diminished, with terrorists less eager to admit to the uniqueness of their violence and more keen to show that their action was no different than the use of traditional military force. The first terrorists to make this transition to "military" ideology were the Irish republicans, who sought Irish independence from Great Britain. Irish republicans had been actively using terrorism against the British state since the 1850s. In 1858, the Irish Republican Brotherhood was formed, a group committed to using violence to overthrow the British in Ireland.[66] Until the twentieth century, however, the IRB had never fashioned itself as an army. Nevertheless, there were instances in its history when its ideologues spoke in greatly contrasting terms to the Russian terrorist theorists. For example, one of its most prominent leaders, O'Donovan Rossa, advocated in 1880 the destruction of English towns and cities by dynamite. When asked of the loss of life this would cause, he stated: "Yes, it is war, and in all wars life must be lost; but in my opinion the loss of life under such circumstances would not be one tenth that recorded in the least of the smallest battles between the South [of Ireland] and the North."[67] In 1919, the IRB changed its

---

63 Frederic Trautmann, *The Voice of Terror: A Biography of Johann Most* (Westport, CT.: Greenwood Press, 1980), 100.

64 For example, Most writes: "Just imagine this bomb had been planted under the table at a high society banquet, or had been thrown through a window onto their table—it would have achieved wonderful results!" (*The Science of Revolutionary Warfare* [El Dorado, AR: Desert Publications, 1978], 14.)

65 *Freiheit*, September 7, 1901.

66 See Charles Townshend, *Political Violence in Ireland: Government and Resistance since 1848* (Oxford: The Clarendon Press, 1983); and Leon Ó Broin, *Revolutionary Underground: The Story of the Irish Republican Brotherhood, 1858–1924* (Totowa, NJ: Rowman and Littlefield, 1976).

67 O'Donovan Rossa, quoted in *Irish World*, August 28, 1880, in Laqueur, *Voices of*

name to reflect this notion of war. It became the Irish Republican Army, claiming to be no longer just a secret brotherhood but the legitimate army of the declared Irish Republic (a Republic that did not, however, yet exist).

The Irish Republican Army, in its various guises, was the most deadly terrorist organization of the twentieth century. In the years 1966 to 2001, the Provisional Irish Republican Army killed 1,778 people, the Official Irish Republican Army 54, and the Real Irish Republican Army 150. The Irish National Liberation Army, an off-shoot of the Provisionals, also killed 150, making the Irish Republican Army and its splinter groups responsible for 2,132 deaths.[68] Many other terrorist groups who operated in the twentieth century also designated themselves armies. These have included, in alphabetical order, the Armenian Revolutionary Army, the Armenian Secret Army for the Liberation of Armenia, the Black Liberation Army, *Ejército Popular de Liberación* (the Popular Liberation Army), *Ejército Revolucionario de Pueblo* (the People's Revolutionary Army), *Ejército Rojo Catalán de Liberación* (the Red Army for the Liberation of Catalonia), *Ejército Secreto Anticommunista* (the Anti-Communist Secret Army), *Fuerzas Armadas de Liberación* (the Armed Forces of Liberation), *Fuerzas Armadas de Liberación Nacional* (the Armed Forces of National Liberation), *Fuerzas Armadas Rebeldes* (the Rebel Armed Forces), *Fuerzas Armadas Revolucionarias* (the Revolutionary Armed Forces), *Fuerzas Armadas Revolucionarias de Colombia* (the Revolutionary Armed Forces of Columbia), the Japanese Red Army, the New People's Army, *Organisation de l'Armée Secrète* (the Secret Army Organization), the Palestine Liberation Army, the Red Army Faction, the Symbionese Liberation Army, the Turkish People's Liberation Army, and the White Patriot Army.[69] This list does not include those who have called themselves Commandos, Brigades, or Fighters.

Terror, 117.

68   David McKittrick, Seamus Kelters, Brian Feeney, and Chris Thornton, *Lost Lives: The Story of the Men, Women and Children who Died as a Result of the Northern Ireland Troubles* (Edinburgh: Mainstream Publishing Company, 1999, 2001), 1495. Before 1970, there was only one Irish Republican Army. In 1969, however, it split into two groups, the Official Irish Republican Army and the Provisional Irish Republican Army. The Real Irish Republican Army and the Irish National Liberation Army were both splinter groups of the Provisional Irish Republican Army.

69   For a brief description of each of these groups, see Sean Anderson and Stephen Sloan, *Historical Dictionary of Terrorism* (Metuchen, NJ: The Scarecrow Press, Inc., 1995).

This trend of terrorists defining themselves in military terms, with their atrocities referred to as acts of war, has continued into the twenty-first century. The group responsible for the attacks of September 11—Al-Qa'ida—is no exception. In 1996, Osama bin Laden issued his declaration of *jihad* against the United States, saying, "Our Muslim brothers throughout the world . . . Your brothers in the country of the two sacred places [Saudi Arabia] and in Palestine request your support. They are asking you to participate with them against their enemies, who are also your enemies—the Israelis and the Americans—by causing them as much harm as can be possibly achieved."[70] Despite this continuity, in many respects bin Laden and his Al-Qa'ida organization have also returned to the nineteenth-century terrorist theorists for their justifications. In a 2002 audio communiqué, bin Laden explains his rationale for terror attacks using logic eerily reminiscent of Karl Heinzen. He first pays homage to peace and justice, calling for the "removal of aggression" and pleading his innocence.[71] Yet, just like Heinzen, he claims that, regrettably, as Western governments have used violence for their aims, so too must the Islamic World: "how long should the killing, destruction, expulsion, and orphaning and widowing continue to be an exclusive occurrence upon us while peace, security and happiness remains your exclusive monopoly?"[72] He concludes that such inequality is "an unfair predicament." Thus, although he claims to seek peace, he believes it has become "high time we were equal in terms of commodities. So as you kill, you shall be killed, and as you bomb, you shall be bombed, and wait for what brings calamity."[73] To borrow some of Heinzen's language, just as the West has murdered, so must the East.

The ideology of terrorism, throughout history, has shown certain consistent characteristics, regardless of its inevitable evolution of rhetoric over the years. The first is the creation of fear. From Heinzen to bin Laden, Morozov to Most, each terrorist theorist has emphasized the production of fear as an essential characteristic of terrorism. The second is the notion that the ends justify the means. If an end goal is considered moral and

70 Quoted in Peter L. Bergen, *Holy War, Inc.: Inside the Secret World of Osama bin Laden* (New York: Touchstone Books, 2001, 2002), 97.

71 Osama bin Ladin, Audio Communiqué broadcast by Al Jazeera, November 12, 2002, in Rohan Gunaratna, *Inside Al Qaeda: Global Network of Terror* (New York: Berkley Books, 2002), xlvii.

72 Audio Communiqué, xlviii.

73 Audio Communiqué, xlix.

righteous, then any means that bring about that end are inherently moral. Finally, there is the lack of restraint when killing civilians. The morality of an ends-only ethic must, by its very nature, include within it a morality of killing civilians. This becomes particularly useful for the terrorist when it has the added effect of producing more fear, thus strengthening the first characteristic of terrorism.

Looking both tactically and ideologically, then, terrorism is a unique form of violence. In its direct and systematic targeting of civilians, its endeavors to inculcate fear, and its philosophy of ends-only morality, terrorism diverges from the violence generally used by the State. Despite this, however, particularly in terms of its tactics, the fragile line between terrorism and non-terrorism grew thinner throughout the twentieth century as newer and deadlier forms of warfare were developed and societal restraints were lessened. While historically terrorism has been an exceptional form of violence, and the terrorists who employed it have held an equally exceptional ideology, in recent years this distinction has become less clear. Targeted bombing, assassination, and the increasing acceptance of collateral damage are examples of relatively recent tactics employed by the State in pursuit of a certain objective.

The ideology of some in the West has also taken a disquieting turn. For example, on February 5, 2002, at a desolate site in Afghanistan forty miles from the Pakistani border, twenty-five men gathered together, representing American Special Forces and the CIA. There they constructed a makeshift tombstone, covering a piece of the destroyed World Trade Center. When they had finished making this tombstone, they said a prayer for those who had died on September 11. Their final words, however, were not *Amen*, but rather, "We will export death and violence to the four corners of the earth in defense of our great nation."[74] Their ends had come to justify their means, and the psychology of terror had triumphed.

There are few today who would doubt the truly horrifying nature of terrorism. It is necessary only to see again the shocking images of the collapsing World Trade Center to realize the gravity of the threat and the necessity for combating it. Despite this, however, what is perhaps just as disconcerting is the recent trend of Western democracies to forego their prior standards of civility and the rule of law in favor of a practice of fighting proverbial fire with fire, no matter the damage this may cause to

----

74 Quoted in Bob Woodward, *Bush At War* (New York: Simon & Schuster, 2002), 351–352.

the larger infrastructure of Western civilization. Indeed, in the *Amnesty International Report 2005*, Amnesty International noted that during 2004, "the 'war on terror' appeared more effective in eroding international human rights principles than in countering international 'terrorism.'"[75] The Secretary General, Irene Khan, warned that this erosion was the direct result of Western inconsistency regarding terrorism: "The USA, as the unrivalled political, military and economic hyper-power, sets the tone for governmental behavior worldwide. When the most powerful country in the world thumbs its nose at the rule of law and human rights, it grants a license to others to commit abuse with impunity and audacity."[76]

This narrowing of the line between the actions of terrorists and non-terrorists should raise alarm to Western governments and their peoples, just as the sickening prospect of more terrorist atrocities itself will. After all, if the very basis of Western culture and society becomes compromised by the security measures erected to protect it, the terrorists will have achieved success in their aims of destroying the Western way of life. Terrorist attacks are inexcusable, and must be condemned in every instance. But in fighting the terrorists, the State must not fall into the trap of adopting an ends-only morality, for it is this lack of restraint and disregard for innocent human life that makes terrorism the unique and contemptible form of violence that it is.

---

75 "Introduction," *Amnesty International Report 2005: The State of the World's Human Rights*, http://web.amnesty.org/report2005.

76 Irene Khan, Secretary General, Amnesty International, "Foreword," *Amnesty International Report 2005*. Kenneth Roth, the Executive Director of Human Rights Watch, made a similar argument in the January/February 2004 edition of *Foreign Affairs* when he wrote, "The Bush administration has used war rhetoric precisely to give itself the extraordinary powers enjoyed by a wartime government to detain or even kill suspects without trial. In the process, the administration may have made it easier for itself to detain or eliminate suspects. But it has also threatened the most basic due process rights . . . In attempting to make America safer, it has made all Americans, and everyone else, less free" (*Foreign Affairs*, January/February 2004, online edition, www.foreignaffairs.org).

INDEX

Adams, John
  French Revolution, 7
Adegbite, Lateef, 192
Afghanistan, 194, 211, 224
Ahmad, Ibrahim Datti, 200
Akaluka, Gideon, 195
Alexander II, Tsar, 156
  assassination of, 168, 177
  emancipation of serfs, 158
Alien and Sedition Acts, 5, 8
Al-Qa'ida, 205–06, 214, 223. See Osama
  bin Laden
American Revolution, 208
Amnesty International, 224
Annan, Kofi, xiv
anti-communism, 77
anti-communist, 18, 101
Appalachia, 23, 32
Argentina, 61
Associated Press, 81, 188
Aziz, Tariq, 113

Baader, Andreas, 138–39
Baader-Ensslin Gang, 141
Baader-Meinhof Gang, 134, 141
Baker, James A., 112, 114–17
Baldwin-Felts detectives, 32, 36
Balkans, 119
Ball, George, 101
Bana, Simon, 199
Bandholz, H.H., 35
Battle of Blair Mountain, 20–21
Bay of Pigs, 79
Biddle, Francis, 15
Biden, Joseph, 122
Bill of Rights, 4, 6, 9
Bismarck, Otto von, 49–52
Black Repartition, the, 173, 178
Blizzard, Bill, 22, 36
  as president of District No. 2, 37
  charged with murder, 39
  death of, 42
Bolivia, 93, 103
Bolshevik Revolution, 12–13

Bolshevism, 32
Bonaparte, Napoleon, 157
Bosnia, 116–17, 119, 125, 127
Bowles, Chester, 84
Brazil, 61, 93
Britain, 158
Bryan, William Jennings, 53, 62, 65
Buchanan, Patrick, 122
Bundy, McGeorge, 77, 85, 87–88
Bureau of Negro Welfare and Statistics, 38
Burma, 102
Bush, George H. W., 107–08, 113, 119–20,
  122
  diplomatic legacy of, 126–7
  Somalia, 124
  Wilsonianism, 109, 129
Bush, George W., 43, 203
  homeland security, x

Cambodia, 102
Cameroon, 102
Cardinal Richelieu, 6
Carothers, George C., 62
Carranza, Venustiano, 45, 47, 61, 65–67, 69
Carter, Jimmy, 95
Castro, Fidel, 78
Chambers, Ed
  death of, 36
Chertoff, Michael, xi
Chief Justice Fuller in *Turner v. Williams*,
  10 n25
Chile, 61, 93
China, 77
CIA, 19, 88–90, 100, 108, 206, 213–4, 224
civil liberties, 6, 9
Civil War, American, 9–10
Clark, Tom, 18
Clausewitz, Carl von, 48, 51
  writings of, 50
Clinton, William Jefferson, 119, 125
Cold War, 17, 77, 105, 107, 111–2, 115, 120
Colombia, 102–03
Communist Party, 13, 18
  and Bolshevism, 12

communist/-ism, 13, 17, 75, 79, 104
Constitution, United States, xv
Constitution, German, 50
counterterrorism, xiii, 205
Crimean War, 158
Croatia, 116
Cuba, 74–75, 77, 98, 104–05

Daniel, Isioma, 181
Debs, Eugene V., 5, 21, 26
    conviction of, 4
    presidential candidate, 3
    prosecution of, 11
democracy, x, xv
Democratic Party, 8, 77
Der Spiegel, 143
Dixit, J.N., 122
Dresden, 210
Dwyer, Lawrence, 35–36

eastern Europe, 110
Ecuador, 93, 102–03
Eisenhower, Dwight D., 76, 86–87, 95
Ensslin, Gudrun, 138, 140, 142–45
Espionage and Sedition Acts, 11–12
European Community (EC), 117
Executive Order 13228, x

Fadlallah, Mohammed Hussein, 213
FBI, 18–19, 206
Federalists, 7
    Alien and Sedition Acts, 7
Felski, Rita, 151, 154
feminism, 154
feminist movement, United States, 150
Figner, Evgeniia, 163–65
Figner, Vera, 159, 163, 166
    arrest and prison sentence, 168
    education of, 160
    flight from Saratov, 166
    life in Zurich, 161
    medical work in Saratov, 164
    opposition to, 165
    participation in the Land and
        Freedom group, 162
    regarding government violence, 167
    sister Lydia, 167
Filipov, Aleksey, 160
First Amendment, 8
Fletcher, Frank, 58

Fodio, Usman dan, 183
Foreign Assistance Act of 1961, 96
France, 158
Franco-Prussian War, 51
Freeman, Orville, 90
French Reign of Terror, 207
French Revolution, 7
Funston, Frederick, 59–60, 68–69, 72

Ganor, Boaz, xiii
Garrison, Lindley M., 53, 59
German-Americans, 11
Germany, 92, 111, 121, 135
Gilpatric, Roswell, 87, 89
Gitlow, Benjamin, 13
Goldberg, Arthur, 90
Goldman, Emma, 10
Gompers, Samuel, 21
Great Depression, 26
Green Berets, 92
Guantánamo, 5, 19
Guatemala, 93, 100, 102–03
Gulf War, 114–15, 119, 128–29

habeas corpus, 9
Hamilton, Alexander, 7
Hamilton, Fowler, 88
Hatfield, Henry, 29
Hatfield, Sid, 32
    death of, 36
Hatfield-McCoy feud, 29, 33
Haymarket Square, 10
Heinzen, Karl, 216–17, 223
Hiroshima, 209–10
Holmes, Oliver Wendell
    conviction of Eugene V. Debs, 4
homeland security, x
    Department of Homeland Security, xi
Honduras, 93, 103
Hoover, J. Edgar, 18
Houston, David F.
    opinion of Woodrow Wilson, 54
Houston, Harold, 26
    and 1919 march, 35
    as attorney of District 17, 31
    as union attorney, mine wars, 36
    retirement, 41
Huerta, Victoriano, 46, 54–55, 61
    USS *Dolphin* incident, 56
Hurricane Katrina, xi

Hussein, Saddam, 111–12, 114, 205
  Gulf War, 113, 115

India, 121
Indonesia, 105
Industrial Revolution
  in Europe, 158
Industrial Workers of the World, 11
  members detained, 12
Inter-American Army Conference of
  1961, 83
Iran, 102
Iran-Iraq war, 111
Iraq, 111, 113, 115, 205
Irish Republican Army, 207, 222

Jackson, Robert
  on civil liberties, 6
Jama'atu Nasril Islam, 193
Jangebe, Buba Bello, 200
Japan, 121
Japanese Americans
  and internment, 14
  and relocation, 16
  Korematsu decision, 17
  relocation of, 15
JCS Memorandum 30-62, 86
JCSM 832-61, 85
Jefferson, Thomas
  election of, 8
Johnson, U. Alexis, 88, 100

Keeney, Frank, 22, 24, 26, 29, 36, 38
  1919 march to Logan County, 34
  and "Devil Anse" Hatfield, 33
  and Kanawha County miners, 41
  and Mother Jones, 25
  and socialist movement, 31
  and the West Va. Mine Workers, 26
  charged with murder. See also
    Mooney, Fred
  death of, 42
  Scots-Irish heritage, 32
Kennedy, John F., 86, 99, 101, 105
  administration of, 74, 94
  and flexible response, 104
  and Latin-American relations, 84
  and Robert McNamara, 85
  and Special Group (CI), 89
  and training of Latin-American

  military, 84
  and U.S. Special Forces, 76
  foreign policy, 77
  inaugural address, 75
  response to communism, 98
Kennedy, Robert, 88
Khan, Irene, 224–25
Khrushchev, Nikita, 75
King Philip's War, 4
Korea, 121
Kovalskaia, Elizaveta, 168, 172–73
  arrest of, 174
  education of, 169
  humanitarian work, 170
Kuwait, 111–5, 121

Laden, Osama bin, 43, 207, 222
Land and Freedom Party, 162, 167
Lansdale, Edward, 80
Lansing, Robert, 65, 67, 69
Laos, 101–02, 105
Latin America, 74–79, 81, 83–85, 93–98,
  101, 103–05
Lawal, Amina, 192
Lebanon, 118, 127
Lejeune, John A., 58
Lemnitzer, L.L., 86, 88
Lewis, John L., 21, 38–39
Libya, 211
Lincoln, Abraham, 9
Lippmann, Walter, 14
Liubatovich, Olga, 177

Maas, Gustavo, 57
Macedonia, 116
Madero, Francisco I., 46
Magaji, Umar Dangaladima, 193
Marwa, Mohammadu, 185
Marxism, 158
Masoaka, Mike, 16
Massachusetts Bay colony, 4
Mayo, Henry T., 55
McCarthyism, 5, 19
McCloy, John, 17
McCone, John, 88
McKinley, William
  assassination of, 221
McNamara, Robert, 78, 85, 90
Meinhof, Ulrike, 139–40, 142
Middle East, 112

Mohammed, Labaran, 200
Moller, Irmgard, 136
Moltke, Helmuth von, 51–52
Montenegro, 116
Mooney, Fred, 22, 25–26, 29, 36
    and socialist movement, 31
    changed with murder, 39
    death of, 41
    Scots-Irish heritage, 32
Morozov, Nikolai, 218–19
Morse, Wayne, 94, 97
Most, Johann, 220
Mother Jones, 24–25, 36, 38
Movement Second June, 152
Muslims, 19
    Conflict in Iraq, 114
    in Bosnia, 118
    in Nigeria, 180
    post September 11, 5
    protest Miss World Beauty Pageant,
    181
Mutual Security Act of 1961, 96

National Guard, xiii
National Industrial Recovery Act, 21
national security, ix, x, xvi, 5, 10, 18–19,
    78, 109
Navy SEALs, 91
Nechaev, Sergei (Sergey), 175, 217–18
Netherlands, 102
New World Order, 107–08, 111–12, 121,
    124–27
    Gulf War, 114
    Legacy, 128
    Somalia, 120, 123
    Yugoslavia, 119
New York Times, 18, 20, 120–21, 212, 214
Nigeria, 179, 194, 196–97
Nigeria-Biafra war, 184-85
Nnaj, Reverend Chijioke, 199
Nobel, Alfred, 208–09
Noriega, Manuel, 83, 110
North Atlantic Treaty Organization
    (NATO), 111
North Korea, 121
North, Oliver, 212–13
NSAM 118, 85
NSAM 131, 88
NSAM 180, 99
NSAM 182, 99–100, 102

NSAM 182 US Overseas Internal Defense
    Policy, 98

Obasanjo, Olusegun, 183, 189
    on sharia, 190
Operation Restore Hope, 125
Operation Enduring Freedom, 205,
    211–212
Operation Iraqi Freedom, 205
Operation Just Cause, 110
Orsini, Felice, 208

Palestine, 223
Palmer, A. Mitchell, 12–13
Panama, 110
Panama Canal, 74
Paraguay, 93
Patriot Act, xv
Pearl Harbor, 14, 16, 19
People's Will, 167, 173, 209, 218
Perovskaia, Sophia, 177
Pershing, John J., 54, 69, 71–73
    military success of, 71
    U.S. Punitive Expedition in Mexico,
    44
Persian Gulf, 111–12
Peru, 93
Philippines, 121
Poos, Jacques, 117
Posse Comitatus Act, xii
Powell, Colin, 110, 118, 125
propaganda, 11, 162, 167, 172
    Soviet, 18

radicalism, 21, 42
    and gender, 138
Realpolitik, 49
Red Army Faction (RAF), 134, 136, 138–
    39, 145, 150–52
Red Scare, 5, 12, 20
rednecks, 20, 40–41
    origin of term, 32
Republican Party, 8
Rice, Condoleezza, 205
Roosevelt, Franklin Delano, 15, 17
    and Japanese internment, 16
Rossa, O'Donovan
    and Irish Republican Army, 221
Rostow, Walt W., 76, 81
Rumsfeld, Donald, 212

Rusk, Dean, 97
Russia, 54, 157, 159, 162, 172
    and terrorism, 156
    military, 158

Sanford, Edward T., 13
Sani, Ahmed, 194, 198
Santa Ysabel massacre, 67
Saudi Arabia, 121, 194, 223
Schelm, Petra, 145
Schenck, Charles, 4
Schiller, Margrit, 135–36, 147–50, 153
Schmidt, Alex P.
    definitions of terrorism, xiii, 204
Schroeder, Edgar, 83
Scott, Hugh L., 52–53, 64, 66, 69
Sedition Act of 1918, 4
September 11, 2001, x, xv, 19, 43, 142, 156,
    178, 204–05, 211–12
    as criminal activity, xiv
    United Nations' attempt to define, xiv
Serbia, 116
Seven Weeks War, 51
Shchedrin, Nikolai, 173
Shinkafi, Mahmoud Dallatun, 193
Shu'aibu, Adamu, 201
slavery, 8
Slovenia, 116
Socialist Party, 3, 25, 28
Socialist/Socialism, 10, 25, 31, 39–40, 158
    in West Germany, 151
Solovyev, Alexander, 166
Somalia, 123–27
Southeast Asia, 98, 102
Soviet Union, 77, 111
    collapse of, 117
Soyinka, Wole, 194
Special Group (CI), 86–87, 93, 98–100,
    102, 104
    and Guatemala, 101
    members of, 88
Stone, Harlan Fiske, 17
Suarez, Jose M. Pino, 46
Suslova, Nadezhda, 160

Taliban, 205
Tarnovski, G., 218–20
Taylor, Francis W., 205
Taylor, Maxwell
    appointment by JFK, 87

terrorism, 135, 146, 153–55, 207–08,
    214–16, 223–25
    and gender in Russia, 157, 159
    definition of, 204, 206
    gender, 133, 143, 150
    in Germany, 137
terrorist/s, xiii, 137, 205, 209–10, 215,
    220, 223, 225
    women as, 135
Thailand, 101, 105
The Times (London), 20
Thomas, Norman, 27
Tiananmen Square, 109–10
Time magazine, 119
Turkey, 158
Turner, Nat, 8

United Arab Emirates, 111
United Mine Workers of America
    (UMWA), 21–22
    Paint Creek and Cabin Creek strike,
    23
United Nations, xiv, 108, 113, 117, 123–25
United States, 5, 18, 43, 46, 48, 50, 54, 65,
    74, 84, 95, 104, 110–11, 113, 119, 121,
    204, 219–20, 223
    Constitution, xv
    military, 81
    military operations, 57
USARCARIB School, 80–84, 103

Vallandigham, Clement, 9
Venezuela, 102–03
Vías, Felipe, 83
Vietnam, 101, 105, 113, 115, 118, 127
    Diplomatic Legacy, 118, 128
Viett, Inge, 136–37, 151
Villa, Pancho, 43, 45, 61, 63, 65, 69, 73
    and Columbus raid, 67–68
    and conflict with Venustiano
        Carranza, 62
    and Mexico City, 64
    and the Constitutionalists, 47
    capture of, 70
    failure of, 63
Vinson, Fred, 17

Wall Street Journal, 82
    on Hurrican Katrina, xi
Warren, Francis E., 44

Washington Post, 20, 120–22, 214
Weigel, Sigrid, 153
West, 22
West Virginia Mine Wars, 21, 39, 41
Wilson, Woodrow, 43, 48, 61, 70, 72
    and civil liberties, 7
    and Huerta regime, 56
    and military commanders, 53
    and Pancho Villa, 62
    and the New World Order, 109
    and U.S. raid on Vera Cruz, 58
    appreciation of Bismarck, 49
    foreign policy, 45–46, 48, 50, 54, 65,
        67, 71, 73
    lack of military experience, 52
    Latin American relations, 47
    military relations, 60
    on Venustiano Carranza, 64
    Wilson administration, 12
Wolfowitz, Paul, 121
World War I, 5, 11, 20, 44, 109, 208
    opposition to, 3
    use of explosives, 209
World War II, 14, 82, 210
    use of explosives, 209

Yemen, 215
Yugoslavia, 118, 211
    Wars of Succession, 116–17

Zasulich, Vera, 172, 174
    and terrorism, 177
    arrest of, 176
    education of, 175
Zimmermann, Warren, 118–19

EDITORS

MELINDA M. HICKS is visiting professor of history at Marietta College in Ohio. In 2005, she received a West Virginia University Foundation Distinguished Doctoral Fellowship, and she was awarded a fellowship with the Gilder-Lehrman Collection in New York in 2006.

C. BELMONT KEENEY teaches history at West Virginia University. He has published one novel, *To Live Again*, and has served on the editorial staff of the *West Virginia Encyclopedia* and *West Virginia History: A Journal of Regional Studies*. Hicks and Keeney directed the 2005 Senator Rush D. Holt History Conference, which had as its theme, "Defining Security in an Insecure World," and from which the essays in *Defending the Homeland* were collected.

CONTRIBUTORS

JOSH ARINZE is a research analyst and graduate student at Georgetown University, Washington, DC.

JEAN K. BERGER is an assistant professor of history at the University of Wisconsin–Fox Valley. Her research focuses on ninteenth-century Russian and women's history.

JAMES DEPALMA is a Ph.D. candidate at West Virginia University, focusing on American diplomatic history. His dissertation deals with American foreign policy in the 1990s.

BENJAMIN GROB-FITZGIBBON (Ph.D.) is Visiting Assistant Professor at Duke University, North Carolina. He has previously published on terrorism in the journals *Terrorism and Political Violence* and *Peace and Change*, and the *Journal of Intelligence History*.

DAVID LAUDERBACK is an associate professor of history at Austin Community College where he specializes in American diplomatic and military history.

MARK MULCAHEY is a Ph.D. candidate at Ohio State University specializing in American diplomatic and military history.

ELLEN SCHRECKER is professor of history at Yeshiva University in New York. Her books include *Many are the Crimes: McCarthyism in America* and *The Age of McCarthyism: A Brief History with Documents*. She is widely recognized as one of the foremost authorities on McCarthyism and political repression in America.

JAMIE H. TRNKA (Ph.D.) is assistant professor at the University of Scranton. Her dissertation on literary representations of Latin American revolution in East and West Germany since the 1960s raises questions about the nature of transnational solidarities and highlights historical interactions between German intellectuals and Latin Americans, including Chilean exiles.